MAKING SPACE

MAKING SPACE

INTERIOR DESIGN BY WOMEN

Jane Hall

Φ

6 Introduction

12 Aino Aalto
13 Elissa Aalto
14 Zeina Aboukheir
15 Lotta Agaton
16 Marella Agnelli
17 Farah Ahmed Mathias
18 Selma Akkari and Rawan Muqaddas
19 Aisha Al Sowaidi
20 Miriam Alía
21 Nebras Aljoaib
22 Paula Alvarez de Toledo and Marine Delaloy
23 Nada Andric
24 Iris Apfel
25 Olimpiada Arefieva
26 Sophie Ashby
28 Laura Ashley
29 Sofía Aspe
30 Valentina Audrito
31 Gae Aulenti
32 Rie Azuma
33 Talitha Bainbridge
34 Neydine Bak
35 Elvira Bakubayeva and Aisulu Uali
36 Claire Bataille
37 Kelly Behun
38 Vanessa Bell
39 Sandra Benhamou
40 Karin Bergöö Larsson
41 Falguni Bhatia and Priyanka Itadkar
42 Natalia Bianchi
43 Sabrina Bignami
44 Justina Blakeney
45 Lina Bo Bardi
46 Cini Boeri
47 Linda Boronkay
48 Muriel Brandolini
49 Sally Breer
50 Sheila Bridges
51 Tiffany Brooks
52 Ester Bruzkus
53 Sigrun Bülow-Hübe
54 Athena Calderone
55 Nina Campbell
56 Cristina Carulla
57 Madeleine Castaing
58 Cristina Celestino
59 Vicky Charles
60 Ghida Chehab
61 Khuan Chew
62 Vera Chu
63 Rachel Chudley
64 Petra Ciencialová and Kateřina Průchová
65 Sibyl Colefax
66 Erica Colpitts
67 Mary Colter
68 Sybil Connolly
69 Gloria Cortina
70 Ilse Crawford
71 Rose Cumming
72 Kana Cussen
73 Aline Asmar d'Amman
74 Barbara D'Arcy
75 Alex Dauley
76 Elsie de Wolfe
77 Pallavi Dean

78	Chiara Di Pinto and Arianna Lelli Mami	143	Nancy Lancaster	212	Brigette Romanek
79	Nicole Dohmen	144	Ruth Lane Poole	214	Catarina Rosas, Catarina Soares Pereira, and Cláudia Soares Pereira
80	Olayinka Dosekun-Adjei	145	Jeanne Lanvin	215	Ruby Ross Wood
81	Dorothy Draper	146	Amy Lau	216	Maye Ruiz
82	Sophie Dries	148	Joanna Lavén	217	Rabah Saeid
83	Nathalie and Virginie Droulers	149	Eleanor Le Maire	218	Tara and Tessa Sakhi
84	Marika Dru	150	Little Wing Lee	219	Teresa Sapey
85	Ray Eames	151	Na Li	220	Laura Sartori Rimini
86	Frances Elkins	152	Xiang Li	221	Katty Schiebeck
87	Eugenia Errázuriz	153	Angela Lindahl	222	Gaby Schreiber
88	Mica Ertegun	154	Katie Lockhart	223	Truus Schröder
89	Stefanie Everaert and Caroline Lateur	155	Hilary Loh	224	Anastasia Schuler
90	Zeynep Fadıllıoğlu	156	Isabel López-Quesada	225	Margarete Schütte-Lihotzky
91	Shahira Fahmy	157	Margaret Lord	226	Gillian Segal
92	Mary Featherston	158	Fiona Lynch	227	Tekla Evelina Severin
93	Claudina Flores	159	Margaret Macdonald Mackintosh	228	Darshini Shah
94	Olga Fradina	160	Elsie Mackay	229	Pamela Shamshiri
95	Kesha Franklin	161	Natalie Mahakian	230	Elodie Sire
96	Emanuela Frattini Magnusson	162	India Mahdavi	231	Halina Skibniewska
97	Dora Gad	164	Yasmina Makram	232	Lena Solovyeva
98	Charu Gandhi	165	Eva Marguerre	233	Maria Speake
99	Hanne Gathe	166	Michèle Maria Chaya and Claudia Skaff	234	Anna Spiro
100	Lauren Geremia			235	Isabelle Stanislas
101	Yasmine Ghoniem	167	Syrie Maugham	236	Sara Story
102	Sandra Githinji	168	Ellen Lehman McCluskey	237	Madeline Stuart
103	Laura Gonzalez	169	Marian McEvoy	238	Ulla Tafdrup
104	Adrienne Górska de Montaut	170	Courtney McLeod	239	Naoko Takenouchi
105	Eileen Gray	171	Eleanor McMillen Brown	240	Rose Tarlow
106	Greta Magnusson Grossman	172	Dorothée Meilichzon	241	Nthabi Taukobong
107	Camilla Guinness	173	Frances Merrill	242	Paola Trombetta
108	Elsa Gullberg	174	Diana Luxton Messara	243	Suzanne Tucker
109	Shabnam Gupta	175	Elizabeth Metcalfe	244	Virginia Tupker
110	Racha Gutierrez and Dahlia Hojeij Deleuze	176	Jeannette Meunier Biéler	245	Rose Uniacke
		177	Yana Molodykh	246	Patricia Urquiola
111	Victoria Hagan	178	Julia Morgan	248	Noura van Dijk
112	Marion Hall Best	179	Charlotte Moss	249	Nelly van Doesburg
113	Rania Hamed	180	Joy Moyler	250	Sarah Vanrenen
114	Olga Hanono	181	Kim Mupangilaï	251	Lella Vignelli
115	Elizabeth Hay	182	Elsie Nanji	252	Nanda Vigo
116	Cecil Hayes	183	Paola Navone	253	Ana Volante
117	Ana Milena Hernández Palacios	184	Tanwa Newbold	254	Vritima Wadhwa
118	Beata Heuman	185	Anna Maria Niemeyer	255	Joyce Wang
119	Briar Hickling and Alex Mok	186	Michelle Nussbaumer	256	Ni Wang
120	Min Hogg	187	Georgia O'Keeffe	257	Kelly Wearstler
121	Nicole Hollis	188	Tola Ojuolape	258	Edith Wharton
122	Kelly Hoppen	189	Tosin Oshinowo	259	Candace Wheeler
123	Rossana Hu	190	Maria Osminina	260	Jialun Xiong
124	Barbara Hulanicki	192	Elisa Ossino	261	Chen Xuan
125	Malene Hvidt	193	Marie-Anne Oudejans	262	Jane Yu
126	Kathryn M. Ireland	194	Laura Panebianco	263	Liane Zimbler
127	Polly Jessup	195	Sister Parish	264	Diana Žurek
128	Eva Jiřičná	196	Luisa Parisi		
129	Betty Joel	197	Sevil Peach		
130	Tamsin Johnson	198	Mónica Penaguião	266	Timeline
131	Melanie Kahane	199	Charlotte Perriand	280	Endnotes
132	Annabel Karim Kassar	200	Brigitte Peterhan	282	Index
133	Celerie Kemble and Mimi Maddock McMakin	201	Kerry Phelan		
		202	Clodagh		
134	Kit Kemp	203	Louisa Pierce and Emily Ward		
135	HRH Anoud Khalid Mishaal bin Saud	204	Sarah Poniatowski		
136	Gertrud Kleinhempel	205	Clara Porset		
137	Florence Knoll	206	Andrée Putman		
138	Sunita Kohli	207	Diana Radomysler		
139	Rita Konig	208	Chessy Rayner		
140	Agata Kurzela	209	Lilly Reich		
141	Joanna Laajisto	210	Suzanne Rheinstein		
142	Roísín Lafferty	211	Katie Ridder		

Introduction

In 1921, Elsie de Wolfe, the world's first professional interior decorator, stood before a New York courtroom, suing a client for unpaid services. When the judge asked her to define her profession, she famously replied, "I create beauty."[1] Her remark highlighted the expressive capacities of the interior as a space for self-determination and artistry at a time when domesticity was both celebrated and contested amid women's growing political influence, having gained voting rights in the U.S. in 1920. Interiors were framed as inherently feminine, if not excluding women from public life outright, at least firmly positioning their social role within the home—a connection Elsie acknowledged in her 1913 book, *The House in Good Taste*, when she noted how, "We take it for granted that every woman is interested in houses."[2] Her comments reveal the deep entanglement of gender and design, and the struggle decorators faced as they tried to reframe interiors not just as sites of domestic labor, but also as spaces for creative potential at a time when decorating was not considered a serious pastime, let alone a professional role. As one contemporary newspaper quipped "whenever a husband dies another interior decorator is born."[3]

Elsie's questioning of the status quo around gender roles was present in her own domestic life; a stage actress turned decorator, she lived on the margins of social acceptability, openly sharing her New York apartment with her female partner, Elisabeth Marbury, while married to someone else.[4] At the same time, she catered to her cisgendered heterosexual housewife clients with whimsical, pastel-colored interiors that were distinctly feminine, demonstrating that even as women leaned into gendered stereotypes to advance professionally, their personal lives often defied societal norms. Born from shifting social forces that both constrained and inspired, this tension between social conformity and individual agency is central to the history of women in interior design, and the diverse spaces they shaped. In a profession where women are overwhelmingly recognized as industry leaders, *Making Space* presents the work of 250 practitioners worldwide, revealing complex narratives such as Elsie's, and underscoring the often overlooked factors—including politics, geography, and, critically, the influence of class and wealth—that shape design history.[5]

Many from the first wave of interior decorators, most of whom were born in the United States at the tail end of the nineteenth century, came from privileged backgrounds, gaining professional opportunities primarily through familial connections. Indeed, Elsie was celebrated as one of the "Great Lady Decorators,"[6] a creative but privileged group which included, among others, east coast socialite Dorothy Draper, whose electric 1946 interiors for the Greenbrier Hotel in West Virginia featured a black and white checkerboard floor, turquoise and white striped walls, and wallpaper printed with oversized magenta rhododendrons.[7] This reliance on wealth and social status not only defined the careers of decorators like Dorothy, but also largely insulated the interior decorating industry from economic downturns. Dorothy's contemporary, Sister Parish, built a business that flourished even during the Great Depression. Her relaxed, American country style featuring patchwork quilts, chintz, and wicker came to define Americana, and accordingly made its way to the White House at the invitation of First Lady Jacqueline Kennedy, following in the footsteps of the original Grand Dame of interior decorating, Candace Wheeler.[8]

However, this "gloss and glamour"[9] wasn't typical of the everyday interiors of most people's homes, and as a result, the "Great Lady Decorators" were often excluded from canonical histories of design.[10] While women were considered to have an innate understanding of the home, gender still limited their professional recognition. After all, decoration was viewed as an extension of unpaid domestic labor. To navigate this, interior decorators like Eleanor McMillen Brown sought to neutralize their gender by adopting more corporate identities; she named her firm McMillen Inc. both to appear more business like and to obscure her identity.[11] In contrast, British decorator Betty Joel centered herself in her brand as a modern woman, appealing to homemakers attracted to her low maintenance interiors, only to lose her name and business after divorcing her husband and co-founder, David Joel.[12] Welsh decorator and textile designer Laura Ashley took this approach a step further, building a global empire upon her own identity as a mother and housewife, aligning this persona with her design services. While her signature florals appeared quaintly feminine, they masked the reality of a shrewd businesswoman who was as much an entrepreneur as she was a tastemaker.[13]

The private nature of interiors led women to devise innovative ways to market their work. In the 1920s, New York decorator Rose Cumming—who famously despised electricity and lit her apartment exclusively with black candles—became the first store owner to leave her shop lights on overnight to attract attention. Similarly, French decorator Madeleine Castaing caused a sensation by painting her Paris store entirely black and mounting bold window displays weekly, her lavish use of leopard print a flamboyant beacon cutting through the drudgery of World War II.[14] As in fashion, interior trends shifted rapidly, responding to cultural shifts and their individual reverberations within the home. This dynamism fed the paranoid misogyny of Viennese architect Adolf Loos, who, concerned about the commerciality of decoration, famously dismissed the discipline along gendered lines, lamenting its reliance on self-expression as evidence of excessive materialism and a lack of aesthetic control.[15] As design historian Penny Sparke explains, "bourgeois taste, linked with that of the display, and, by implication, the aesthetic of feminine domesticity, provided an image against which modernist architects could react."[16]

In the first quarter of the twentieth century, modernism emerged across central Europe, which resulted in a turn away from traditional decoration in favor of the functional and mechanical. Monochromatic, planar surfaces replaced stuffy, over-furnished interiors, with women like Dutch pianist and dancer Nelly van Doesburg emerging as an exemplar of the movement. In 1931, Nelly designed the interior of the studio she shared with her husband, artist Theo van Doesburg, in Meudon, France. Featuring a boxy, red acrylic sofa and blue velvet curtains carefully set within an entirely grayscale room, their design brought the geometric abstraction of the De Stijl art movement to life in three dimension.[17]

Their contemporary, writer Til Brugman, engaged with De Stijl differently, commissioning artists like Piet Mondrian to paint rooms in her Hague apartment to explore the relationship between color and space, following Theo's mantra that "without color, architecture is without expression."[18] However, it was Truus Schröder who not only had the vision to commission architect Gerrit Rietveld to create her eponymous home, but also had deep involvement in designing its De Stijl-inspired interior. Through such contributions, women played a central role in the avant-garde, elevating the interior to sit alongside architecture as a legitimate site of design.

Not all modernist designers embraced the industrial materials of the machinic age—both at the time associated with traditional notions of masculinity. Eileen Gray's squishy Bibendum chair (1926) weaponized comfort as a feminist retort to modernism's sleek designs.[19] The chair was integral to Gray's sculptural, materially rich interiors, the fantastical rooms of which created physical and psychological realms for exploring inner subjectivity. Her moveable partitions, screens, and folding tables were among a number of designs that offered a queer, bohemian challenge to heteronormative spatial organization, rejecting fixed rigidity and functionality.[20]

Finnish couple Aino and Alvar Aalto deviated from mid-century modernism by incorporating a traditionally upholstered armchair into their own home's otherwise modern living room for comfort.[21] Their extensive use of wood resulted in surfaces that were warm to the touch. By softening modernism's harder edges, the duo embraced the naturally decorative properties of bent plywood, using its textural striations to humanize their space. While not overtly feminist, the organic quality of their brand of modernism subtly prodded gender norms at a time when discomfort and a lack of decoration intended to erase feminine domesticity from the home's interior altogether.

Erasure of women's contributions is a recurring theme within design history, in both physical spaces and archival records. Interiors, unlike buildings, are inherently ephemeral, often stripped, dismantled, and remade over time.[22] Brazilian textile designer Regina Gomide saw much of her colorful, abstract interior designs from the 1920s and 1930s vanish simply because her fiber materials were vulnerable to the intensity of the Brazilian sun, bleaching away over time.[23] This instability likely explains why designers strive for timelessness in their work, a pursuit that, while aligned with ecological sustainability, also resists the historical association of perishability with the interior and of femininity itself.[24]

Another reason women interior designers often go unnoticed is that their ambition—unlike that of their male counterparts—is frequently characterized as a form of exuberance, which was viewed as a threat to masculinity and led American designer Melanie Kahane to wryly observe that "when a man's wife is a decorator, he frequently gets the compulsion to assert himself."[25] As a result, women's work has often been sidelined, sometimes even by female contemporaries. Mica Ertegun and Chessy Rayner, who established their studio, MAC II, in 1967 out of Chessy's New York brownstone, were labeled "the girls," dismissed by the decorating establishment on the basis that, as Sister Parish remarked, "Chessy is a nice girl and Mica does not have to work."[26] Such internalized misogyny highlights how, for many, decorating was a lucrative, free-market enterprise; notoriety lay in its commercial nature, and by the latter half of the twentieth century, it was part of a competitive service industry.

Disrupting this trend, in the 1960s, two Barbaras redefined department store displays, leveraging them to engage a postwar, consumption-driven mass audience. Barbara Hulanicki's 1964 launch of Biba in London transformed retail spaces into immersive environments; her graphic prints, mirrored surfaces, and maximalist furnishings captured the psychedelic spirit of the flower power generation.[27] Meanwhile, at Bloomingdale's in New York, Barbara D'Arcy curated staged showrooms, including one made entirely of cardboard, transforming interior spaces into realms of fantasy.[28] Both women shifted the focus of their profession from domestic servitude to imaginative personal expression, positing interiors as works of art, and as such vehicles for cultural commentary.

These designs—inspiring, yet unattainable in most homes—align with the feminist practice of using fantasy as a tool for envisioning alternate worlds and possibilities for the embodied experience of womanhood. They upended traditional uses of space, enacting Dorothy Draper's earlier and prescient idea that interior decorating responds to a "yearning to be lifted momentarily out of our own lives into the realm of charm and make-believe."[29] While it would be misleading to claim that women inherently design differently from men, female interior decorators often embraced so-called "womanly intuition" as a professional service, challenging the rationalism valued in male-dominated design industries, particularly architecture.[30] Contrastingly, this kind of empathy was, for Italian modernist Lella Vignelli, a reason to avoid residential interiors altogether. She worked mostly on corporate projects, stating that she didn't want to be a therapist nor go shopping with her clients.[31]

In the early 1960s, when Lella began her career in the United States at the architecture and interiors giant Skidmore, Owings & Merrill (SOM), corporate offices were male-dominated. However, it was a woman, Florence Knoll, who revolutionized the work environment by reimagining every detail, designing custom furniture to create light, modern, and flexible interiors. While Knoll's dominance in design literature overshadows her lesser-known American contemporaries, designers like Maria Bergson and Eleanor Le Maire also dedicated their careers to workplace design. Maria used time-motion studies to create partitioned workstations that were the precursor to open-plan offices, while Eleanor introduced new colors to the interiors of Studebaker's Land Cruiser car model, targeting a previously untapped market of aesthetically oriented female vehicle owners.[32]

What unites these ingenious designers is their ability to bring fresh ideas to prosaic, everyday objects and spaces. When Czech architect Eva Jiřičná proposed a staircase made entirely from glass, she single-handedly defined a high-tech aesthetic for retail and hospitality interiors, an arena her more famous male peers had overlooked. Eva's ghostly and almost absent materialism played with delicacy to invoke a contradictory feeling of strength. Her designs, created over a career spanning six decades, were highly influential for Steve Jobs as he developed the retail side of his Apple brand.[33] Eva's successes rest on her ability to integrate her work as an architect with her explicit concern for the interior, intertwining the two disciplines, in tandem with the larger profession's trend away from the term "decoration" toward "interior design" (and now, "interior architect") in the last quarter of the twentieth century.

Home lifestyle magazines played a pivotal role in this slow shift, and women were instrumental changemakers in their roles as editors, commissioners, and authors. Influential figures include Ruby Ross Wood, Iris Apfel, Marian McEvoy, and more recently Katie Ridder and Virginia Tupker.[34] When renowned editor Min Hogg founded *Interiors* (later renamed *The World of Interiors*) in 1981, she used the pages of her magazine as an engine to reorient consumer preferences, prioritizing offbeat, unusual gems over conventionally overdesigned spaces to assert her thesis that taste transcends excess. Her own disheveled Knightsbridge apartment exhibited her delight in cluttered, worn, yet convivial spaces, which *Interiors* dubbed "shabby chic," unintentionally launching a whole new interior design genre.[35] French designer Andrée Putman embraced Min's view of blending high and low culture, taking pride in her ability to defy the conventions of the decorating establishment.[36] By juxtaposing luxurious, historically significant pieces with mass-produced, everyday objects, she challenged traditional hierarchies of taste.

This approach echoed early Chilean modernist Eugenia Errázuriz's minimalist interiors and humble aesthetic of raw finishes and whitewashed walls. It also finds resonance in the contemporary designs of Lebanese designer Aline Asmar d'Amman, whose love of antique markets is in striking opposition to her opulent renovation of the Hôtel de Crillon.[37] All three designers share a connection to Paris, a city where romanticism and the suspension of disbelief blur beauty, fantasy, and materialism. Their work also raises questions about the democratization of design, and the authenticity of repackaging objects of low culture as aspirational.

Brazilian architect Lina Bo Bardi invoked simple materials for a very different reason, to resist colonial legacies of design. Blending modern industrial processes with indigenous craft practices, at SESC Pompéia, a leisure complex in São Paulo built in the late 1970s, she designed intentionally uncomfortable wood theater seats to keep audience members upright.[38] Completed during the final decade of Brazil's military dictatorship, her interiors expressed her view that comfort was a privilege tied to an emancipated society. Historical examples like this highlight interior design's dual role as a tool for both liberation and domination. In American author Jacquelyn Ogorchukwu Iyamah's compelling essay "Interior Race Theory," she frames interior space as a site of resistance to race-based oppression, urging consideration of the provenance of the objects we live with.[39] Her concept of "political placemaking" explicitly references African American feminist social critic bell hooks's 1990 text, *Homeplace (A Site of Resistance)*, where bell describes her grandmother's home as a sanctuary against cultures of whiteness—a gendered space providing "warmth, comfort, shelter, and nurturing for the soul."[40]

In the present day, designer and Philadelphia native Sheila Bridges exemplifies this resistance in reimagining traditional toile wallpaper, a staple of the European decorative arts. By weaving in imagery that confronts the colonial legacy of slavery in America, she critiques stereotypes deeply embedded in African American history. As she explains, her Harlem Toile de Jouy wallpaper "lampoons" these tropes, transforming the surfaces of a room to envelop inhabitants in a cultural commentary.[41] Reimagining and reclaiming cultural narratives is also evident among young designers who seek to bring their heritage to the forefront. Tola Ojuolape's interiors for The Africa Centre in London celebrate African culture through the use of regionally specific materials including Ghanaian kente cloth, while Sandra Githinji, working from Australia, explores the global history of the African diaspora through her narrative-driven designs. Her tables reference the traditional Kikuyu *giturwa* (stool), historically crafted for women and central to the *nyumba* (home). Through such objects, Sandra's interiors become sites of decolonization that tell stories of the fluidity of identity and heritage, of which gender forms just one part.[42]

Shaping interiors has long been a powerful expression of identity, and ongoing efforts to increase diversity within the profession continue to reshape the industry. British designers Sophie Ashby and Alex Dauley founded United in Design to offer education and networking for young designers of color, while American designer Little Wing Lee's initiative, Black Folks in Design, advocates a similar mission.[43] In today's social media-driven world, designers can cultivate their own agency by amplifying their voices on digital platforms, rather than relying on traditional print magazines. Justina Blakeney launched her design career through her lifestyle blog, *Jungalow*, which has since attracted more than one million followers, while Kim Mupangilaï has built a strong audience of admirers by sharing images of her signature carved wood furniture, inspired by her Congolese heritage. Swedish designer Tekla Evelina Severin is known for her striking, color-blocked interiors that photograph to produce vivid imagery, becoming just as much a part of the work as the spaces themselves. Similarly, Mexican designer Maye Ruiz modernizes Spanish baroque architecture with her confident application of color. Her fresh perspective resonates with an Instagram generation eager to bring her aesthetic into their own homes, regardless of location.

At the same time, advancements in artificial intelligence have expanded the possibilities of interior design, fueling a heightened appetite for fantasy in real-world spaces. This is epitomized by Shanghai-based designer Xiang Li, whose bookshop in Shenzhen transforms the act of browsing into an immersive experience, with improbable spiraling walkways and gravity-defying bookshelves. Likewise, Rania Hamed's Orijins cafe in Dubai envelops visitors in a cavernous, monolithic marble and travertine interior, where every surface appears sculpted from stone. Although both designers studied in the U.K. and U.S. respectively, where design education is dominant, their work, located outside the Global North, signals a shift away from the design hubs of Western Europe and the U.S. toward markets in the U.A.E. and China. Design culture continues to evolve as it globalizes, while designers seek to balance local specificity with personal narrative. Now marks a significant moment for women who make interiors, as a broader awareness dawns around the intersectionality intrinsic to shaping creative practice. A feminist history of interior design, as revealed in this curated selection of work by women worldwide, is a reminder that the interior is never neutral—it is shaped by those who create and occupy it, expanding the possibilities for reimagining the self and *Making Space*.

Endnotes

1. Elsie de Wolfe quoted in Ruth Franklin's "A Life in Good Taste." *New Yorker*. September 19, 2004. First accessed March 12, 2025.

2. Elsie De Wolfe. *The House in Good Taste*. The Century Co. 1913.

3. Florence Davies. "Making More Money." *Buffalo News*. March 16, 1921.

4. Elisabeth Marbury and Elsie de Wolfe Residence. *NYC LGBT Historic Sites Project*. First accessed March 12, 2025.

5. Oliver Vallerand. "Uncovering Structures: Making Visible Hidden Biases." *Journal of Interior Design*. 2024. Vol. 49(1) 3–7, p.5.

6. Adam Lewis. *The Great Lady Decorators*. Rizzoli. 2010.

7. greenbrierwv.com/editorials/dorothy-draper-the-greenbrier-decorator.

8. Eric Pace. "Sister Parish, Grande Dame of American Interior Decorating, Is Dead at 84." *New York Times*. September 10, 1994.

9. Penny Sparke quoted in eds. Susie McKellar and Penny Sparke's *Interior Design and Identity*. Manchester University Press. 2004. p.1.

10. Isabelle Anscombe. *A Woman's Touch*. Elizabeth Sifton Books. Viking. 1984. p.11.

11. Carol Vogel. "Eleanor Brown Is Dead at 100; Interior Designer Pioneered Field." *New York Times*. February 1, 1991.

12. Charlotte Hopkins. "The London years of designer Betty Joel." *London Archives*. August 6, 2024. First accessed January 10, 2025.

13. Nicola Bryan. "Laura Ashley 30 years on: Memories of the girl from Dowlais." *BBC News*. September 29, 2015. First accessed January 10, 2025.

14. Anon. "From the archive: an interview with Madeleine Castaing (1966)." *House & Garden*. July 10, 2020. First accessed January 10, 2025.

15. Boris Groys. "The Obligation to Self Design." *E-flux Journal*. Issue #00. 2008.

16. Penny Sparke quoted in John Potvin's "The Materials of Shame: Decoration, Masculinity, and the Birth of Modern Interior Design." *Art Bulletin*. 106:1. 2024. pp.7–19. p.7.

17. Ellen Himelfarb. "De Stijl Distilled." *World of Interiors*. May 4, 2024. First accessed March 9, 2025.

18. Theo van Doesburg quoted in Ellen Himelfarb's "De Stijl Distilled." *World of Interiors*. May 4, 2024. First accessed March 9, 2025.

19. www.eileengray.co.uk/products/bibendum.

20. Katarina Bonnevier. "A Queer Analysis of Eileen Gray's E-1027" in eds. Hilde Heynen and Gülsüm Baydar's. *Negotiating Domesticity*. Routledge. 2005.

21. www.alvaraalto.fi/en/architecture/the-aalto-house.

22. Vlad Ionescu. "The interior as interiority." *Palgrave Communications* 4, 33. 2018.

23. Indeed, Regina could not be featured more extensively in this book due to the lack of available images of her work. Maria Alice Milliet. "Desafios da modernidade. Família Gomide-Graz nas décadas de 1920 e 1930." MAM.

24. Leslie Weisman. *Discrimination by Design: A Feminist Critique of the Man-Made Environment*. University of Illinois Press. 1994. p.95.

25. Susan Heller Anderson. "Melanie Kahane, 78, a Designer Known for Colorful Rooms, Dies." *New York Times*. December 24, 1988.

26. Mitchell Owens. "Chessy Rayner, 66, Decorator and Fashion Icon, Dies." *New York Times*. February 28, 1998.

27. Sophie Laybourne. "Biba's Back in Style." *Daily Telegraph*. January 29, 1993.

28. Estelle Ellis. "Interview with Barbara D'Arcy. Bloomingdale's Barbara D'Arcy Oral History." Fashion Institute of Technology. November 5, 1986.

29. Dorothy Draper quoted in Paxton Place Design's blog post, www.paxtonplacedesign.com/blog/dorothy-draper.

30. John Potvin. "The Materials of Shame: Decoration, Masculinity, and the Birth of Modern Interior Design." *Art Bulletin*. 106:1. 2024. pp.7–19. p.12.

31. Melissa W. M. Seiler, Pat Kirkham and Lella Vignelli. "Lella Vignelli on Vignelli: Design History, Concepts, and Collaboration." *Studies in the Decorative Arts*. Fall–Winter 2000–2001, Vol. 8, No. 1. pp.139–152. p.145.

32. Anon. "Studebaker Brings New Trend to Automotive Color Styling." *Sunday News*. November 22, 1953.

33. Magali Robathan. "Interview Eva Jiřičná." *Spa Business*. 2019. First accessed January 10, 2025.

34. John Potvin. "The Materials of Shame: Decoration, Masculinity, and the Birth of Modern Interior Design." *Art Bulletin*. 106:1. 2024. pp.7–19. p.15.

35. Jonathan Dawson. *Evening Standard*. November 9, 1994.

36. Karen von Hahn. "French design pioneer Putman woman of firsts." *Toronto Star*. February 2, 2013.

37. Ibid.

38. Zeuler R. M. de A. Lima. *Lina Bo Bardi*. Yale University Press. 2013.

39. Jacquelyn Ogorchukwu Iyamah. "Interior Race Theory: Using Interior Objects to Resist Harmful Racial Conditioning." *Journal of Interior Design*. December 2023.

40. bell hooks. "Homeplace (A Site of Resistance)." *Yearning: Race, gender, and cultural politics*. South End Press. 1990.

41. www.sheilabridges.com/product/harlem-toile-de-jouy-wallpaper-samples.

42. Interview with Sandra Githinji via email. November 1, 2024.

43. www.blackfolksindesign.com.

Aino Aalto

1894, Helsinki, Finland
1949, Helsinki, Finland

Paimio Sanatorium, Paimio,
Finland, 1932

Aino Aalto was the driving force behind many iconic designs created with her husband and business partner, architect Alvar Aalto. Known for her diligent and understated nature, Aino served as creative director, and later managing director, of Artek, the furniture design company the Aaltos co-founded. At Artek, she shaped its aesthetic direction and produced furnishings for their architectural projects, stating "We wish to make what we call social furniture,"[1] with the goal of making their designs accessible to a wide audience. Aino's designs reflected the principles she studied at the Helsinki University of Technology, emphasizing material quality, sustainability, and attention to ergonomics. She often led the design of interior commissions, aiming to create furniture that was "comfortable, cheap, and easy to clean."[2] This simplicity did not detract from the elegance and poetry of their forms, as they pioneered innovative techniques to mold plywood into inventive shapes. Artek was established to mass-produce furniture primarily for their projects, including in notable works like the Viipuri Library and the Paimio Sanatorium. In the latter, interior design played a crucial role in physical health and patient recovery, incorporating sunlight and ergonomic furniture as design elements. Aino's interest in botany and landscape was evident in Artek's seamless blend of interior and exterior spaces, especially in the Aalto family home, the Riihitie House in Helsinki.

Elissa Aalto, the second wife of renowned architect Alvar Aalto, played a crucial role in developing and preserving the Aalto architectural legacy. She began her studies during World War II at the Helsinki University of Technology, where she was part of a cohort with equal numbers of men and women, reflecting Finland's progressive stance on gender and equality in architecture—Finland was the first European country to have a licensed female architect. She joined Aalto's office and became deeply involved in significant projects, including the Säynätsalo Town Hall, the Muuratsalo Experimental House, the Aalto Theatre in Essen, and the Maison Louis Carré. The interiors of the latter unfold toward the landscape outside, with Artek furniture complementing the use of warm building materials such as brick and wood. A photo of Elissa inspecting the Lappia Town Hall construction site shows her hands-on approach and eye for detail, stylishly dressed in a neat suit, oversized sunglasses, and a hard hat. Continuing Alvar's legacy for combining technology with natural materials, she completed his projects while pursuing her own, focusing on human-centered designs. Elissa managed the office for twenty years alongside Alvar, and continued for another twenty after his passing. She tirelessly pursued the conservation of his buildings and the preservation of his office's drawings. Her interests also included textile design and she created patterns such as H55, Pisa, and Patio.

Elissa Aalto

1922, Kemi, Finland
1994, Helsinki, Finland

Maison Louis Carré, Bazoches-sur-Guyonne, France, 1959

Zeina Aboukheir

1949, Lebanon

Al Moudira, Luxor, Egypt, 2002

Photographer and interior designer Zeina Aboukheir is the creator of Al Moudira, a hotel that opened over two decades ago in Luxor, Egypt. This hotel has become a sought-after getaway for travelers seeking authenticity and luxury. Zeina's design demonstrates her eye for opulence and eclectic glamour while reflecting her cross-cultural background, with dusty pinks, ochres, and deep oranges standing in for the varied landscapes of her childhood; with roots in Lebanon and Italy, she spent time across the Middle East and Europe. Zeina traveled around the Middle East seeking antiques and artworks to enhance Al Moudira's charm, working with architect Olivier Sednaoui to ensure the property would evoke the faded past and cultural heritage of Egypt. The serene atmosphere belies the strong personality of its creator. During the hotel's construction, Zeina spent three years managing over 150 artisans and workers, earning the nickname "Al Moudira," which means "the boss lady," a name she passed on to the hotel.[3] Al Moudira is not Zeina's first interiors project. She designed a riad in Rabat and a bistro in Beirut, where she acquired a 1940s house in the Mar Mikhaël neighborhood, which then suffered damage after a catastrophic explosion in the neighboring port. Like at Al Moudira, Zeina transformed the guest house, the Zanzoun, with vintage and modern furniture acquired from countries across the Middle East.

Stockholm-based interior designer and stylist Lotta Agaton founded the Swedish interiors magazine, *Residence*, before establishing her own design studio in 2004. Agaton's passion for design was influenced by her architect father, and she gained early experience working for him after leaving school. Growing up in an eclectic home filled with floral patterns, bright colors, and lively antiques, she eventually developed a sleek, minimalist aesthetic in sharp contrast to her childhood environment. Agaton's designs take shape through desaturated tones and a refined use of texture, using soft furnishings, rugs, and curtains to add interest to an otherwise restrained color palette. Her background as an interior stylist honed her eye for composition and fine detail, emphasizing the importance of scale and the selection of even the smallest items, such as toothbrushes, for her clients. Agaton's minimalist interiors have set trends in Stockholm and across the world, featuring stark white spaces with strong black accents mixed with natural, durable materials like cotton, linen, jute, and wood. Her airy aesthetic and emphasis on light are inspired by the need for illumination during long Scandinavian winters. Using this luminous backdrop, Lotta's own home artfully blends sculptures with iconic furnishings to arrive at a space that has as much depth as it does light.

Lotta Agaton

1970, Stockholm, Sweden

Lotta's home, Stockholm, Sweden, 2022

Marella Agnelli

1927, Florence, Italy
2019, Turin, Italy

Marella's home, Alzipratu, Corsica, France, c.1990s

Marella Agnelli's fame was cemented when Truman Capote dubbed her the "Last Swan" among his elite group of high society ladies he called "the Swans," which included C.Z. Guest and Lee Radziwill. The youngest and only European of the group, Marella gained prominence in 1953 when she married Giovanni (Gianni) Agnelli, head of the Fiat empire, then known as Italy's richest man. Already accustomed to wealth, Marella was a Neapolitan princess whose upbringing in Florence influenced her love of interior and landscape design. Before her marriage, Marella trained at the Académie des Beaux-Arts and Académie Julian in Paris, and worked for French *Vogue* and Erwin Blumenfeld in New York as a photographer and model. She also modeled for Andy Warhol and Richard Avedon, whose portrait of her emphasized her elegant neck, reinforcing her Capote-given nickname. Flouting a life of leisure, Marella was industrious and peripatetic in her designs for several iconic rooms in her ten homes across three continents. Known for her love of wicker, floral pattern, and vibrant color, she collaborated with designers like Gae Aulenti, with whom she restored a villa in Marrakesh and co-published *The Last Swan*, detailing Marella's designs. Marella's work transcended mere tastemaking; she was an avid gardener, published author, and a philanthropist, supporting the Italian Environmental Fund and serving on the board of the Museum of Modern Art.

Bengaluru native Farah Ahmed Mathias moved to the U.S. to study photography and political science at Northwestern University and initially pursued a career in advertising in New York. Compelled by her interest in interior design, she moved to Milan to study design, and earned a master's degree from the Istituto Marangoni. Returning to India in 2011, Farah co-founded FADD Studio in Bengaluru with her business partner, Dhaval Shellugar. Together they have built a reputation for bold, well-crafted projects for private homes and restaurants that integrate their architecture with high-impact, well-chosen artworks. At the Clermont Residence in Bengaluru, Farah combined two separate apartments into a single intergenerational family home. Introducing curves throughout by way of furniture and even carved patterns on the ceiling, the apartment's walls take on the appearance of a continuous wave. The design for her own ground-floor apartment showcases more traditional features, including white painted ceilings and ornate cornice moldings. A contemporary color palette brings a new lease of life to her husband's ancestral home, which she remodeled into a modern residence for her family. Blush pink and powdery blues along with decorative flourishes, such as an abundance of floral murals, contrast with her eclectic furniture choices, which mix artisanal Indian items with Bauhaus-inspired pieces.

Farah Ahmed Mathias

1983, Bengaluru, India

Clermont Residence, Bengaluru, India, 2023

Selma Akkari and Rawan Muqaddas

1991, Montreal, Canada
1992, Kuwait City, Kuwait

Amity Street Residence, New York, NY, USA, 2022

Muqaddas Akkari Studio (MA Studio) is led by Selma Akkari and Rawan Muqaddas. Having studied architecture together at New York's Pratt Institute, Selma and Rawan began their careers working at the same architecture office. They soon realized their shared affinity for working with natural materials, particularly woods and marble, and the detail-work essential to interior design. Their first project—Amity Street Residence, an apartment in New York's Cobble Hill neighborhood—allowed them to establish MA Studio, which now has offices in Dubai and London. For this project Selma and Rawan wanted to invite a dialogue between old and new, creating curved arches to frame room openings in the 1910 apartment that hadn't been touched since the 1960s, while introducing modern materials, such as reflective but understated brushed aluminum-clad cabinetry in the kitchen, which they paired with a striking gray streaked marble countertop "to warm it up."[4] Their style combines the simplicity and clarity of minimalism with an inviting warmth, achieved through the thoughtful use of natural materials, soft tones, and tactile, often raw, finishes that celebrate the patina of age. Drawn to renovation projects, the duo embraces the existing fabric of a building, updating interior spaces to feel modern while preserving their sense of history. In order to achieve this, they work closely with artisans, prioritizing local and women-run businesses with the aim of promoting traditional methods of making.

Interdisciplinary designer Aisha Al Sowaidi studied graphic design in Doha, graduating from VCUarts Qatar. Her design practice is deeply rooted in her engagement with Doha, where she explores the city's heritage through the lens of home, childhood, and memory. Amid a rapidly changing urban environment, Aisha's projects blend traditional elements with contemporary design. She designed Townhouse 8 as part of Doha's Culture Pass Club, a members' arts club in the design district of Msheireb Downtown, founded by Her Excellency Sheikha Al Mayassa Bint Hamad bin Khalifa Al Thani. Aisha's project within the complex, which features a suite of townhouses designed by a group of international design luminaries, conveys evolving notions of everyday Qatari home life. Furniture referencing *majlis*, a traditional low seating arrangement used in a hospitality setting, is reimagined as a modular system made from alpaca wool and walnut. A monochromatic color palette of white tones is offset by colored patterned inlays in tables inspired by traditional Arabic motifs, while a series of copper pipes adorns the walls distributing scent throughout the room, artfully updating a traditional system in a contemporary material. In addition to her design practice, Aisha is involved in developing Doha's artistic sector as director of Liwan Design Studios and Labs, a creative organization run by Qatar Museums.

Aisha Al Sowaidi

1983, Doha, Qatar

Townhouse 8, Msheireb Downtown, Doha, 2022

Miriam Alía

1983, Madrid, Spain

Private residence, Madrid, Spain, 2023

Miriam Alía's modern interiors favor geometries and colors reminiscent of the 1970s. She unifies her designs through generously applied swathes of pastel pinks, juicy oranges, and acid greens covering every surface. Combining these tones with experiments in pattern and shape results in spaces that have a unique energy, such as in her design for a home in Madrid which she describes as "an escape into the retro world of the 70s, with a modern edge."[5] Miriam states that her designs are a direct reflection of her optimistic personality filled with "harmony, color, light."[6] A flair for interior design runs through Miriam's family. Her mother studied interior architecture, and the designer Tomás Alía is a distant relative. Miriam obtained her master's degree in interior architecture from IADE Escuela de Diseño in Madrid, and worked for several design studios before setting up her own company in 2015. Drawn to the interplay of soft and hard forms, and with a self-confessed "rock and roll" attitude, Miriam confidently and playfully combines vintage furnishings, always making sure to disrupt or undermine her own designs by inserting an unusual, seemingly out-of-place element, often through a fluorescent accent.[7]

Nebras Aljoaib founded her firm Nebras Aljoaib Creative Studio in 2015. Based in Riyadh, Nebras's design philosophy blends tradition with modernity, creating spaces that are carefully curated yet familiar. She often incorporates unique elements such as antique Byobu screens, admired for their intricate artistry, and vintage ceramics collected from her travels. These pieces contribute their own stories, adding depth and character to the spaces she creates. Inspired by the art and music of the 1950s and 1960s, Nebras has developed a personal aesthetic that celebrates "the unexpected beauty of vintage pieces" alongside clean, contemporary lines.[8] A defining feature of Nebras's work is her passion for marble. From homes to wellness destinations, Nebras collaborates closely with both local and international craftspeople and quarries and makes creative use of the many colors and patterns that can be found in natural stone. "In my creative process, marble is how I set the stage," she states, emphasizing how it embodies "restraint and luxury, all at once."[9] Her design for the FOURSPA IV in Riyadh epitomizes her confident use of the material, with its central Norwegian rose pink marble bar and an Italian arabescato marble on the floor and walls. Her designs have a graphic quality, offset by the inclusion of rough materials such as unfinished raw textured walls against delicate, decorative elements like a vintage mural of an English garden.

Nebras Aljoaib

1988, Dhahran, Saudi Arabia

FOURSPA IV, Riyadh, Saudi Arabia, 2021

Paula Alvarez de Toledo and Marine Delaloy

1987, Marseille, France
1987, Aix-en-Provence, France

Mandel apartment, Paris, France, 2017

Jaune Architecture, founded by Marine Delaloy and Paula Alvarez de Toledo, is a boutique interior design studio based in Paris. Its name—the French word for yellow—evokes the sunshine of Marseille, where both founders grew up. Marine discovered her interest in interiors during her architecture studies at the École Nationale Supérieure d'Architecture de Marseille and while earning her master's degree at the campus in Paris La-Villette. Fascinated by the play of light and the relationship to materiality and detail, Marine refined her experience through designing theater sets, developing a narrative approach, which she translates in her interior design practice. Paula's interest in interiors started in childhood, when she would constantly rearrange her bedroom, discovering how design could impact her mood. She studied interior architecture at Penninghen and the École Camondo. Marine and Paula met through a mutual friend while working at Studio KO and Joseph Dirand respectively.[10] Together their designs prioritize the use of natural materials, working with wood to create partitions in space and textured stone to introduce patterns, while their use of reflective surfaces for cabinets and tables bounces light around a room. In their Haussmannian apartment, Mandel, the graphic veining of a large marble kitchen island brings a sculptural quality to the calm, light-filled space. Their work has expanded to commercial and hospitality projects, including The Baja Club hotel in La Paz, Mexico.

Nada Andric emigrated from Yugoslavia to the U.S. without family support after seeing a lecture about the Chicago School while studying architecture at the University of Belgrade. When she arrived at the architecture firm Skidmore Owings and Merrill (SOM) in Chicago in 1992, they did not have any openings in architecture, so she joined the interior design team, without any training in the discipline. She promised her family that she would only stay for six months. Since then, she has led large-scale projects worldwide, including the Hong Kong Convention and Exhibition Centre and the Hyatt Global Headquarters in Chicago. In 2010, the Burj Khalifa, built by Emaar Properties in Dubai, became the world's tallest building. As the lead interior designer, Nada wanted the interiors to reflect the building's wavy exterior and so incorporated undulating forms in public areas with curved ceilings and walls connecting spaces across levels. Working closely with a graphic designer, Nada introduced Arabic script on the floor. She chose a material palette inspired by the local context, drawing on the fine sand and pearls that have been harvested in the region for centuries. These references are made manifest through glass, stainless steel, polished dark stone, and silver travertine flooring. As an associate director at SOM, Nada worked on many high-profile developments in Saudi Arabia, Malaysia, and China, among other countries. She was inducted into the Interior Design Hall of Fame in 2011.

Nada Andric

Belgrade, Yugoslavia

Burj Khalifa, Dubai, UAE, 2010

Iris Apfel

1921, New York, NY, USA
2024, Palm Beach, FL, USA

Apfel's apartment, Park Avenue,
New York, NY, 2016

Born in Queens, New York, Iris Apfel studied art history at New York University and briefly taught before becoming a journalist for *Women's Wear Daily*. In 1952, Iris and her husband, Carl Apfel, founded Old World Weavers, a textile company specializing in fabricating, selling, and restoring textiles. Their textiles were included in the redecoration of the White House throughout nine presidential terms, with Iris often clashing with First Ladies—except Mrs. Nixon, whom she found cooperative. From the 1950s onwards, Iris designed interiors for notable private clients, including Greta Garbo and Estée Lauder. Though they sold Old World Weavers and retired in 1992, Iris continued to consult for the firm. The Apfels traveled the world, collecting unique textiles and adding to their extensive personal wardrobes. Exposed to fashion from a young age through her mother's fashion store and her father's business, Iris met glamorous figures like interior decorator Elsie de Wolfe. Surrounded by wealth and style, Iris developed her own distinctive sense of style, known for mixing couture with flea market finds. She famously stated, "style is all a matter of how you wear it and your attitude."[11] In 2005, the Metropolitan Museum of Art showcased her wardrobe, marking the first time the Met exhibited a living individual's personal clothing. The exhibition's success solidified Iris's status as a style icon, leading to book deals and a modeling contract with IMG Models that lasted well into her 90s.

Olimpiada Arefieva has emerged in Moscow as a leading residential interior designer. After graduating from Saint Petersburg Academy of Arts as an architect, she trained in interior design under Veronika Blomgren, founder of Russia's interior design school, Details. Olimpiada assisted Veronika in designing the interiors for several large-scale residential projects before founding her own studio, Well Done Interiors. Her process begins with a focused conversation with her clients, interpreting their needs and desires exclusively through hand drawing.[12] She has since established a reputation for her contemporary take on the traditional family home. This is realized to great effect in her project, Artistic Apartment, situated on the Moskva River in a modern industrial building. Here Olimpiada embraced the dramatic 16-foot (5-meter) high ceilings by filling the spaces with detailed patterns and colors, introducing a wall of mirrors and an array of contemporary furniture. This interior showcases Olimpiada's ability to create comfortable, practical spaces that enliven traditional architectural motifs through the use of deep, sophisticated colors including midnight blue in the narrow hallway and burnt orange for the living room's ceiling. Olimpiada's designs are expressive through their playful moments, with large pendant lights, unusually proportioned table lamps, and placement of unusual objects adding warmth and vitality.

Olimpiada Arefieva

1980, Saint Petersburg, Russia

Artistic Apartment, Moscow, Russia, 2022

Sophie Ashby

1989, London, UK

The Blewcoat School, London, UK, 2022

Sophie Ashby is a London-based interior designer whose practice has an emphasis on curation, combining a deep knowledge of design history and an eye for impactful art pieces with a fresh approach to styling. After earning a degree in art history from the University of Leeds, she pursued her passion for interiors at Parsons School of Design in New York. At only twenty-five years old and with just a single client, Sophie founded Studio Ashby, quickly establishing herself as a sought-after designer. Her design philosophy is rooted in the belief that home is deeply connected to identity. This perspective is shaped by her childhood, spent between the United Kingdom and South Africa, where the rich colors and textures of the landscape bear a lasting impression on her work. Sophie's projects often feature a nod to South African hues. In one project, she was inspired by the green, dark teal blues, and reddish brown from the Bushveld, a woodland area in South Africa. Applied to soft furnishings throughout the property, she seamlessly blended regional motifs with contemporary design's clean lines and graphic shapes. For a home in Paris, Sophie reimagined classical features like parquet wood floors and wood-paneling pairing them with contemporary furniture from her own line, Sister, and flea market antiques. In addition to Studio Ashby, Sophie along with fellow designer Alex Dauley founded United in Design, a charity focused on promoting diversity in the design industry.

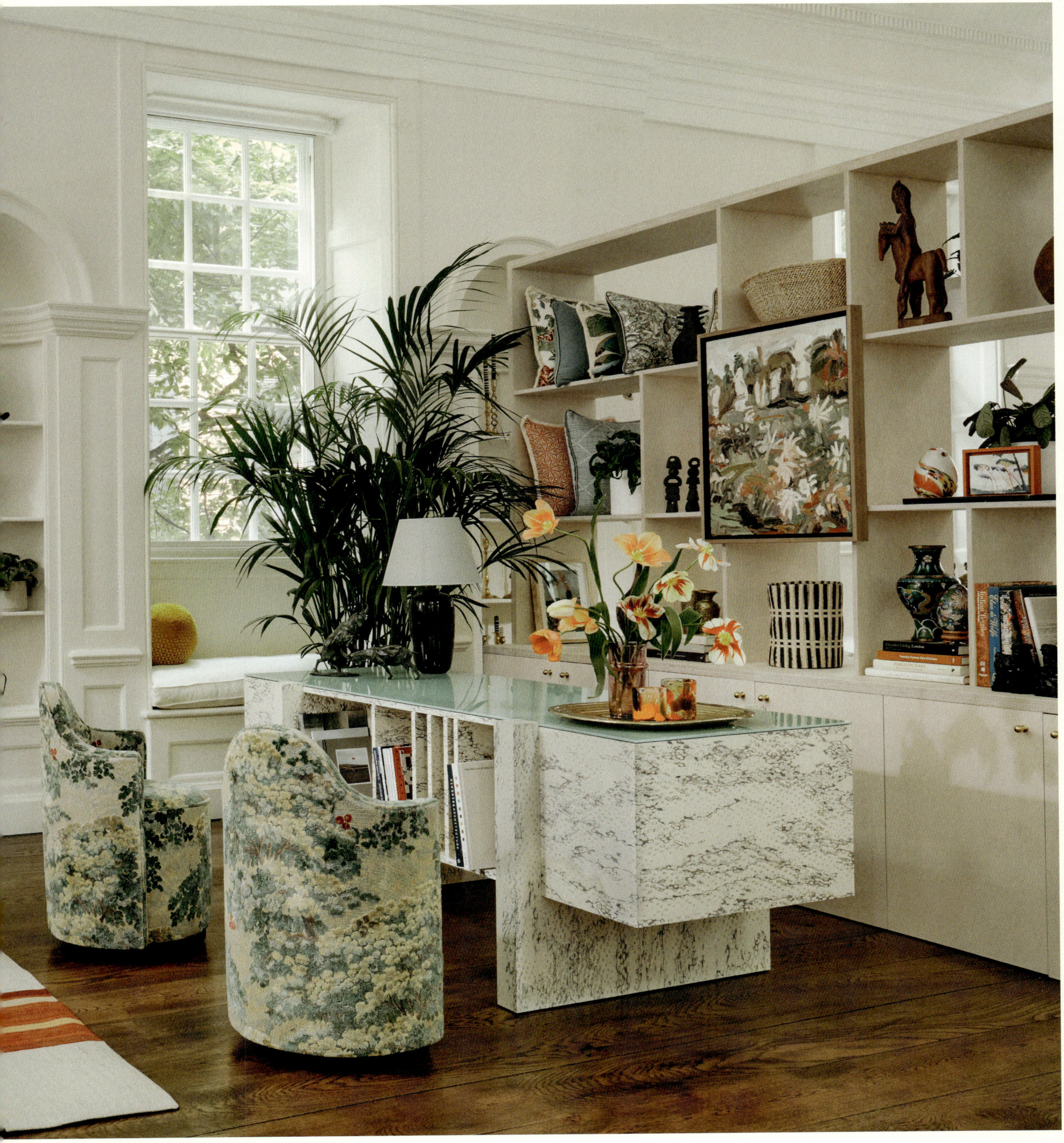

Laura Ashley

1925, Dowlais, Merthyr Tydfil, UK
1985, Coventry, UK

Artist's studio featuring the Bloomsbury Room collection, London, UK, 1987

When Princess Diana announced her engagement to Prince Charles, it was her sartorial choices, not her new status, that captured headlines. Photographed in a floral Laura Ashley skirt that turned translucent in the sunlight, she cemented her image as a modern English Rose, a distinctly pastoral, romantic British aesthetic exemplified by Laura Ashley's fashion designs and homewares. Laura convinced young women to embrace conservative, longer-length dresses even when Mary Quant's miniskirts were all the rage. Inspired by a Women's Institute exhibition at the Victoria & Albert Museum, Laura began hand-printing fabric at her kitchen table in the early 1950s. While her name became the brand, Laura's husband Bernard was a vital partner, inventing a continuous printing machine to produce fabric by the yard. By the 1980s, Laura Ashley had expanded to 200 stores worldwide, with all production centralized in the couple's factory in Wales. Laura released several books on interior decorating, expressing her love for "faded and mellow" rooms. This is evident in designs featured in her *Book of Home Decorating*, where she emphasizes natural light and the interplay between patterned china and decorative fabrics. Laura Ashley style has made a resurgence with younger audiences who have dubbed its lace, ruffles, and floral patterns "cottagecore" for its influences from the British Arts and Crafts Movement.

Sofía Aspe

1975, Boston, MA, USA

Private residence, Madrid, Spain, 2024

Raised in a family that appreciated the decorative arts, Sofía Aspe fondly remembers playing with the miniature furniture she collected, found at local markets and gifted to her by her father from his trips abroad. Despite nurturing an interest in the arts from a young age, Sofía initially studied business management in Mexico City, followed by training in the culinary arts in Chicago. She then spent eleven years as president of ChildFund México before her unexpected entry into the world of interior design. Her design career began when a friend invited her to design an office in a historic house in the Polanco neighborhood of Mexico City, a project that sparked subsequent residential design commissions. Sofía has completed 200 projects in Mexico, the United States, and Spain. She is known for her fearless use of color and a mix-and-match approach to covering surfaces with wallpaper and fabric, creating visually stimulating designs and always prioritizing comfort and tactility. She incorporates artisanal, handmade pieces to infuse her spaces with character and her exuberant, maximalist style is informed by the mood and personality of her clients. Her designs expertly blend antiques with contemporary textiles and furnishings. For example, plum-colored walls and ornate ceiling cornicing for a dining room in a house in Madrid give a sophisticated, regal feel, contrasted with an array of modern light shades, each different from one another, which hang dramatically above a circular dining table. In addition to her interiors practice, Sofía advises clients on their art collections, and has published two books articulating her design philosophy.

Valentina Audrito

1972, Turin, Italy

Seascape villa, Lembongan island, Indonesia, 2018

Born in Turin, Italy, Valentina Audrito earned a degree in architecture from the city's Polytechnic University. Valentina grew up steeped in design; her father is prominent Italian designer Franco Audrito, who designed the iconic Bocca Sofa, resembling a pair of red lips. She is also associated with the architecture and design practice, Studio65, founded by her father and mother, Athena Audrito, which has offices in Italy and Saudi Arabia. In 1998, she left Italy for Bali, where in 2004 she established Word of Mouth House, an architecture and design studio. Known for her playful approach, Valentina blends her minimalist architectural style with bold, maximalist interiors, following her mantra that "anything goes, as long as it fits."[13] Her Lembongan island villa, Seascape, merges with its ocean surroundings through a palette of whites and blues, featuring geometric lines and circular shapes cut into walls throughout, harmonizing with the island's natural beauty. She contrasts her ultra-modern take on bohemian seaside-chic with hand-painted ceramic lights, woven natural fiber rugs, raw wood, and wicker furniture, drawing on the island's rich craft traditions. One of her notable creations, the Sunny Shag Up Rug, displays her whimsical flair and forms part of a series of furniture she made inspired by eggs. She exhibited this series of egg-shaped furniture pieces, titled Le Uova di Leon, at the Salone de Mobile, Milan's furniture fair in 2006. Valentina's Word of Mouth headquarters in Bali serves as an atelier as well as an exhibition and performance space.

Gae Aulenti initially studied to be a pianist, but switched to architecture at age seventeen. A rare trailblazing women architect and public intellectual of her generation, she addressed critical claims of her work being "masculine" by stating, "People think that intelligence is a male characteristic. There is no difference between the architecture of men and women."[14] Gae believed in combining theory with practice, lecturing at the Venice School of Architecture and editing for the Italian magazine Casabella for over a decade. At the 1976 International Women in Design Conference in Ramsar, Iran, she was among the few women who had her own office that did not include a male partner. The project that solidified her career was the Musée d'Orsay in Paris, where she created large, unified spaces while preserving the Beaux-Arts features of the old railroad depot. The ornate design split opinion and crystalized Gae's reputation as a provocateur.[15] She was known for bold design gestures that showcased her vast knowledge of a range of materials she could harness to arrive at surprising and singular forms. She gained fame designing showrooms for Olivetti and Fiat, notably renovating the Palazzo Grassi in Venice. Ahead of her time, she championed industrial reuse and building renovation before sustainability was widely recognized, a principle that guided her design for Altana Palazzo Pucci in Florence, in which reflective sheet metal covers every surface, enveloping the walls and furniture.

Gae Aulenti

1927, Palazzolo dello Stella, Italy
2012, Milan, Italy

Altana Palazzo Pucci, Florence, Italy, 1971

Rie Azuma

1959, Osaka, Japan

Tsukihashi Maisonette, Hoshinoya, Kyoto, Japan, 2009

Immersed in architecture and design from a young age, Rie Azuma was heavily influenced by her father, architect Takamitsu Azuma. She grew up in the Tower House, the famous compact home he designed in central Tokyo in 1966. Rie first studied architecture at Japan Women's University before pursuing postgraduate studies in architecture at the University of Tokyo and Cornell University. In 1983, she joined her father's architecture firm and worked with him to design private homes and public buildings across Japan, ranging from nursery schools to university departments. One of Rie's most notable collaborations is with the luxury resort brand Hoshinoya, known for modern resorts that incorporate traditional construction techniques. For their resort in Kyoto, Rie refurbished the hotel whose history dates to the Meiji period, emphasizing its historic timber structure through the installation of paper screens, traditional tatami mats, and Karakami wallpaper, made from the fiber of mulberry trees featuring delicate gold patterns made locally. Allowing visitors to discover Japanese architecture, she artfully weaves these handcrafted elements together with contemporary furniture, such as a sleek curved bamboo sofa by the Japanese furniture factory Hinoki Kogei.

Talitha Bainbridge

1989, Lörrach, Germany

Talitha's home, Rümmingen, Lörrach, Germany, 2020

Talitha Bainbridge recalls the care her mother took in creating and decorating living spaces, all crafted from D.I.Y. and handmade decorations. This effort to make the home feel special left a lasting impression on Talitha, who realized the importance of taking pride in one's home, and that rooms evoke emotions as spaces of "love and care."[16] Talitha studied integrated design with a focus on spatial design, followed by a degree in interior design. Her first design opportunity came when friends asked her to design the interiors of their apartment, which led to a much larger commission to also design the cafeteria at their company. Founding ZWEI with her partner, Michael Bainbridge, in 2018, Talitha works closely with each client to gain a clear understanding of their style, with color and materials forming the basis of her designs. Sustainable design is central to Talitha's ethos, and in her work she seeks to use and promote the availability of circular materials and economies. When it comes to interior furnishings, Talitha prioritizes vintage pieces, or reusing items from her client's existing collection. This practice has led to ZWEI Finds, an initiative within her studio dedicated to buying and reselling vintage and antique furniture, art, and objects. For the interiors of her own home, Talitha mixed her own custom-made pieces with European classic furniture including an olive green velvet Ligne Roset Togo sofa and Utrecht chair by Gerrit Rietveld for Cassina in pale gray, which she states she loves to look at and sit in as it gives her "so much joy and a sense of calm."[17]

Neydine Bak

1985, Pretoria, South Africa

Flamingo Room by tashas, Dubai, UAE, 2017

Neydine Bak met her life and business partner, Dewald Struwig, at the University of Pretoria, where they both studied architecture, going on to work for large architecture firms in Johannesburg upon graduation. In 2015, they relocated to Sydney, and founded their design studio, Verhaal, a year later. The studio's name originates from the Afrikaans word for "a well-told tale – a narrative beyond literal fact."[18] Growing up, Neydine was deeply influenced by her mother's love of hosting, which Neydine translates into her designs by adding a touch of the surreal to simple forms to create hospitable and entertaining spaces. Verhaal works globally, with projects across Australia, and more recently in the Middle East. Their designs weave together historical references, cultural themes, and modern silhouettes, creating a style Neydine describes as "classic, but with a personal touch."[19] Neydine's design for the Flamingo Room at the Jumeirah Al Naseem hotel in Dubai showcases her ability to draw on cultural references from across the globe. Pairing African safari aesthetics with tropical, nature-inspired motifs, Neydine adorned the soft furnishings with flamingo pink velvet upholstery and cushions emblazoned with images of the pink birds, accented by occasional chairs upholstered in bold zebra stripes. A canopy of sculpted decorative bronze palm leaves backdrops the bar, the muted metallic patina of which joins the soft pink and turquoise color palette to unite the lavish space.

Elvira Bakubayeva and Aisulu Uali founded their interior design studio, NAAW, in Almaty, Kazakhstan's largest city and former capital. The pair conduct thorough research into the history of a location, using their architectural training to thoughtfully consider volume, light, and materiality. Their designs are dynamic and joyful, reflecting their instinctive use of color. From a bright blue ceiling and oversized terrazzo floor for the interiors of Bitanga, a restaurant in Alamaty, to a shop outfitted with full-length eggplant curtains, Elvira and Aisulu demonstrate an inspired ability to make daring choices in color, material, and form that pay off with high impact in their designs. Their interior for FIKA cafe, located in the historic TurkSib Railway Workers' House dating to 1953, draws thoughtfully on the building's Soviet-era history. With the project, Elvira and Aisulu intended to "engage in a meaningful dialogue with the building's rich historical layers" through careful preservation of original plasterwork encountered during demolition, as well as thorough restoration of the facade's arched windows, setting these elements against the simplicity of raw concrete and cheerful yet streamlined Danish furnishings.[20] As designers, they are not attached to one fixed style, allowing them to be agile and reactive to new sites, materials, and ways of working, evidenced by their use of mycelium panels—a highly sustainable material grown from mushroom fungus—to clad the interior walls and make custom tables and lighting for a small coffee shop in Oxford, United Kingdom.

Elvira Bakubayeva and Aisulu Uali

1992, Almaty, Kazakhstan
1990, Almaty, Kazakhstan

Fika Café, Almaty, Kazakhstan, 2024

Claire Bataille

1940, Antwerp, Belgium

Private apartment, Brussels, Belgium, 1968

Claire Bataille, a distinguished Belgian interior architect, built her career in collaboration with furniture designer Paul Ibens, with whom she both studied and worked in Antwerp. She graduated from the Henry van de Velde Institute in Antwerp in 1962, however, she began her career making furniture due to the lack of demand for interior and architecture projects. Concurrently, she taught drawing at La Cambre art school in Brussels while advancing her career as a designer. Claire found early success by securing second place in a *Daily Mirror* furniture design competition for designing an armchair. This achievement marked the beginning of a prolific partnership with Paul Ibens, creating work defined by simplicity and a minimalist visual language composed of geometric shapes and sleek surfaces. Their meticulously controlled and detailed aesthetic has been applied to a variety of spaces, ranging from homes and shops to offices. In 1995, the pair founded BVBA Ibens & Bataille, a firm dedicated to delivering a range of furniture and objects embodying their shared design philosophy. Their residential interiors eschew traditional decoration, instead centering on architectural forms to fulfill central functions, like storage. The curvilinear metal wall storage unit Claire designed for Madame Zucker's apartment on Avenue Brugmann in Brussels shows off the disciplined elegance and refined minimalism that went into these architectural interventions that made each of her projects distinctive.

Kelly Behun's approach to interior design, much like her path to becoming a designer, veers toward the unconventional. Born and raised in Pittsburgh she graduated from the Wharton School with a degree in Economics before moving to New York where she joined the in-house design studio for Ian Schrager Hotels. While there she trained under Romanian architect Anda Andrei, collaborated with renowned French designer Andrée Putman, and was an integral part of the design team that created iconic properties such as the Delano in Miami, the Mondrian in Los Angeles, and the Royalton, Paramount, Morgans, and Hudson hotels in New York City. Once on her own, she forged a style that eschews easy characterization, preferring to treat each project as a unique opportunity to collaborate and elicit a client's true style. Her interiors are distinguished through an interplay of carefully selected artworks and deftly mixed vintage and modern furnishings. This can be seen in her pairing of Mathieu Lehanneur's Familyscape seating with a vintage Nombe carved throne chair in the living room of a house in La Jolla. Known as the Razor House, it is an architectural marvel made even more compelling through Kelly's warm and soulful interiors. The home, dramatically perched on a cliff overlooking the Pacific Ocean and comprised of sweeping concrete walls and large curtain walls of glazing, is a highly personalized example of Kelly's signature layering of textures and furnishings.

Kelly Behun

Pittsburgh, PA, USA

Razor House, La Jolla, CA, USA, 2021

Vanessa Bell

1879, London, UK
1961, Lewes, UK

Charleston House, Lewes, UK, c.1916

Best remembered as a painter, Vanessa Bell also made textiles, ceramics, and furniture, all of which coalesced in the home she created at Charleston House, a sixteenth-century farmhouse in East Sussex. Moving there in 1916 with her husband, art critic Clive Bell, Vanessa made Charleston more than a home; it was a studio and a space for exploring new forms for domestic life. Vanessa, Clive, and their friend Duncan Grant created free-flowing rooms that changed uses, reflecting their fluid interpersonal relationships. This lifestyle extended ideas from the Bloomsbury Group, of which Vanessa was a central figure. Her social circles, starting from her time at the Royal Academy Schools, included artistic, politically liberal, and socially privileged early twentieth-century luminaries. Notable figures included Roger Fry, who set up the Omega Workshops, an artist-led avant-garde interior design shop that influenced Charleston's aesthetic. The Omega Workshops promoted art as part of everyday living, and Charleston's interiors were adorned with playfully painted surfaces that embraced an intentionally naive aesthetic. Every object held significance, and each, from the utensils to the wallpaper, was designed by group members, including Vanessa. She used her own body to make imprints on the walls, creating impressions in a freehand painterly style emblematic of a Bloomsbury Group interior.

Sandra Benhamou

1973, Paris, France

Manor House, Tourgéville, Normandy, France, 2022

Sandra Benhamou, a graduate of the École Supérieure des Sciences Economiques et Commerciales, a business school in France, and self-taught interior designer, moved to the U.S. where she began her design career by building her family country house in the Hamptons. In 2010, she opened her own design agency in Paris while transforming a dilapidated Haussmann apartment into her home. Seeking to create a "joyful place,"[21] with a contemporary feel while retaining the historical features of the apartment, Sandra refurbished the original wood flooring and moldings, as a backdrop against which to display her personal collection of artworks. This showcased her curated collection of furniture and her collage-like approach to composing interiors, which she replicates in her home in Normandy. Sandra's seaside home has a more serene and sensual feel. For this project she selected sleek, vintage 1970s wood furniture, softening each space with sofas and curtains drawing from a palette of navy blue, moss green, and mustard yellow. Before her career in interior design, Sandra worked in the film industry in New York. As a result, her designs are cinematic, infused with a sense of storytelling. While she has completed both residential and hospitality projects, Sandra also produces her own furniture line. Influenced by her Italian-Tunisian family history and life in Paris, Sandra's work draws on the great Italian architects of the 1920s and 1930s, including Carlo Scarpa and Gio Ponti, as well as Bauhaus masters like Josef Albers and the textile artist Sheila Hicks.

Karin Bergöö Larsson

1859, Örebro, Sweden
1928, Sweden

Carl Larsson-gården, Sundborn, Sweden, 1912

Artist Karin Bergöö Larsson significantly influenced her husband, Carl Larsson, whose paintings of Swedish country life anticipated the Swedish Modern. Karin enjoyed a comfortable upbringing as the daughter of a wealthy businessman who encouraged her artistic interests. She studied handicrafts and later painting at the Royal Swedish Academy of Fine Arts before moving to a Swedish artist colony near Paris, where she and Carl first met. When they married in 1883, Carl expected Karin to give up her artistic career to support him and raise their eight children. After moving between France and Sweden, the couple settled in Lilla Hyttnäs, purchasing a cottage to raise their family. Resigning herself to her new role as mother and housewife, Karin channeled her artistic talents into creating a unique family home inspired by Carl's idealized paintings of country life. Her design aesthetic, now iconic in Sweden, was radical at the time. Drawing from the British Arts and Crafts movement and Japanese motifs, Karin crafted bright, folksy interiors whose rustic charm used vivid colors in a naive, abstract style. She rejected heavy dark wood furniture—then common in Swedish homes—in favor of informal, bright, child-friendly spaces. Karin also designed textiles, embroidery, furniture, and even clothing for her family. While she never achieved personal success as an artist, the home she created remains a popular Swedish attraction, open to the public as Carl Larsson-gården.

Falguni Bhatia and Priyanka Itadkar became friends while studying together at Lokmanya Tilak Institute of Architecture and Design Studies in Mumbai before founding their design studio The Act of Quad, which is named for the four elements of air, earth, fire, and water. Based in a former public library, the white studio is a blank canvas for their projects. Priyanka's father, a sculptor, allowed them to test materials in his studio, and they have since developed a hands-on approach of salvaging materials and minimizing waste through reuse. Priyanka and Falguni's refined sensibility blurs the lines "between practicality, beauty, and emotion" through their innovative use of color and material to arrive at striking spaces.[22] For one residential project, they combined two apartments into a multi-generational home for a family inspired by traditional Japanese architecture. The pair worked closely with the family, documenting their daily routine to inform the layout. Introducing gentle curves and spherical objects into their design, Priyanka and Falguni arrived at a "soft minimalism" that combines bold graphic and architectural gestures with eased edges.[23] The cream-colored walls create a calm backdrop for an array of spirited, geometric touches, from a sweeping curved rose-gold mirror to wiggly floor-to-ceiling sculptural columns to pops of bright color, all of which imparts the studio's unique twist to conventional furnishings.

Falguni Bhatia and Priyanka Itadkar

1993, Mumbai, India
1995, Mumbai, India

Mumbai Apartment, Ghatkopar, Mumbai, India, 2021

Natalia Bianchi

1967, Milan, Italy

Private residence, Milan, 2023

As a child, Natalia Bianchi enjoyed rearranging the furniture in her bedroom, and even in hotel rooms when she traveled. Her passion for composing objects in space, seeking qualities such as proportion, balance, and beauty, led her to study architecture at the Politecnico di Milano, where she specialized in interior design. She cites fashion designer Yves Saint Laurent as a key influence, admiring his ability to elevate personal taste and aesthetics. Natalia's work reflects her interest in the elegance of twentieth-century design, but characterized by taking an experimental and transgressive approach to mixing materials and redefining the original style of furniture—such as adding fine black and white stripes to antique pieces. In 1997, she founded her eponymous studio in Milan, developing an eclectic and ever-changing style marked by attention to cultural context. Her designs for private residences in Milan showcase her ability to layer intricate patterns on every surface, from walls to furniture, sculpting each space by harnessing natural light and bold colors to create elegant maximalist interiors. The dynamism of Natalia's interiors is often emphasized by her signature use of a feature wall painted in bold, candy-box colors. Natalia believes that an interior designer, in addition to having an artist's eye and a poetic imagination, must have passion and patience to truly understand the client's way of living.

Sabrina Bignami

1967, Florence, Italy

Casa Orlandi, Prato, Italy, 2008

The main task of architect Sabrina Bignami's restoration of an eighteenth-century palazzo in Prato—which had been derelict for twenty years—was to bring back to life the frescoes covering every wall surface in the home. Originally painted by the Tuscan painter Luigi Catani, each room of Casa Orlandi had been covered in white paint, which Sabrina painstakingly stripped away to reveal the rich colors and ornate illustration beneath. As a counterpoint to the historic nature of the palazzo, to furnish the guest house, Sabrina chose contemporary, minimal objects and well-known icons of modern furniture design, such as Saarinen dining chairs, artfully placing them so as not to obscure the frescoes. Born in Florence, Sabrina trained as an architect at the University of Florence before undertaking two master's degrees, one in architectural restoration and hotel design, and the second in Architectural Office Management and Strategies in Milan. Now based in Prato, Sabrina runs an architecture studio called b-arch with her partner and husband, Alessandro Capellaro. The studio specializes in architecture, restoration, and interior design for the residential, hospitality, and commercial sectors. Among its clients are renowned brands such as Ginori 1735 and Ruffino. In 2012, Sabrina founded Extradesign Selection, a gallery featuring a carefully curated selection of design objects, often unique vintage pieces, sometimes custom-made in limited editions.

Justina Blakeney

1979, Berkeley, CA, USA

Jungalow by the Mountain, Altadena, CA, USA, 2022

Justina Blakeney is an artist and designer renowned for her ability to "harmonize vibrant colors and bold patterns."[24] Her designs are inviting and unconventional, and are always infused with a touch of wild bohemian flair. Growing up in a large, multicultural family with Black and Jewish European roots, Justina came of age in a colorful household filled with African art, batik textiles, and collected objects her family brought back from travels all over the world. Having lived in Switzerland and Italy as a teenager, she studied World Arts and Cultures at UCLA before moving to Florence, where she studied fashion with her sister, Faith Blakeney, and worked at a literary agency. The sisters stayed in Italy for seven years, running a vintage clothing and home goods boutique. Justina then returned to the U.S. and freelanced as a magazine editor and stylist. During this time, she started posting to her lifestyle blog, Jungalow, and soon realized she had garnered over a million followers on Pinterest. This revelation prompted her to pay more attention to her online presence, leading to collaborations with various brands, including Anthropologie, Target, and Mattel, for whom she designed a room in Barbie's Dreamhouse, drawing inspiration from the Barbie archives. Justina's own home in Altadena functions as a collage of her signature design elements, mixing intricate floral prints with soft, earthy colors to set the scene for her vast collection of tropical houseplants.

Surrounded by tropical fauna, the Casa de Vidro (Glass House) stands on slender blue pilotis, blending with the trees around it. Architect Lina Bo Bardi built it as her home in 1951 in São Paulo's Morumbi suburb. The house's full-length glazing allows light to filter through the trees, creating a sun-dappled interior. The long sitting room overlooks surrounding rolling hills, with furnishings positioned throughout the space as if on display in a gallery. This house was an emblem for Lina's belief that everyday objects held as much value as museum artifacts, and should be displayed with equal consideration. She wrote passionately about Brazilian folklore and tradition, promoting interiors layered with diverse materials, textures, and forms in her magazine *Habitat*. Lina arrived in Brazil from Italy in 1947, quickly becoming captivated by the Indigenous crafts of the northeast. She sought to integrate these artisanal elements into industrial processes and commercial products for middle-class homes. Naturalized in 1954 as a Brazilian citizen, Lina, in partnership with her husband Pietro Maria Bardi, the art critic and director of the São Paulo Museum of Art, developed a career spanning five decades. She designed furniture, exhibitions, museums, and urban plans. Although her career was stymied by Brazil's military dictatorship in the 1960s and 1970s, this period of restriction further politicized her designs. This is evident in her large-scale projects like the leisure center SESC Pompéia where she foregrounded everyday life, creating a joyous public space for collective gatherings.

Lina Bo Bardi

1914, Rome, Italy
1992, São Paulo, Brazil

Casa de Vidro, São Paulo, Brazil, early 1950s

Cini Boeri

1924, Milan, Italy
2020, Milan, Italy

Casa nel Bosco, Osmate, Lombardy, Italy, 1969

Cini Boeri stands out among a generation of Italian women who made a name for themselves as architects and designers. She studied architecture at the Politecnico di Milano and did an internship with iconic Italian designer Gio Ponti after graduating in 1951. She also worked for Marco Zanuso for 12 years, specializing in interiors. Encouraged by architect Franca Helg, Cini established her eponymous studio in 1963. Cini's architecture and interiors challenged traditional familial structures through home designs with very few—often moveable—walls that unified rooms to encourage collaborative living. Modular design elements became the decor, resulting in her signature essential and functional style that always adapted to the needs of the users of the spaces. She advocated for a dynamic way of living free from established norms, stating, "when you want to change the room, you change the furniture."[25] Her book, *The Human Dimensions of the House: Notes for a Design That Is Attentive to the Physical and Mental Needs of Man*, outlined a humanistic approach to living that rejected standardization in favor of adaptation. Cini embraced modernity and wanted people to engage with their environments to "open them up to each other and the world."[26]

Linda Boronkay

1982, Budapest, Hungary

Richmond residence, London, UK, 2024

Linda Boronkay's interiors exude theatricality with their fantastical, escapist environments. Her aesthetic sensibilities were shaped by global travels as a young fashion student as well as her design-suffused upbringing by an architect father and art collector mother. Transitioning from fashion to interiors was seamless for Linda, as both fields require a keen eye for concepts, colors, and textures to craft immersive experiences. She studied interior design at London Metropolitan University, where she won Best Emerging Interior Designer before graduating. Seeking industry experience, Linda worked with British designer Tom Dixon and architecture studio Woods Bagot before joining Soho House, where she learned the importance of integrating service, food, drink, and music with design to enhance one's experience of hospitality. Linda founded her studio after receiving a commission from a friend to design a mansion in Bel Air, leading to more projects, including a hotel outside Sydney. Her distinctive approach to design is characterized by meticulous detail, layering, and craft. She is known for her bold use of color, her striking juxtapositions of contemporary pieces with vintage icons, and her sense of drama. Linda works internationally on residential and hospitality projects, with headquarters in London, Los Angeles, and Sydney.

Muriel Brandolini

Montpellier, France

Private residence, Hampton Bays, NY, USA, 2022

Raised in Vietnam's most populous city, Ho Chi Minh City, interior designer Muriel Brandolini draws inspiration from her Vietnamese upbringing, which informs her signature blend of modernist and tropical themes. After moving to Martinique with her family, she dropped out of high school and was sent to Paris by her mother to train as a secretary. Unfulfilled by the prospect of a desk job, Muriel made her way to New York, where she began her career in fashion, working for Deschamps and Cacharel before securing a job as a stylist for *Vogue*. During this time, she discovered her passion for interior design, which included designing her own home and those of friends. She regularly plays around with furniture and objects, placing high-end furnishings among pieces thrifted from antique stores and flea markets. Attentive to final details, Muriel incorporates handmade elements to add comfort and warmth to a space. Her intuitive approach to design is evident in her work for a home in the Hamptons, where she wrapped the walls and ceilings with richly colored deep green, striped fabric to create a continuous three-dimensional surface. This technique has not only made her an icon in the interior design world, but has also solidified her reputation for achieving exuberant elegance through experimentation.

Self-taught designer Sally Breer was raised in an artistic household. A New York native who spent time in her youth living in Paris, she discovered a passion for interiors after attending an antiques fair while living in Texas. In 2010, Sally moved to Los Angeles where she established her studio, Sally Breer World, which focuses on residential and commercial projects infused with her love of modern art. Often ahead of American decorating trends, Sally honed her skills with her previous company, ETC.etera, where she crafted functional furniture with elegant silhouettes. Her texture-driven approach and love of color reflect her talent for creating personal, livable environments. Moving from a downtown loft to a 1950s ranch-style property in the East LA neighborhood of Eagle Rock, Sally wanted to create a family home that was both beautiful and practical. Light-flooded rooms are filled with bespoke furniture designed by Sally. Sofas take on unusual, undulating shapes, while the spaces exude warmth through a muted palette of pastel-colored walls and hand-painted murals. She contrasts upholstered leather furniture with textured fur rugs and metal bedside tables to create an edgy, modern, but nonetheless cozy feel. Sally's distinctive use of materials that embrace imperfection and patina results in striking, unique spaces that still foster a sense of ease and comfort.

Sally Breer

1988, New York, NY, USA

Sally's home, Los Angeles, CA, USA, 2022

Sheila Bridges

1964, Philadelphia, PA, USA

Hudson Valley Cottage, Hudson River Valley, NY, USA, 2011

A Philadelphia native, Sheila Bridges has become among the most successful and sought-after interior designers in the United States, earning many accolades including a spot on *Forbes' 50 over 50 2023* list. By her mid-thirties, she was already recognized as a rising star, having been commissioned to design former President Bill Clinton's offices in Harlem. Considered a creative visionary and design tastemaker, Sheila's design expertise was showcased in her television show, *Sheila Bridges: Designer Living*, on the Fine Living Network, and in her 2002 book, *Furnishing Forward: A Practical Guide to Furnishing for a Lifetime*. During her time at Temple University's Tyler School of Art and Architecture, Sheila studied in Rome where she was first exposed to design. She further honed her skills at Parsons School of Design in New York, and later launched Sheila Bridges Design, Inc. She targeted an African American clientele, aiming to provide access to affordable yet culturally relevant home design. Her interiors are celebrated for their vibrant, multi-layered approach, often informed by architecture and historical references. Notably, she created the iconic Harlem Toile de Jouy wallpaper, which subverts seventeenth-century French pastoral motifs, and "lampoons some of the stereotypes deeply woven into the African American experience."[27]

Few successful interior designers have an entry story into the design world as unlikely as Tiffany Brooks's. As part of her job working in luxury real estate as a property manager, Tiffany staged homes on shoestring budgets, including for a model apartment that she transformed with only three thousand dollars. Her boss was so impressed with the outcome that he submitted the project for an award, which Tiffany won. This early success motivated her to give up her day job and pursue interior design as a full-time career. Offering free design services on Craigslist, Tiffany quickly built up her portfolio and became known for her quirky style, which she describes as "classic with a twist."[28] Her design, featured in *House Beautiful* magazine's 2020 Whole Home Concept House, showcases her talent for surprising and delighting through bold choices. In the living room, she covers the walls with fabric wallpaper featuring a pattern reminiscent of black ink pooling in water. She carries a mauve and pink color palette throughout the space, while also introducing a breakfast nook. Her adventurous designs have won her further accolades, including the winning title for Season 8 of HGTV's *Design Star*. Now a household name, Tiffany regularly brings her design perspective to the screen, including in shows like HGTV's *Smart House* and HGTV's *Rock the Block* and she has acted as a judge on the network's *Barbie Dreamhouse Challenge*.

Tiffany Brooks

1979, Waukegan, IL, USA

House Beautiful Whole Home Concept House, Franktown, CO, USA, 2020

Ester Bruzkus

1975, Haifa, Israel

The Green Box, Berlin, Germany, 2020

Ester Bruzkus founded her Berlin-based international Architecture and Interiors practice, Ester Bruzkus Architekten, in 2002. Ester is known for her signature approach, balancing minimalism and opulence, cool and warm, edgy and comfortable, with a bold use of color. She adopts an interdisciplinary approach, blurring typologies by mixing expertise learned in hospitality, workspace and residential design. An early notable project that garnered her significant attention was her design for the Amano Hotel in Mitte, Berlin. Here, she brought a sense of modernity to the grand hotel concept by mixing and matching textiles and furnishings from different eras, featuring a dramatic collage of more traditional patterned carpets grounding sumptuous chocolate brown leather sofas. Riffing on a building's history and her clients' tastes, Ester hones in on compelling material and spatial contrasts to shape interiors that draw on modernist lines and volumes set against energetically disruptive, bright visual cues. This approach is exemplified by her design for The Green Box apartment, for which she inserted a deep green volume into the middle of the home containing all the core amenities. This is complemented by furniture that introduces an aray of green tones, such as a corduroy sofa and a dramatic reflective brass fireplace shroud.

Sigrun's creativity was shaped by her mother, a sculptor, and her father, a town planner for the Swedish city of Malmö. However, the influence of Kaare Klint, her tutor at the Royal Danish Academy of Art, oriented her toward prioritizing function in design, inspiring an interest in traditional furniture typologies alongside Arts and Crafts ideals. Adopting his teachings, she spent summers apprenticing in a furniture factory in Sweden, aspiring to become an artist and designer. After graduating in 1935, Sigrun returned to Sweden, working on church restoration projects and, through her father's contacts, found work with the Swedish government. She became chief designer for the interiors of Malmö City Theater and during this period, Sigrun developed an interest in housing standards, receiving several awards for her work, including the Gold Medal at the Exhibition on Urbanism and Housing in Paris in 1947. As the popularity of Scandinavian design grew in North America, a fellowship from the American-Scandinavian Foundation brought Sigrun to the U.S. for a year to research housing design and furniture production. In 1950, she emigrated to Montreal, where she first worked as an interior consultant for T. Eaton Company. She later founded and directed the AKA Furniture Company, specializing in modern Scandinavian furniture design and construction.

Sigrun Bülow-Hübe

1913, Linköping, Sweden
1994, Canada

12 Habitat Suites, AKA Furniture Company, 1967

Athena Calderone

1974, Long Island, NY, USA

Brooklyn Townhouse, Cobble Hill, New York, NY, USA, 2018

Athena Calderone is the founder of Studio Athena Calderone, a multidisciplinary design studio based in New York. With storytelling at the core of her creative process, Athena's work is defined by her ability to blend historical and contemporary styles. She is renowned for her use of bold natural stone and layered neutrals, a signature approach that has been widely emulated. Athena attended interior design classes at Parsons School of Design before embarking on several home renovations that deepened her passion and fluency in design. Her refined and elegant approach to interiors became instantly recognizable with the design of her Brooklyn Townhouse. Athena preserved key Greek revival details, including two black marble fireplaces, gold framed mirrors, and select ceiling mouldings, heightening the grandeur of the rooms. In the living room, she used wood herringbone flooring to anchor a triangular white marble coffee table, shot through with gray streaks, and a sumptuous neutral low sofa, exuding comfort. Every detail of the design was documented in the digital publication "You Asked For It," outlining how to achieve and where to purchase every part of the home's interiors.[29] In 2011, she launched the lifestyle media platform, EyeSwoon, focusing on food, style, and home decor and is the author of two best-selling books: *Live Beautiful* a volume on interior design, and *Cook Beautiful*.

Nina Campbell has led her London-based design studio, Nina Campbell Interiors, for more than fifty years. Renowned for her work with royalty and high-profile clients, she has designed the American Bar at the Savoy Hotel and refurbished its Art Deco lobby, among many other prestigious commissions worldwide. At nineteen, Nina trained with John Fowler of Colefax and Fowler, soon after establishing her own decorating company, which in its initial stages oversaw the redecoration of Annabel's, a private members' club. There she reintroduced rich, dark colors and decorative wallpaper, building rooms around found objects sourced by her client, Mark Birley, including a Buddha sculpture that became the centerpiece of a lounge room painted entirely in red lacquer. Her collaboration with Birley continued when they opened a luxury furniture shop, Campbell and Birley, in 1970. Nina's style is synonymous with the English Country aesthetic, and she aims to bring color into her clients' homes, remarking that it is "so sad that people are scared of colour."[30] Today, Nina Campbell Interiors is a family-run business, with Nina's son Max and daughter Alice joining the firm, while her other daughter, Rita Konig, works as a successful designer under her own name. Nina has published numerous books on design, including *Nina Campbell Interior Decoration: Elegance and Ease* (2018) and *A House in Maine* (2023).

Nina Campbell

1945, London, UK

The Buddha Room, Annabel's, London, UK, c.1965

Cristina Carulla

1984, Spain

Private country house, Cruïlles, Girona, Spain, 2024

Cristina Carulla renovated her country home in Cruïlles as a retreat from city life. The interiors of the traditional farmhouse, parts of which date back to the twelfth century, are warm and rustic, featuring solid wood furniture. Cristina enhances the farmhouse's traditional charm by incorporating natural fibers such as jute rugs, wicker lamps, and linen tablecloths. At the same time, she skillfully modernizes the interior with contemporary elements, like a pair of plush white bouclé armchairs. Based in Barcelona, Cristina's studio has been designing residential and commercial spaces since 2015. She began her career as a political reporter at Spain's most widely read newspaper and later moved to Mexico, where she worked as a correspondent for a leading fashion and lifestyle magazine. Immersed in a new creative landscape, she opened a furniture store in the capital, which naturally evolved into interior design commissions. Seeking to deepen her expertise, she relocated to New York to study at Parsons School of Design before returning to Spain to work with Lázaro Rosa-Violán. She went on to establish her own studio, blending journalistic curiosity with a refined aesthetic sensibility. Cristina's style is deeply rooted in a sense of history. She highlights this by incorporating historical references into her furniture choices. Just as in her country home, she ensures her designs feel modern through her color palette—often featuring bold greens, bright oranges, and deep navy blues—to create elegant yet relaxed atmospheres. This approach is evident at Servicio Continuo restaurant in Barcelona, where lux materials like brass and olive wood bring warmth and a distinct character to the space.

Few interior designers match Madeleine Castaing's depth of research, for which she insisted on living with clients for two weeks to truly understand their personalities so she could uniquely tailor their spaces to them. Despite the bleakness of World War II, her Parisian business flourished in the 1940s, with vibrant store window displays that showcased her imaginative ideas. She frequently rotated her window displays, staging different interior styles weekly. New concepts found expression almost as soon as they came to her, and she sparked controversy by painting the interior of her store black, a radical move that later inspired others to follow suit. Madeleine sourced furniture herself, longing to travel to England for new pieces. She believed in collaging interiors from the different historical periods, choosing "the best bits from each," from the English for comfort and the French for taste.[31] Her theatricality possibly stemmed from her brief silent film career, which was cut short by her marriage to art critic Marcellin Castaing, allowing her to pursue a career in design. Her favorite palette of red, sky blue, and garden green, often mixed with leopard print carpets and upholstery, defined her signature style, as can be seen in the decor of her country house, La Maison de Lèves, just outside Chartres. For Madeleine, interiors were dreamy, opulent, and joyful portraits of their occupants.

Madeleine Castaing

1894, Le Mans, France
1992, Paris, France

La Maison de Lèves, outside Chartres, France, 1940s

Cristina Celestino

1980, Pordenone, Italy

Framing Life, Rome, Italy, 2023

Cristina Celestino's designs evoke a refined world of sculpted forms and sophisticated pastels, balancing elegance with a playful edge: geometries, materials, and color are functional elements that shape a space beyond mere decoration. Cristina studied architecture in Venice and spent time in Florence and Rome. Eventually, she settled in Milan, Italy's design capital where she officially launched her own studio in 2013. She is a meticulous researcher and keen observer, qualities that enable her to reinterpret traditional forms in her work. This is evident in her recent tile collection, which draws inspiration from Euclidean geometry and transforms it into a two-dimensional intersecting marbled design. Her collaborations with brands like Fendi and Fornace Brioni highlight her interest in a feminine sensibility embracing curvaceous forms and her ability to work across different scales, always prioritizing small details—a trait evident in her design for a 1930s apartment in Rome. The serene apartment's muted color palette is accented by Cristina's signature colors, and pays homage to the original space's Rationalist architecture through artfully composed arrangements of geometric furniture. Cristina's fusion of design eras across time results in a retro-futuristic aesthetic drawing on historical and contemporary references from art and fashion alike.

Vicky Charles

1975, Gloucestershire, UK

Private residence, Beverley Hills, CA, USA, 2020

Soho House has become synonymous with a look that is equal measures glamorous and understated, elegant yet always well-worn and comfortable. Much of this aesthetic owes to Vicky Charles, the club's design director for twenty years. After graduating from the University of Exeter with a degree in fine art and literature, her initial jobs waiting tables had little to do with design. However, working at Cafe Boheme in Oxford, owned by Soho House proprietor Nick Jones, led to a job with the company, and she quickly worked her way up. Moving to New York, Vicky honed her design skills under interior designer Ilse Crawford. She helped export the Soho House brand globally, starting with her first design role: creating the bedrooms at the Miami branch of the club. After Amal and George Clooney stayed at Soho House in Berlin, they invited Vicky to design their home, becoming her first residential client. With her company, Charles & Co., Vicky has developed her own aesthetic of luxurious yet livable comfort, believing that homes should express and be enriched by the wear and tear of living. Vicky credits her lack of formal training and her unconventional path into the interior design world with her ability to challenge industry conventions. She is known for leaving building materials like brick exposed, devising pared-back interiors that are nonetheless enriched by luxurious textiles such as velvet, often in deep, earthy tones.

Ghida Chehab

1994, Beirut, Lebanon

Ganache Dubai Hills, Dubai, UAE, 2024

Ghida Chehab remembers how traces of her native Lebanon impacted her in her youth and inspired her career in design, from exploring the narrow streets of Beirut's city center to taking family road trips to the mountains. She studied at the American University of Beirut before moving to Dubai, where she worked at waiwai and Nakkash Design Studio. Her first major project was Aptitude, a café at the Louvre Abu Dhabi, where her design sought to connect to the nature of U.A.E.'s rich sandy textures. Ghida founded Studio Baab in 2022 alongside the debut of major projects for artisan chocolatier Ganache in Dubai. She named her studio after the Arabic word for "door," an opening to a new area as well as a new experience of a space, the baab imminently revealing what is on the other side. With each design, Ghida's ambition is to craft an individual personality, something she achieves through careful consideration of materiality. Her project, Ganache Dubai Hills, borrows from the varied color palette of different chocolates, creating a warm atmosphere. A sculptural chocolate station stands in the center of the space while a curved textile light feature hangs above, creating a sensory experience that uses natural textures and tones to set the mood.

Khuan Chew, hailing from an artistic Chinese family, studied music at the University of London. Soon after completing her degree, she found her way to interior design through music, in particular her love for opera and its theatrical staging. She worked as Creative Director for David Hicks, and with hospitality pioneers Dale Keller and Associates before founding her own studio, KCA International, in London in 1988, quickly becoming known for her dramatic, opulent designs. She participated in a competition to design the interiors of the Chicago Beach Resort Development Project in Dubai, which became the Jumeirah Beach Hotel and the Burj Al Arab—both of which she won, consecutively. These projects embrace the spectacular, with design schemes inspired by the four elements of water, fire, earth, and air. These elements find form through a water fountain that projects water 262 feet (80 meters) high into the air, the generous use of vivid reds, deep oranges, watery blues, and verdant greens, and the integration of layered geometric patterns and Arabic calligraphies which weave historical and cultural references into the surrounding futuristic landscape of Dubai's tallest buildings. Describing the Burj Al Arab as "quintessentially designed as a modern Arabic palace," Khuan's contribution to the iconic site remains an emblem for her luxurious style. This success led to continued work in the U.A.E. and her establishment of a KCA International Dubai office in 2000.[32]

Khuan Chew

China

Burj Al Arab, Dubai, UAE, 2021

Vera Chu

1971, Taiwan

Green Massage Lujiazui, Shanghai, China, 2021

Vera Chu is the co-founder and Lighting Design Director of Vermilion Zhou Design Group, a premier interior design firm in Shanghai. With a Master of Fine Arts in architecture and lighting design from Parsons School of Design, Vera began her career in New York, working as a lighting designer at prominent firms like Leni Schwendinger Light Projects and Gary Gordon Architectural Lighting. During this time, she also contributed to interior design magazines in Taiwan as a columnist. Returning to China in 2002, she co-founded Vermilion Zhou with Ray Chou, fusing her lighting design expertise together with Eastern aesthetics and the requirements for functional, modern interiors. Vera's projects range across diverse applications, from public spaces to commercial and residential interiors throughout East Asia. For the Green Massage spa in Shanghai, she collaborated with lighting designer Chia Huang Liao to create an immersive environment. Inspired by faint cave lighting, the spa's dark interiors feature textured walls softly illuminated by subtle water ripple reflections. The minimalist lighting design gently reveals natural textures and deepens shadows, evoking a serene cavern. Drawing from Wuxing (Five Elements), black symbolizes water, blending into deep Chinese ink tones that signify inclusivity. The interplay of delicate illumination and darkness sharpens the senses, creating a tranquil, mysterious ambience for relaxation. *Chasing Cloud*, a multimedia video artwork by Yong Yang Liang, provides a dramatic interlude. Depicting two Chinese dragons soaring through mist and clouds, the installation adds a dynamic, immersive layer to the overall spa experience.

With an art history degree from The Courtauld Institute of Art in London, British designer Rachel Chudley applies her interest in composition and her love of narrative and history to her projects. Having also studied at the Interior Designers Institute in California, she worked in the United States before founding Rachel Chudley Interior Design in East London in 2015. Rachel is a keen observer of the layers of history that make up a building or room. Her passion for interiors began at a young age when she had the chance to see her grandmother decorate a hotel. Rachel was influenced by the intuitive way her grandmother blended a miscellany of objects and furniture to immerse and inspire guests. She was particularly captivated by the welcoming symbol of pineapple-themed wallpaper in the hotel's hallway. Rachel's style, which she describes as both "eclectic" and "distorted," comprises a wide range of periods contributing to the "Modern Baroque" feel of her interiors.[33] Rachel amplifies the drama of her spaces by carefully pairing colors and playing with contrasts, creating moody dark spaces alongside dreamy, light-filled rooms, using the layering of animal patterned prints on walls and other sumptuous textiles to convey different atmospheres. From wallpaper that looks like fabric drapery to high-gloss painted ceilings, velvet-covered walls, and a freestanding papier-mâché faux Doric column with a kink in it, Rachel's introduction of the surreal within her own home subverts the traditional meaning of a domestic setting.

Rachel Chudley

1985, Kettering, UK

Wanstead Villa, London, UK, 2022

Petra Ciencialová and Kateřina Průchová

1993, Prague, Czech Republic
1993, Prague, Czech Republic

Apartment by the Colonnade, Karlovy Vary, Czech Republic, 2023

Founders of Plus One Architects, Petra Ciencialová and Kateřina Průchová met while studying Architecture and Urbanism at the Czech Technical University in Prague. Discovering shared sensibilities and collaborative ease, they founded their own studio in 2020, focusing initially on interior design projects including the renovation of a small contemporary gallery in the city center together. Their projects emphasize the inherent, preexisting qualities of a space—whether previously visible or hidden—and enhance them with new interventions that serve the necessities of contemporary living. They frequently collaborate with young Czech designers, incorporating both existing and bespoke products to add a fresh, local touch to their projects. A prime example of their work is the 1902 apartment renovation in Karlovy Vary where they featured the work of Czech studio, JanskyDundera, whose minimalist furniture creates tension with the historic setting. The duo reinstated some of the apartment's original features, streamlined circulation by removing doors, and undid outmoded additions from a previous renovation that they estimate date to the late 1970s. The revamped interior boasts a bright, airy atmosphere with natural sunlight streaming through large windows, leaving exposed original paintwork on walls and ceilings. The effect is a series of rooms that all bear the patina of their previous use, with the marks of the locations of walls removed during renovation left visible and the mottled texture of the old paintwork acting as a kind of wallpaper, contrasting with new areas of pinky plaster, left raw, creating a coherent feel throughout.

Sibyl Colefax

1874, London, UK
1950, London, UK

Argyll House, London, UK, 1920s

Sibyl Colefax spent her early childhood in India before being drawn, as a teenager, into the circle of British expatriate intellectuals living in Florence. Later, as a young woman in London, she married Sir Arthur Colefax and swiftly became a glamorous and notorious socialite, admired for her seemingly effortless gift for entertaining.[34] Virginia Woolf preferred her company away from the bustle of dinner parties, while H.G. Wells reportedly begged her to leave him alone. Yet others, like Vita Sackville-West, cherished Sibyl's friendship and loyalty. Sibyl's passion for entertaining spurred her interest in interior decorating, beginning with the decoration of her own eighteenth-century house on the King's Road in Chelsea. Argyll House became a study in relaxed elegance featuring ivory walls, vivid rugs, and chintz-covered furniture creating a convivial yet refined atmosphere. Alongside her friend Peggy Ward, she launched the Colefax brand in the wake of the 1929 Wall Street Crash, quickly earning a reputation for impeccable, classic taste. After Arthur's death, Sibyl partnered with the painter John Fowler to establish Colefax and Fowler. During World War II, the pair developed a distinctive restrained yet richly layered aesthetic that came to define the English country house style. Elegant without ostentation, their interiors had a true sense of lived-in comfort. In 1944, after just six years and struggling with ill health, Sibyl sold her share to the interior designer Nancy Lancaster.

Erica Colpitts

1980, Vancouver, BC, Canada

Colwood House, Vancouver, BC, Canada, 2021

For Erica Colpitts, interior design is a family affair. Fond memories of reading home decor magazines with her grandmother nurtured her interest in design. As a teenager, while her friends shopped for clothing and makeup, Erica could be found in home stores enamored with beautiful objects. She pursued her interest in design at university, developing an interest in hospitality design throughout her studies at the British Columbia Institute of Technology, from which she graduated in 2006. An early project of hers involved designing a gastropub for her brother. For The Watson, one of four venues she designed for him, Erica developed a sophisticated modern take on a Victorian aesthetic installing forest green wood paneling on the walls, a mirrored arch, and pendant lights that hang dramatically over the space, achieving what she describes as a "gritty" and "moody style" that is "romantic with an edge."[35] Erica is now sought after for translating her commercial projects' bold concepts into residential spaces. She characterizes her style as modern with a touch of "whimsy."[36] This is evident in Colwood House, a home designed by architecture firm Olson Kundig, where Erica devised a rich, romantic mid-century modern interior pairing caramel-colored leather seating with dramatic deep charcoal tones. Situated within a forest of mature cedar trees, the home's interior feels luxurious but practical. Mixing organic textiles and beautifully crafted furniture, she layers the natural patinas found in wood, metal, and stone, embracing their wear over time to imbue the space with character and a sense of history.

Mary Colter spent her teenage years in Minnesota before studying at the California School of Design (now the San Francisco Art Institute). After years working as a drawing teacher and editor for a local paper, Mary found success as the main architect for the Fred Harvey Company, which operated stores and hotels along railroads in the Southwestern United States. Mary would often sketch ruins to document an overlooked part of American history at a time when the country sought modernity and erasure of its Indigenous past. Inspired by the landscapes of Arizona and New Mexico, and dedicated to making her projects regionally appropriate, Mary completed more than twenty Harvey Houses that deployed Native American building practices and employed Indigenous builders. Her style embraced the kitsch aesthetics of burgeoning tourism and the romanticism of the Southwest, incorporating handicrafts and Mission-style furniture. Mary aimed to create new versions of traditional designs, but has faced accusations of pastiche and plagiarism. Accordingly scholars have sought to diminish her authorship, highlighting the precarious status of women's professional achievements in an era when women were not encouraged to professionalize, making way for a climate where women had to self-authorize to claim credit for their work. Despite this, four Grand Canyon National Park structures, including Hopi House, remain protected as part of her legacy.

Mary Colter

1869, Pittsburgh, PA, USA
1958, Santa Fe, NM, USA

Hopi House, Grand Canyon National Park, AZ, USA, c.1905

Sybil Connolly

1921, Swansea, UK
1998, Dublin, Republic of Ireland

Merrion Square House, Dublin, Republic of Ireland, 1978

After training in London, fashion designer Sybil Connolly returned to Ireland in 1939 when World War II broke out. She initially assumed an executive role in a Dublin fashion shop before moving into a creative position, where her designs caught the attention of Carmel Snow, the influential American publicist and editor of *Harper's Bazaar*. Snow was impressed by Sybil's inventive use of traditional Irish fabrics like Donegal tweed and Belfast linen, which Sybil accomplished by working directly with women weavers to innovate a combination of fibers that could achieve the fine, light fabric she envisioned. Snow shared Sybil's designs with her American audiences, which led to many new American clients traveling to Dublin to purchase Sybil's creations. Her full-length red Kinsale cape and white crocheted evening dress were featured on the cover of *Life Magazine*, further boosting her popularity in the United States. She favored bright colors such as lime green and orange. A major career highlight came when American First Lady Jacqueline Kennedy's chose a Sybil Connolly design for her official White House portrait. Sybil's Georgian townhouse on Merrion Square, known affectionately as "the house that linen built," became both a showroom for her couture as well as for her interior designs, which included textured fabric-like wallpapers and antique furniture.[37] Sybil believed clothes should be well-loved, not trend-driven, and as tastes shifted toward the rise of miniskirts, her influence in fashion waned. Sybil pivoted to focus on interiors, penning books on Irish homes and gardens and Irish craft traditions, and designing tableware for Tiffany & Co. as well as glassware for Tipperary Crystal.

Furniture, lighting, and interior designer Gloria Cortina has been passionate about design since childhood. From a young age, she constantly rearranged her own bedroom, and displayed curiosity about how others decorated their homes. She works with light and shadow to create highly conceptual interiors, as can be seen in her project, Acut, where she has selected sculptural furniture with hard lines made from reflective materials like metal and velvet in a dramaturgy of light and space. Much of the furnishings in her interiors are her own pieces, influenced by various sources from Mayan artifacts to Mexico's Arts and Crafts heritage including her Golden Universe Obsidian table and stone-based spherical dining table. Her designs are sensually sophisticated and emotionally engaging, with beautifully crafted individual pieces that have significantly raised international awareness of Mexican culture in contemporary design. This deep appreciation for balance and beauty in her work can be traced back to her husband's great aunt, Inés Amor, the legendary founder of the Galería de Arte Mexicano, Mexico City's first gallery of modern art. Inspired by Inés, Gloria moved to New York, studied at the Parsons School of Design, and worked with architect David Ling. At her salon spaces in Mexico City and New York, Gloria focuses on expressing a Mexican aesthetic language with sculptural furnishings crafted from bronze, obsidian, and quartz.

Gloria Cortina

1972, Bethesda, MD, USA

Acut residence, Mexico City, Mexico, 2018

Ilse Crawford

1962, London, UK

Ett Hem Hotel, Stockholm, Sweden, 2012 and expanded 2022

Studioilse, founded in 2003 by designer Ilse Crawford, is renowned for blurring the lines between art, architecture, and design. With little formal training apart from having grown up in a bohemian household, Ilse entered the design world through stints copy-editing for magazines like the *Architects' Journal*. She later became an editor at *The World of Interiors*, eventually rising to deputy editor. Ilse went on to become the founding editor for the British version of *Elle Décoration*, where she employed unorthodox methods like conducting photoshoots in the streets rather than the studio. She quickly built a reputation as a designer who could mix the affordable with the special, eliciting beauty from everyday things. Ilse's career took her to New York, where she led and inaugurated Donna Karan's home division, catching the attention of private member's club Soho House's owner Nick Jones. Nick invited her to redesign the interiors of Babington House in Frome, Somerset. Ilse applied her signature style to Ett Hem hotel in Stockholm, infusing the space with her easygoing yet crisp aesthetic, combining carefully sourced antiques with her own custom furniture to choreograph an experience that "goes way beyond interior design to make a strong emotional impact."[38] Her work has always focused on the well-being of the people who use it, a philosophy she taught for twenty years as the leader of the Man and Wellbeing course at the Design Academy Eindhoven.

Rose Cumming, the last of an era of lady decorators, hailed from humble beginnings on a sheep farm in Australia. Despite her background, she developed a taste for splendor, creating vibrant rooms rich in color and texture, often punctuated by a surrealist twist such as birdcages, images of snakes, and Indian parasols used as lampshades. In 1917 she moved to America with her sister Dorothy, a silent film actress, through whom she met *Vanity Fair* editor Frank Crowninshield, who introduced her to decorating. When asked if she wanted to be a decorator—without knowing what it entailed—Rose embraced the challenge, and soon opened a decorating and antiques shop on the corner of Park Avenue and 59th Street. This shop, which also served as the headquarters for her decorating business, remained under her leadership for over forty-five years. Rose was an innovator with a flair for marketing. She was the first New York shopkeeper to keep her store lights on at night, though she distrusted electricity and lit her townhouse entirely with black candles. Her theatrical interiors were as spirited as she was, mixing baroque Gothic, Venetian, Austrian, and East Asian elements. Bold colors and patterns defined her work, such as in her own home library which boasted emerald green walls, scarlet lacquered chairs, and a peacock blue satin sofa. She was also the first to invent metallic wallpapers, including the "zebrine" paper used at New York's El Morocco nightclub.

Rose Cumming

1887, NSW, Australia
1968, New York, NY, USA

Cumming Residence, New York, NY, c.1929

Kana Cussen

1982, Santiago, Chile

Casa FOA, Santiago, Chile, 2017

Kana Cussen is a designer and co-founder of Grisanti & Cussen, a prominent interior design studio based in Santiago. Founded in 2007 with architect Hugo Grisanti, the studio has developed an impressive portfolio, designing spaces across a range of industries including hospitality, retail, corporate, cultural, and residential projects. Kana's approach to design centers on blending contrasting elements to create spaces that tell unique stories. In one project, Casa Foa, Kana and Hugo merged the concepts of a library and a bar, transforming the space into a functional yet artful environment, complete with deep green walls and blue velvet furnishings that they describe as feeling "like an art installation."[39] The duo's interiors are often immersive, with high octane, bold aesthetics, that draw on the color-blocking techniques of the Italian Memphis Group, while also paying homage to the elegance of Art Deco and the eclecticism of Postmodernism, by including playful shapes throughout their spaces. They state that part of their design philosophy is to prioritize "experience via the senses," approaching each project with a focus on how it will create an experience that resonates with users and their bodies.[40] Rather than adhering to a specific style, Kana incorporates elements from past and present, crafting interiors that surprise and engage, each one boasting a distinctive personality aimed at fostering a memorable connection between people and their surroundings.

Aline Asmar d'Amman

Beirut, Lebanon

Salon Marie Antoinette, Hôtel de Crillon, Rosewood, Paris, France, 2017

Lebanese and Parisian designer Aline Asmar d'Amman is known for her luxurious interiors. Born in Beirut, Aline trained as an architect at the Lebanese Academy of Fine Arts, graduating top of her year. Her success garnered her attention, and her love for French culture led her to move to Paris. After a collaboration with a prestigious French architect Jean-Michel Wilmotte she founded her own design studio Culture in Architecture in 2011. Within two years, Aline was invited by the owner of the Hôtel de Crillon, Rosewood Paris, to oversee the renovation of its eighteenth-century interiors. The historic hotel, overlooking the Place de la Concorde, appealed to Aline's extravagant design sensibility. As the artistic director for the renovation, she collaborated with celebrated fashion designer Karl Lagerfeld, among others, to create a lavish, palatial setting inspired by Marie-Antoinette's "sense of whimsy."[41] Precious materials—particularly Aline's favorite, marble—adorn every surface, with no expense spared, including a swimming pool lined with gold tiles. While Aline's tastes tend toward refined artistry with a narrative force, she is an avid seeker of beauty everywhere, and can be found hunting for treasures in Paris's antique markets on weekends with her family.

Barbara D'Arcy

1928, New York, NY, USA
2012, Southampton, NY, USA

Cardboard Room, Bloomingdale's, New York, NY, USA, 1973

Growing up near Bloomingdale's, Barbara D'Arcy developed a keen eye, influenced by walks through the city with her parents admiring antique furniture. In the early 1960s, Bloomingdale's was a hub for fashion-forward New Yorkers seeking the latest interior decorating trends. Barbara, with an art degree from the College of New Rochelle, joined the company as a fabric consultant, and quickly succeeded Henrietta Granville in creating model rooms featuring furniture from all over the world, in the process attracting a sophisticated clientele and becoming one of the most accomplished visual merchandisers of our era. Barbara popularized modern furnishing trends such as glass-topped tables and decorating rooms with orange and purple. In her 1974 book, *Bloomingdale's Book of Home Decorating*, she famously stated, "I like Lavender and Orange. Together."[42] She developed furniture collections and sourced ideas from France, Italy, and India, often distressing new pieces to mimic the patina of antiques. Her most notable design was for Bloomingdale's black marble interior, inspired by the Lake Palace Hotel in Udaipur, India. Barbara's room designs were often cinematic, including one space made entirely of cardboard with the architect Frank Gehry. The drama and consistency of her designs made them effective backdrops for displaying products. Barbara remained with Bloomingdale's for forty-three years, becoming vice president before retiring in 1995.

Alex Dauley

1983, Cardiff, UK

South London Home, London, UK, 2022

British interior designer Alexandria Dauley moved to London at age nineteen and built a successful early career in property management, which exposed her to beautifully designed homes across the city, before transitioning into design in her thirties. Originally from Wales, as a child she was inspired by her stylish mother's independent fashion sense and interest in furniture, which nurtured Alex's own passion for design. After renovating her own home and working on projects for family and friends, Alex pursued formal training at the KLC School of Design in London. She benefited greatly from the mentorship of her design tutor, Evey Dunbavin-Hands, for whom she later worked. Alex's South London home project exudes sophisticated warmth. Dark-toned walls create a striking backdrop for a mix of modern and vintage furniture. Emphasizing the home's Edwardian features, Alex incorporates contemporary silhouettes and adds playful touches such as a white fur-upholstered armchair. In 2020, Alex co-founded United in Design with designer Sophie Ashby, an organization aimed at making interior design an accessible career choice for those from underrepresented backgrounds, stating that "We want to open doors, educate, and create a truly inclusive industry that celebrates people from all ethnic backgrounds. Design is for everyone and all should be welcome."[43] Additionally, Alex is a presenter on Channel 4's *The Great Home Transformation*, for which she redecorates homes across the United Kingdom.

Elsie de Wolfe

1865, New York, NY, USA
1950, Versailles, France

Tea House, Planting Fields, Oyster Bay, NY, USA, 1916

At the turn of the twentieth century, successful Broadway actress Elsie de Wolfe reinvented herself as a pioneering interior decorator. Known for her individuality and colorful personality, at the height of her fame Elsie published *The House in Good Taste*, though it was ghostwritten by fellow decorator Ruby Ross Wood. Elsie's signature style rested on creating light, intimate spaces that brought a romantic touch to modern design. She is credited with professionalizing the role of the interior decorator and stirred controversy, often due to her private life. Despite being married, Elsie lived openly with theatrical and literary agent Elisabeth Marbury. Her first interior project in 1896 was the redecoration of their home together on East 17th Street. Advocating for a simpler and more coherent approach to decorating, many of Elsie's early projects were spaces frequented by women, such as the Colony Club and Brooks Hall. She became known for using practical yet eclectic furniture, signaling her interest in maintaining continuity with the past. Male critics rejected her framing of interiors as feminine spheres, and she wrestled with the criticism of her attachment to romantic and historical styles. Elsie had a keen eye for branding. She cleverly used an image of a wolf to promote her work and appeared in *Vogue*. Historicized as the founder and matriarch of the interior decorating industry, Elsie's appeal lay in her accessibility to the many women who modeled themselves on her success.

Pallavi Dean's interior design career draws influence from her rich and diverse cultural background. With roots in India, Pallavi grew up in the U.A.E., before going on to study in the U.S., and subsequently beginning her career in London. She studied architecture at the American University of Sharjah and interior design in the U.S. at the Savannah College of Art and Design. Her fascination with the ways in which architecture can shape human behavior, chiefly discovered through observing religious spaces, laid the foundation for her design philosophy, which is centered around a deep understanding of the user experience within buildings. This empathetic perspective was so important to her that she even hired a psychologist for one of her projects. After gaining experience in London, she returned to Dubai and founded her own studio, originally named Pallavi Dean Interiors, which she later renamed ROAR to emphasize collaboration within the team. ROAR is known for its scientific evidence-based and data-driven research, which it expresses artistically through design. This can be seen in the design of ORA, Nursery of the Future where Pallavi referenced research that suggested that children learn in calmer environments, without bold colors. For ORA she balanced a minimal aesthetic with textured cork and concrete surfaces, creating areas for analog activities as well as "digital play."[44] Typical of her designs, the space engages the senses and prioritizes well-being.

Pallavi Dean

1981, Mumbai, India

ORA, Nursery of the Future, Dubai, UAE, 2018

Chiara Di Pinto and Arianna Lelli Mami

1975, Desio, Italy
1976, Milan, Italy

Private residence, Milan, Italy, 2020

Multidisciplinary design duo Arianna Lelli Mami and Chiara Di Pinto bring a fresh, contemporary aesthetic to their work, reimagining Italian mid-century modern design for the twenty-first century. Having both studied at the Politecnico di Milano, they reconnected after graduation serendipitously in a chance meeting while on separate vacations in Mexico, and decided to explore collaborating upon their return home founding Studiopepe. Arianna and Chiara started to conceive cover stories for renowned interior magazines in Italy and abroad and to collaborate as creative directors for design brands.[45] After a few years the studio opened a new branch specializing in interior and product design, imagining iconic pieces and exquisite interiors for brands and private clients. Together they have evolved their design aesthetic by experimenting with playful, unusual juxtapositions of form and color. Their design for a Milan apartment features a chair upholstered in light pink and a fluorescent orange patterned rug set against walls painted dark brown. Surprising detailing such as gold-leafed casework to frame the living room entryway hearken to the 1930s, while a salon-like arrangement of artworks on the walls shows their skill at styling spaces. As in many of Arianna and Chiara's projects, the apartment features bespoke furniture pieces alongside design classics, demonstrating their reverence for Italian design.

Nicole Dohmen

1972, Limburg, The Netherlands

Private residence, outside Amsterdam, The Netherlands, 2022

Amsterdam-based interior designer, Nicole Dohmen honed her recognizable style by first refurbishing her own home, then designing interiors for her friends, who were impressed by Nicole's work on her own space. In 2018, with no formal training in design, she founded her studio, Atelier ND Interiors. Transitioning from a career in fashion—working with brands like Diesel and Adidas—to interiors, she credits her knowledge of photography for her richly saturated, colorful, and layered aesthetic. For the home of actors Carice van Houten and Guy Pearce, located just outside Amsterdam, Nicole created a kaleidoscopic interior, covering every surface in color and pattern, ranging from avocado green carpeting and deep eggplant walls to sunshine yellow cupboards and psychedelic floral wallpapers. She embraces bold contrasts juxtaposing graphic stripes with luminous candy pink and olive sofas and striking artworks, creating playful interiors that are both witty and understated, but always luxurious. She loves to foreground her spaces with warm hues, pairing dusty pinks, bright corals, brick reds, and cinnamon browns, to ensure a cozy, inviting atmosphere. Combining these robust color selections with organic forms and vintage finds, Nicole articulates, "I want to make interiors softer, with fewer hard lines."[46] Textiles play a significant role in creating her signature warmth, from wall coverings and carpets to framed tapestries and prints.

Olayinka Dosekun-Adjei

1987, Lagos, Nigeria

BAMBU Beach House, Ilashe, Lagos, Nigeria, 2023

Founder of Nigerian architecture and design practice Studio Contra, Olayinka Dosekun-Adjei has an international background, having studied classics at the University of Oxford and architecture as a Kennedy Scholar at Harvard University's Graduate School of Design. Olayinka began her career as a financial analyst in London before making the transition to architecture, and gained experience working at large firms including Barkow Leibinger in Berlin and MASS Design in Boston. While working at acclaimed architecture practice Sheppard Robson in London, Olayinka met her partner Jeffrey Adjei, with whom she would go on to form Studio Contra, their joint practice aimed at disrupting and challenging design norms. They established their studio in Lagos, drawn to the dynamism of the city, and have since built an extensive portfolio of projects across both the residential and public sectors. Olayinka's designs are rooted in the intersection of culture and craft, taking special interest in the synthesis between African architectural traditions and contemporary material and technological innovations. The interiors of BAMBU beach house include carefully crafted, modern furniture made from a range of local woods which contrast the minimal lines of the home's architecture. In addition to her studio practice, Olayinka has been a visiting faculty member at her alma mater, Harvard's GSD, and a guest critic at the University of Johannesburg GSA.

Dorothy Draper

1889, Tuxedo Park, NY, USA
1969, Cleveland, OH, USA

Greenbrier Hotel, White Sulphur Springs, WV, USA, 1948

Dorothy Draper, known for her exuberant and daring colors, established the first professional interior design company in the United States, the Architectural Clearing House, in 1923. Born into wealth, she sought to break from the period styles of her upbringing. Despite having no formal training, her unique "Modern Baroque" style quickly gained recognition, earning her prestigious commissions from clients such as the Metropolitan Museum of Art and the Quitandinha Palace in Brazil.[47] Dorothy disrupted gender norms by transforming interior decorating into a respected career for women. However, she found domestic projects restrictive due to her clients' demanding tastes and preferred designing public spaces. Her best-known work was in hospitality, where she created sumptuous hotel lobbies, restaurants, and bars employing the maximalist, multi-color schemes for which she became famous. Her signature bold color combinations included eggplant and pink, turquoise and vermillion, and her favorite: dull white with shiny black. She also loved to pattern-mix, pairing graphic stripes with decorative chintz. Her company, later rebranded as Dorothy Draper & Company, thrived as she became a tastemaker of the 1920s and 1930s, a role which found form and a wide audience in her regular column for *Good Housekeeping* magazine. Her grand, surreal interiors were visually stunning yet comfortable, with a design philosophy centered on enhancing a room's mood through play and whimsy. This style was epitomized by the 1948 renovation of the Greenbrier Hotel in West Virginia, where a vibrant red-and-green palette was festooned with large-scale plaster ornamentation, culminating in a lavish three-day opening party and an iconic interior style that endures to this day.

Sophie Dries

1986, Paris, France

Sophie's home, Paris, France, 2021

Paris-based designer Sophie Dries gained extensive experience working for celebrated designers, including Jean Nouvel, Pierre Yovanovitch, and Christian Liaigre, before founding her eponymous studio in 2014. She studied architecture at École Nationale Supérieure d'Architecture de Paris-Malaquais and contemporary art at the École du Louvre. However, it was her move to Finland to study at Aalto University that shifted her interest toward interior and furniture design. Inspired by the country's handcraft-steeped design history, she began working in an experimental way with ceramics, wood, and glass, continuing to foster close relationships with artisans to realize her designs. Sophie associates her approach to materials with her early childhood interest in chemistry, likening design to a chemically transformative process. This is reflected in the interior of her own home, a classic Haussmannian apartment, where Sophie makes use of the space's archetypal features, including floral ceiling moldings and wall paneling as a backdrop for her family's collection of contemporary furniture. The apartment feels akin to an art gallery, with each object acting as sculpture to emphasize the negative space between them. Her work echoes historic art movements such as Arte Povera, which Sophie cites as inspiration for her use of humble, natural materials like raw wood, stone, and metal. Sophie's success has allowed her to expand into producing her own range of rugs and ceramics.

Nathalie and Virginie Droulers

1973, Milan, Italy
1973, Milan, Italy

Private residence, Milan, Italy, 2021

The iconic sixteenth-century Hotel Villa d'Este on Lake Como, owned by Nathalie and Virginie Droulers's family, provided the backdrop for the twins' design education. Surrounded by rich fabrics and handcrafted furniture, the pair both chose to pursue careers in design, inspired by their mother's care for the interiors of the villa.[48] Virginie studied graphic design at Parsons School of Design in New York, while Nathalie moved to Milan to study architecture at the Politecnico di Milano. After a stint working together in New York, the sisters decided to found their studio, Droulers Architecture, together in Milan, joining their complementary creative forces: Nathalie interprets the architectural qualities of a space while Virginie artfully curates the details. Their strong and often opposing points of view allow the twins to contribute different qualities to a project, finding common ground in the exchange of ideas. Having grown up in the midst of some of Italy's most famed architecture, from Como's Rationalism to Villa d'Este's Classicism, Nathalie and Virginie mix styles from different eras and from across the world. The interiors of their project in Milan deploy a warm palette of soft pinks, with oversized sofas anchoring walls clad in an effulgent floral wallpaper. In this project, Nathalie and Virginie offset their classic aesthetic with a large fluorescent pink artwork by Anish Kapoor that hangs above the fireplace, demonstrating their ability to layer old and new.

Marika Dru

1980, Paris, France

Henri Martin II, Paris, France, 2023

Understated luxury defines the interiors of Marika Dru, founder of the Paris-based studio Atelier MKD. After graduating from the Penninghen architecture school in Paris, she worked for six years at interior design firm GBRH in Paris and Studio Charlotte Macaux Perelman in New York before establishing her own practice, Atelier MKD, in 2008. Marika's design philosophy centers on clean lines, uncluttered volumes, and classical symmetries. In her project, Henri Martin II, an apartment in Paris, Marika played with the scale of the windows and tall ceiling heights, emphasizing its Art Deco features while introducing tall curved alcoves throughout to update and soften the space. She achieves her serene atmospheres by using warm beiges, whites, and chocolate tones as a neutral backdrop for the natural wood millwork and furniture that detail each space. Her designs maintain coherence through the repetition of materials, patterns, and textures. This is evident in her tactile furnishings, such as the voluminous bouclé-covered cream armchairs, honey-colored wood chairs and graphically veined marble coffee table that recur in her projects. While primarily known for her residential interiors, Marika has also made her mark in the fashion world. She designed the Paris showroom for Uruguayan-American fashion designer Gabriella Hearst, incorporating cashmere from Gabriella's clothing line into the display cases.

Given the number of retrospectives celebrating Charles and Ray Eames, it is astonishing that Ray is often overlooked as the author of their most recognizable works, from their playful Eames Elephant chair to their iconic Plywood Group furniture. When they moved to Los Angeles in the late 1940s, Charles worked as a film set designer for MGM while Ray refined their technique for bending plywood. This innovation earned them a contract with the U.S. Navy making plywood medical splints for use in World War II. With access to enhanced military technology and manufacturing resources, the Eameses further honed their skill with the material, leading to the creation of their acclaimed bent plywood chairs. Ray was instrumental in designing *La Chaise*, featured in MoMA's 1951 *Good Design* exhibition, although Charles was the only one credited. Ray trained at the Art Student League of New York and the Cranbrook Academy, where she met Charles and rejected disciplinary boundaries. This ethos coalesced in the design of their home, Case Study House 8, part of a series of low-cost homes sponsored by *Arts & Architecture* magazine. Their house outside Santa Monica became an expression for their shared vision for modern living, featuring an interior where modularity and moveability were central. Students would visit at night to admire it, so Charles and Ray left a note on a bookcase explaining that they were still working on the layout, and would correct the position soon.

Ray Eames

1912, Sacramento, CA, USA
1988, Los Angeles, CA, USA

Case Study House 8, Los Angeles, CA, USA, 1949

Frances Elkins

1888, Milwaukee, WI, USA
1953, San Francisco, CA, USA

Casa Amesti, Monterey, CA, c.1919

Frances Elkins, an influential West Coast decorator, was inspired by her extensive travels across Europe with her older brother, David Adler, who at the time was studying architecture at the École des Beaux-Arts in Paris. Together, they explored the continent's cathedrals, castles, and stately homes, befriending many European avant-garde artists along the way. After three years abroad, Frances returned to the United States and settled in Monterey, California, where she renovated her new marital home, a nineteenth-century manor house called Casa Amesti. Collaborating with her brother, who had established an architecture office in Chicago, the siblings created dramatic interiors swathed in saturated colors, including Frances's favorites, blue, yellow, and white. They blended French and English period furniture with classical American detailing such as molded cornicing and redwood floors. Casa Amesti showcased Francis's skills as a decorator, leading to commissions from wealthy families in Pebble Beach. By the 1920s, she was the go-to consultant for style and decoration, advising clients on everything from table settings to flower arrangements. Through her brother's connections, Frances began designing interiors for projects in the Midwest and opened a workshop to produce her designs. David and Frances continued to travel together throughout their lives, becoming the first to import French country antiques to the United States.

Eugenia Errázuriz

1860, Bolivia
1951, Santiago, Chile

Eugenia's home, Paris, France, c.1900

Eugenia Errázuriz, a patron of modernism in Paris during the Belle Époque, was the matriarch of simplicity, famously declaring, "Throw out and keep throwing out."[49] When she was five, her family moved from Bolivia to Chile, where she grew up in a wealthy household and was educated by English nuns in the Chilean hilltop town of Valparaíso. In 1882, she married and moved to Paris, where she pioneered interiors focused on elegance and comfort. She stripped back historic moldings, left walls bare, and incorporated iron garden furniture into upper middle class drawing rooms. Her Biarritz home, with its whitewashed walls and terracotta tiles, inspired celebrities like photographer Cecil Beaton, who credited Eugenia with inventing the modern interior. Part of an artistic avant-garde, Eugenia was admired by painter John Singer Sargent, for whom she sat, and was also close with Pablo Picasso, supporting him as a patron and showcasing his work in her interiors. Fashion designer Elsa Schiaparelli also benefited from Eugenia's eye, using a shocking pink tone Eugenia shared from Chile in her collection. A minimalist ahead of her time, Eugenia's home on Avenue Montaigne was featured in *Harper's Bazaar* in 1938, showing her austere tastes that concealed rather than displayed bourgeois "bric-a-brac."[50] Despite her wealth, Eugenia preferred her home to look "very poor."[51] She commissioned Le Corbusier to build her a house in Chile, but the project was unrealized.

Mica Ertegun

1926, Bucharest, Romania
2023, Southampton, NY, USA

Private residence, USA, c.1970s

Vanity Fair dubbed Mica Ertegun the "virtual definition of sophistication."[52] However, her ascent to interior design as a doyenne and New York socialite was not without its trials. Fleeing postwar communism as a Romanian refugee, Mica lost her aristocratic status and wealth. She supported herself through modeling in Paris and, with the help of friends, emigrated to Canada, where she worked as a chicken farmer. Despite her poverty, Mica strived to make her home attractive, believing personal taste trumped wealth—although ironically, her later designs would be defined by opulence and luxury. She later married Ahmet Ertegun, founder of Atlantic Records, and moved to New York to enroll in decorating school. In 1967, she founded her interior design company, MAC II, with her friend Chessy Rayner. For more than forty years, they designed luxury homes across the Americas, Europe, and the Middle East, using unusual materials like straw and fabric on walls. Mica favored blocked colors, creating elegant interiors designed more like art galleries to serve as backdrops for large-scale artworks. MAC II also designed commercial spaces, including the redecoration of Saks Fifth Avenue's fifth floor, which entailed the installation of an interior "street" of shops. Deeply influenced by her knowledge of history, music, languages, and literature, Mica generously donated her amassed wealth, including a $41 million gift to Oxford University, earning her a CBE (Commander of the British Empire) honor in 2017.

Stefanie Everaert and Caroline Lateur

1975, Aalst, Belgium
1975, Brugge, Belgium

Lotje, Roeselare, Belgium 2023

Stefanie Everaert and Caroline Lateur are the founders of Doorzon Interior Architects. Their approach to interior design is rooted in interior architecture and they steer away from decorative excess to focus on the essence of spatial form. Both trained as interior architects—Stefanie at KASK School of Arts in Ghent and Caroline at KU Leuven Faculteit Architectuur Campus Sint Lucas Gent (formerly Sint-Lucas)—and met while working at the studio of renowned Belgian designer Maarten Van Severen. There, they gained hands-on experience crafting furniture and objects, which fostered their tactile understanding of materials and encouraged a broader awareness of design's social impact. Their studio name, Doorzon, is inspired by "Doorzonwoning" meaning "sun through," a Dutch modernist housing typology that maximizes sunlight by allowing it to pass through spaces fully, a principle reflected in their work.[53] Their interiors are defined by a sophisticated balance of modern and graphic elements, combining clean, minimal lines with an offbeat touch. Stefanie and Caroline are known for playing with contrasts, often bringing together poured polished concrete floors, natural woods, and soft textiles. Their bathrooms—an example of which can be seen in their project, Lotje—are particularly playful, featuring free-standing shower and sink elements finished in sky blue tiles, bold color blocks, and sculptural bathtubs that add surrealist touches to functional spaces. Alongside their practice, Stefanie and Caroline teach at KU Leuven, Ghent, Belgium and the Swiss Federal Technology Institute (EPFL) in Lausanne, sharing their expertise with the next generation of designers.

Zeynep Fadıllıoğlu

1955, Yeniköy, Turkey

Şakirin Mosque, Istanbul, Turkey 2009

Zeynep Fadıllıoğlu, a renowned Turkish interior designer, grew up in an Italian Palazzo in Yeniköy, on the European shore of the Bosphorus, surrounded by high-end objects and locally crafted pieces that sparked her love for fabrics and textures—a passion inherited from her family, who were deeply involved in the textile industry and antique collecting. She was encouraged by her father to pursue a career in design, so she studied art history and design at the Inchbald School of Design in London. Her career took off—she designed more than twenty restaurants and clubs for her husband, Metin Fadıllıoğlu, then a key figure in Istanbul's modern dining scene. These successes gave her the footing to found her own design company, Zeynep Fadıllıoğlu Designs, or ZF Designs, in 1995. Zeynep's work spans private residences, yachts, retail spaces, and office buildings. She is the first woman to design a modern mosque in Turkey (and possibly the world), the Şakirin Mosque in Istanbul. This modern, minimalist structure—nominated for the 2010 Aga Khan Award for Architecture—features glass layered with metal patterns inspired by the Qur'an rather than walls, allowing light to stream in and surround worshippers, and cast sun-shadows of the patterns throughout the space. She prioritized the prayer space for women, providing them the best view of the mihrab below a dome filled with light. Zeynep's design approach is nuanced and cross-cultural, blending Eastern and Western influences. Her work, from the Şakirin Mosque to luxury hotels and international restaurants, is timeless, impactful, and resonates with both local and universal appeal.

Architect Shahira Fahmy's design for the interiors of Lucida restaurant in Cairo exemplifies her interest in using organic materials deployed by local artisans to express the historical and cultural significance of a project. The restaurant's undulating palm-leaf structure, which adorns the walls of the space, washes the space in a pink glow and gives the interior a sculptural quality. This feature was completed by Cairo's Fel Warsha Studio, with all the finishes sourced locally. Shahira's mother was an interior designer, which influenced Shahira's interest in design. After training at the Faculty of Engineering at Cairo University and earning a master's degree in architecture, Shahira became a Loeb Fellow at the Harvard Graduate School of Design in 2015, later winning two additional fellowships there. More recently, after being asked to design a film set, Shahira developed an interest in acting, which she thinks of as parallel in practice to architecture. In her view, both disciplines involve understanding human behavior and how people move through space, and using this understanding to set a scene and tell a story. This perspective led to a successful renovation of the theater at the American University of Cairo, a career-making project that allowed her to establish her own office. A sensitive restoration of old mud-brick buildings into a boutique hotel for The Royal Commission for AlUla followed, solidifying her reputation as a leading design figure in Egypt.

Shahira Fahmy

1974, Cairo, Egypt

Lucida, Cairo, Egypt, 2023

Mary Featherston

1943, London, UK

National Gallery of Victoria, Melbourne, VIC, Australia, 1968

After migrating to Australia from England with her family in 1953 Mary Featherston studied at The Royal Melbourne Institute of Technology while working in the design studio of renowned furniture designer Grant Featherston, whom she later married. Together, they focused on creating furniture for mass-production, developing expertize in plastic molding and manufacturing. Their high-profile projects include the entire interior design for Australia's National Gallery of Victoria as well as various interior design projects for which they conceived and crafted the majority of the furniture. Mary's career took a significant turn when she became involved with the Community Child Care Association. She began designing child-centered learning environments that were research-based, involving extensive participatory design practices. Mary developed a model for an enriched play and learning environment that was home-like, with a kitchen at the core, linking together interconnected education and play spaces that each offered unique experiences. In 1972, she applied for a Commonwealth Fund to study children's play and learning environments. Her dedication to this field led to the creation of Australia's first museum for children in 1985. The Reggio Emilia Australia Information Exchange followed in 1995, and cemented her legacy in exploring the relationship between young people, modern learning theories, and the design of supportive physical environments.

Claudina Flores

1983, Guadalajara, Mexico

Arts and Crafts Workshop, Mexico City, Mexico, 2024

Claudina Flores's furniture and interiors come together through her sensitive use of material and color, deploying traditional craft techniques to create spaces that are "an invitation for reflection."[54] After gaining a degree in business and marketing, Claudina embarked upon design studies across the world: first, industrial design at Tecnológico de Monterrey in Guadalajara, followed by architecture and environmental design at The University of New South Wales in Sydney, and finally architectural and object lighting at Universitat Politécnica de Catalunya in Barcelona. She founded Estudio Claudina Flores in 2012, which excels at hospitality and residential interiors creating concepts that transform spaces into meaningful experiences. One of Claudina's standout projects, the Arts and Crafts Workshop, celebrates Mexican craftsmanship by highlighting the value of process and the integrity of raw materials. It honors traditional artisanship while inviting people to engage in a hands-on creative practice. The space fosters human connection, as crafting by hand sparks reflection and transforms reality. This project featured in "Design House" during Design Week Mexico, where architects and interior designers were invited to transform old properties into extraordinary spaces. Working primarily with natural materials, her designs prioritize context and function while also being engaging and tactile, and are often made locally. In addition to leading her design studio, Claudina has held teaching positions at the Tecnológico de Monterrey and the Escuela Superior de Arquitectura in Guadalajara.

Olga Fradina

1975, Kyiv, Ukraine

Dzen Space Club, Kyiv, Ukraine, 2020

Ukrainian designer Olga Fradina designs like a curator, layering fabrics, textures, unique furniture finds, and muted colors to make her spaces. Her keen eye for composition comes from a background in graphic design. She worked for a newspaper in Kyiv before joining the design studio Kolo, where she was able to hone her skills as a designer. With co-founder Lidiya Pfayfer, Olga started her own design studio Pfayfer & Fradina. Since 2014 she has completed residential interior design projects solo, including the reorganization of a compact apartment located on the top-floor in an ex-Soviet building in Kyiv. Olga united the spaces with dramatically dark, charcoal-colored walls, and furnished the apartment with her own mid-century modern-inspired furniture designs. The flow of the spaces, achieved by thoughtfully removing walls to create large open-plan rooms, is enhanced by traditional Ukrainian craft items. This design fosters a meditative atmosphere, making it an ideal home for wellness entrepreneur Kateryna Bakhirka. Kateryna also commissioned Olga to design Space, her wellness center in Kyiv. Here, monochrome interiors are accented by textured materials, including non-uniform tiles and rough plaster walls, enriching the space devoted to healing. Olga has recently diversified her interests, applying her skills as a designer to making ceramics, and has also become increasingly involved with digital art.

Rearranging the interiors of her room regularly from a young age, New Jersey-based designer Kesha Franklin was brought up surrounded by her father's vast collection of now iconic copies of *GQ* and *Architectural Digest*, crediting her parents for instilling in her an awareness of, and appreciation for, design. She worked as a backstage manager and wardrobe stylist for fashion houses, including Donna Karan, Vera Wang, and Lanvin, as well as being the production manager for Victoria's Secret Fashion Show for four years. Alongside her successful career in events and fashion, Kesha took on interior design commissions, eventually dedicating herself full-time to her studio, Halden Interiors, which creates designs that take inspiration from art and fashion. Early in her interior design career, she was tasked with designing the home of professional football quarterback Colin Kaepernick. Creating a place where he could entertain family and friends, she first thought that she would be designing what she refers to as an "ultra man cave."[55] However, upon meeting the sports star, she recognized his own eye for design, and quickly recalibrated her ideas to create an airy yet bold, eye-catching home filled with interesting furniture pieces, including a sculptural bronze coffee table to complement the home's daring color palette.

Kesha Franklin

1974, Brooklyn, NY, USA

Private residence, San Jose, CA, USA, 2015

Emanuela Frattini Magnusson

1959, Milan, Italy

Vineyard Family House, Tuscany, Italy, 2019

Based in New York, multifaceted Italian architect Emanuela Frattini Magnusson is the principal of her architecture firm EFM Design, which she founded in 1992. Specializing in residential and corporate interiors, Emanuela's expertise extends across various design disciplines including industrial and graphic designs. In addition to leading her own practice, she has served as the Global Head of Design at Bloomberg and founded the furniture company Artìcolo Studios. Born in Milan, Emanuela graduated in architecture from the Politecnico di Milano and holds an MBA from New York University's Stern School of Business. She has also served as a visiting faculty member at notable American schools of design including Parsons School of Design. Emanuela's design understanding is informed by her branding savvy, allowing her to use the spaces she designs to build the foundation for a brand's identity. In 2018, Emanuela collaborated with architect Pietro Todeschini on the design for a single-story villa in Tuscany built using local materials, including locally sourced Alberese stone. In contrast to the traditional vernacular of the exterior, the interiors are modern and sparse, featuring blocks of color and built-in oak paneled cabinetry. The stark simplicity of the interior has a graphic quality, with decorative elements introduced through handcut irregular terracotta tiles ("tozzetti") set in cement mixed with Carrara marble chips, inspired by a traditional Venetian flooring technique known as "seminato."

Dora Gad, born in Romania, graduated from the Technical University of Vienna in 1934. Two years later, she emigrated to Tel Aviv where she embarked upon numerous high-profile projects, including designing the interiors for the Knesset and the Israel Museum in Jerusalem. Dora's designs introduced an intimate, human scale to the monumental Knesset setting, conveying her signature simple and modest style through a reduced palette of materials and colors. Emerging as a leading design figure during the British Mandate and early years of the foundation of the Israeli state, her work played a crucial role in shaping the nation's image. She drew inspiration from local craft culture, deploying materials like wool, straw, and felt to make modern sculpted forms influenced by her European training. While mindful of the many different peoples coexisting in the state, her designs frequently invoked Zionist and biblical symbols. Throughout her career, Dora was a prolific collaborator. Initially, she worked with her husband, Heinrich Yehezkel Goldberg, and after his death, she partnered with her employee, Arieh Noy. Together they designed interiors for a wide range of clients, from luxury hotels to ships for Zim, Israel's commercial shipping company, as well as several airplanes for El Al. Dora's career peaked in 1966 when she received the Design Prize Regulo d'Oro from the Italian design magazine *Domus*, and became the first woman to win the Israel Prize in Architecture.

Dora Gad

1912, Câmpulung Moldovenesc, Romania
2003, Ceasarea, Israel

Chagall State Hall, Knesset, Jerusalem, Israel, 1966

Charu Gandhi

1979, Delhi, India

The OWO Raffles Residences, London, UK, 2023

Charu Gandhi, born in Delhi and educated in Singapore, was inspired to pursue architecture after witnessing the work of a female architect who designed her family home. Charu studied architecture at the Architectural Association in London, and worked with large international firms in her early career. However, it was her experience working for the developer Candy & Candy on London's One Hyde Park development that led to her interest in interior design. Launching her studio, Elicyon, in 2014, she has completed over one hundred projects. Her studio's name derives from blending the words "elysian" and "halcyon" to denote a sense of bliss and peacefulness. This philosophy is reflected in her work where pops of color are thoughtfully introduced through furnishings while large-scale artworks and objects frame different areas of a room; she is inspired by the history of the properties she designs and the unique personalities of those who inhabit them. Charu's designs embrace the decorative arts and have an affinity for the intricacy of details, often present in singular antiques she sources from around the world. Charu's keen eye for fine art and artisanal crafts makes for imaginative interiors that weave narrative and encourage fancy through compelling objects. Unencumbered by any one particular style, Charu favors designs that eschew trends, evident in the quiet and calm interiors of The OWO Raffles Residences in Whitehall, where she enlivened a serene living room with a 1940s inspired chandelier and a careful curation of artworks on paper.

Hanne Gathe

1982, Oslo, Norway

Hanne's home, Oslo, Norway, 2024

Norwegian designer Hanne Gathe studied Interior and Spatial Design at Chelsea College of Art and Design in London. She gained extensive experience while working for large-scale architecture firms, including Foster + Partners, where she designed villas, a yacht, and even a private jet. After spending eleven years in London and two in South Australia, she returned to Oslo and founded her own interior design studio. Later, she merged her company with Linda Gram Egede-Nissen to form their joint practice Gathe + Gram. Focused on high end residential and hospitality projects, Hanne is passionate about creating spaces that feel personal and cozy. Her style is international with Scandinavian influences, reflected through her use of restricted tonal color palettes, whether in neutral or more vibrant shades. Hanne prefers unique furniture, so she often designs and makes bespoke items or sources antique pieces, incorporating a variety of textiles in her interiors, including wool, velvet, leather, and silk. This approach can be seen in her own home, a classic building from 1898 featuring 10-foot (3-meter) high ceilings, original cornicing, and two wood-burning fireplaces. Using four different shades of white throughout, Hanne created the majority of her own furnishings, including the dining room table which she paired with reupholstered chairs from the 1960s.

Lauren Geremia

1982, Wallingford, CT, USA

Lauren's studio, San Francisco, CA, USA, 2023

San Francisco-based multidisciplinary designer Lauren Geremia brings a painterly approach to her interior designs. After studying painting at the Rhode Island School of Design, she began her career as an assistant to a film producer who also had an interior design company. There she quickly became adept at making selections and commissioning friends for fabrication and furniture making. Transitioning into the world of interiors, Lauren views design as a way to combine her passions for art, color, and photography, skills she has applied in corporate office projects for Silicon Valley startup clients like Dropbox, Instagram, and Lumosity. She installed sculptural light fixtures for these technology spaces and crafted custom furniture to enhance workplace ergonomics. At Lumosity, she included artworks sourced from artists working with the Creative Growth Art Center, a non-profit organization supporting artists experiencing disabilities. In her residential projects, Lauren starts with a narrative, often inspired by a specific artwork, aiming to infuse her designs with warmth and personality. She prioritizes function in her designs and layers art and furniture to create unexpected compositions. A significant aspect of her practice is her art consultancy, helping clients build art collections as a holistic part of planning their interiors. As an art collector herself, Lauren has a deep connection to the personal and conceptual nature of art, using her work to support a wide network of artists and makers.

Yasmine Ghoniem

1981, Kuwait City, Kuwait

Polychrome House, Cronulla, Sydney, NSW, Australia, 2018

Yasmine Ghoniem grew up in Kuwait, Saudi Arabia, and Sydney before moving to the United States to undertake postgraduate studies in interior design at the Savannah College of Art and Design. She went on to work in Portland, Oregon for an interior design studio, focusing on boutique hotels and private residences. Moving to Sydney, she initially pursued a music career, forming a band and supporting herself by working for an interior design studio by day. However, her growing success in design led her to partner with her sister, a landscape architect, to establish their own practice. In 2020 she launched her eponymous solo studio, YSG. Specializing in residential and hospitality design, Yasmine infuses spaces with whimsy, playing with dramatic proportions, assertive colors, and layered patterns. Her Polychrome House features her signature style, characterized by vibrant artwork, bespoke furniture, and colorful rugs. Black crazy pavers, usually an outdoor material, are deployed inside, creating a porous relationship between interior and exterior, while textured materials, including goat's hair, white cork, and clay brick are juxtaposed with large surfaces in primary colors. Yasmine's ability to unite these seemingly disparate objects is further evidenced by her inclusion of modular mid-century furniture to complement the 1960s architecture, exposing the existing brickwork to create a backdrop to set off the vibrant sofas and chairs in the home.

Sandra Githinji

1993, Kenya

CB2, Black in Design Collective, 2023

Sandra Githinji's curiosity in spatial design was shaped by her mother, who ran a family owned furniture store. Initially interested in painting and aspiring to a fine arts degree, Sandra was encouraged by her mother to pursue a more normative and stable career in design. She found a middle ground by studying interior design at RMIT University, blending vocational design with art history. Her interdisciplinary approach weaves together ethical, social, and political perspectives to create "intentional and impactful spaces." This results in a multifaceted practice that encompasses design, pedagogy, and research, all of which she explores as she pursues a practice-based PhD at RMIT University, where she also teaches as a sessional lecturer. Her teaching focuses on representing Black African women in academia and design, evolving an understanding of how decolonizing design can challenge colonial legacies. She was invited to contribute to CB2's Black in Design Collective, for which she designed furniture, lighting, and sculpture that are both functional and deeply symbolic, drawing from adornment, architecture, and stories of liberation. Inspired by the traditional Kikuyu *giturwa* (stool), crafted for women and central to the *nyumba* (home), the dome coffee table honors this heritage with a contemporary sensibility. For Sandra, personal identity is a key aspect of the designer's role, and she advocates for a pluralistic approach in what she calls a "constellation."[56] Resisting a singular narrative, her projects challenge the dominance of a "western-centric perspective […] through cultural expressions that centre an African perspective."[57] Her work artfully explores the fluidity of identity and belonging across a global Afrodiaspora.

Laura Gonzalez

1983, Paris, France

Gallery and showroom, New York, NY, USA, 2024

Classic, romantic, and fairytale atmospheres define Laura Gonzalez's design style, influenced by her upbringing in Cannes, where she was immersed in art and antiques, as well as by her father, a hotelier and restaurateur with Algerian roots. She founded her design studio while still a student at the Ecole Nationale Supérieure d'Architecture Paris-Malaquais, with time spent in China and studying in Venice also shaping her young business. Her first major commission was for the nightclub, Le Bus Palladium, where she showcased her trademark bohemian style and drew on her knowledge of hospitality interiors. Laura has imbued her diverse cultural influences into interiors for luxury brands such as Christian Louboutin and Cartier, including the redesign of Cartier's historic Fifth Avenue store in New York. In partnership with Cartier, in 2021 she designed the facade panels of the Women's Pavilion in Dubai, a monumental expanse of glittering geometries inspired by traditional mashrabiya latticework, meant to evoke the starry night sky. Laura describes her expressive maximalism as "chic mix and match," achieved through wall coverings like floral print cloth, playful neoclassical motifs, and bold washes of color, all of which can be seen in her own home, a nineteenth-century manor in Normandy in France.[58] She encourages other designers to be daring in mixing patterns, eras, styles, and cultural influences, which she demonstrates in her gallery and showroom in New York's Tribeca and on Paris's Left Bank, where she displays her own furniture. Her self-titled book was published in 2024.

Adrienne Górska de Montaut

1899, Moscow, Russia
1969, Beaulieu-sur-Mer, France

Tamara de Lempicka's residence, Paris, France, c.1930

In her early twenties, Adrienne Górska moved to Paris to study at the École Spéciale d'Architecture under modernist architect Robert Mallet-Stevens. Influenced by his functionalist approach, Adrienne began redesigning cinemas across France, working closely with her husband, Pierre de Montaut, whom she met at the French firm Molinié et Nicot. Embracing the materiality and aesthetics of the industrial age alongside Art Deco fashions of the day, Adrienne and Pierre referenced architecture for factories, cruise ships, and silos to create curved volumes for Cinéac movie theaters as emblems of technical progress. The cinemas featured advanced systems to maximize user comfort, reflecting a concern for environmental design. A notable design element was the visible projection area, enclosed in a glass booth to highlight the technical event inside. In 1931 Adrienne designed a residence and art studio for her sister, artist Tamara de Lempicka, featuring a custom bar replete with walnut furniture and polished nickel fixtures. Adrienne's austere style was showcased at the Union des Artistes Modernes exhibition in 1932. She presented a building she had designed in Neuilly, which critics described as "a neat job and a little cubist."[59] Adrienne narrowly escaped the Nazis when they invaded Poland in 1939. Little is known of her work after this date, but her designs remain significant for injecting industrial modernity into familiar interiors to achieve a progressive aesthetic.

Eileen Gray

1878, County Wexford, Ireland
1976, Paris, France

E-1027, Roquebrune-Cap-Martin, France, 1929

Eileen Gray was a twentieth-century polymath, skilled in painting, lacquer work, cabinet making, furniture design, and architecture. Raised in Ireland and educated at the Slade School of Art in London, Eileen moved to Paris seeking creative stimulation. There she met Evelyn Wyld, with whom she established a weaving studio in 1910, followed by her own gallery, Jean Désert, where she showed under a male pseudonym to disguise her gender. At the gallery, Eileen displayed her own designs, which included furniture and early lacquer work made with Eyre de Lanux, who, like Eileen, was a queer designer at the center of the city's flourishing modern art scene. Eileen's interiors broke conventions, as in her introduction of Japanese lacquer techniques to European silhouettes, and she shocked Paris with her entry of an entirely white lacquered boudoir to the 14th Salon des Artistes Décorateurs in 1923. Her first professional commission was a design for Madame Mathieu-Lévy's (also known as Suzanne Talbot) home at Rue de Lota. She layered lush textiles and furniture to achieve a sumptuous interior setting. In her forties, influenced by her partner and art critic Jean Badovici, she turned to architecture, creating her Mediterranean seaside villa masterpiece, E-1027. Eileen believed that the "house is only a shell of a man," emphasizing that the integration of interior elements makes it human in the most profound sense, challenging Le Corbusier's notion of a house as a machine for living.[60]

Greta Magnusson Grossman

1906, Helsingborg, Sweden
1999, San Diego, CA, USA

Trousdale House, Palm Springs, CA, USA, c.1948

Prominent in Los Angeles's celebrity social scene, Greta Magnusson Grossman is often remembered as an interior designer for Hollywood's elite. Moving to California in the early 1940s, Greta opened Studio, a store selling Scandinavian designs, including her own. The name was borrowed from her first store in Stockholm, where she had been a successful designer before emigrating to the United States. Her designs combined wood with metal, blending European modernist and traditional Swedish furniture-making traditions. Her interiors, such as for the Trousdale House featured on the cover of *House Beautiful* in 1949, appeared conservative but had unique, eccentric touches. Greta believed objects collected over time enriched any interior, emphasizing history and a sense of place. Her success lay in creating commercial yet creative interiors, advancing modernist ideas for the general public. Her talent shone in her room sets for Barker Brothers department store, where she designed model rooms that demonstrated whole-home designs for customers, rather than focusing on individual pieces. Greta promoted a lifestyle where home and work life overlapped, a concept ahead of its time that necessitated moveable furniture that could adapt spaces for different uses. She believed functionality, especially having ample storage, should pair with "happy colors," an approach that equated the importance of usability and joy in the home.

Camilla Guinness's interiors are known for their cozy, bohemian, and quintessentially British charm. She blends English countryside traditionalism with sun-soaked Tuscan influences, borrowed from the many years she spent living in Italy. This intermingling is best seen in her own home, a once-neglected property in the Tuscan countryside where her daughter Amber runs Arniano, a painting school. The simple, rustic furnishings and original architectural features exhibit Camilla's interest in comfort, as she states, "not in the luxury way but in the convivial sense."[61] Her style is cosmopolitan yet deeply romantic and whimsical, with an air of aristocratic tradition. Camilla began working with furniture after taking a restoration course in Florence. She brought to this discipline a keen eye for pattern and color, developed as a child watching her artist and fashion designer mother, Sally Uniacke, in her workshop. As a teenager, Camilla befriended Isabella Blow, who became a renowned magazine editor and style icon. The two shared an aesthetic kinship, and Camilla redesigned Isabella's London apartment, incorporating dramatic purple accents in an already colorful and texture-filled space. Theatrical touches, including baroque furniture and a family heirloom chandelier, contrasted with contemporary art and a neon text wall sculpture, making for a memorable, highly personal place.

Camilla Guinness

1963, London, UK

Isabella Blow's apartment, London, UK, 2006

Elsa Gullberg

1886, Malmö, Sweden
1994, Vaxholm, Sweden

Wood-paneled office, Sweden, c.1960s

Elsa Gullberg, a modernist reformer, was dedicated to making good design affordable to working-class people, believing everyone deserves access to beautiful things. Her extensive travels across Europe, including visits to the Wiener Werkstätte and Deutsche Werkstätten in Hellerau, inspired her to replicate artisan aesthetics through modern industrial processes. In 1917, she participated in the reorganization of the Swedish Society of Crafts and Design, fostering relationships between artists and manufacturers and promoting everyday objects made using emerging technologies. Elsa began her career as a textile designer at age seventeen. Seeking conventional employment, she moved to Stockholm to study at Konstfack, Sweden's leading design school, qualifying as a drawing instructor. She gained essential knowledge as an assistant to textile designer Lilli Zickerman, which afforded her trips throughout Europe. By the early 1920s she had become a successful textile designer and in 1927, she founded Sweden's first interior design studio, Elsa Gullberg Textil og Inredningar AB, which focused on carpet design, but crucially offered full interior design services, as Elsa understood clients needed to be able to situate her rugs within the larger context of a cohesive design. Her exhibits at high-profile events such as the World's Fair in New York in 1939 garnered international acclaim, establishing hers as one of Sweden's leading interior design firms.

Shabnam Gupta has become renowned for her interior designs for illustrious clients, including many Bollywood stars. Her first client was Bollywood producer-director Vidhu Vinod Chopra, followed by Aditya Chopra, the chairman of Yash Raj Films. Shabnam studied Interior Design at the L.S. Raheja School of Architecture in Mumbai, where she is also based. She began her career working for an architect before founding her own firm, The Orange Lane, in 2003. Although her approach is collaborative, Shabnam has always embraced a non-conformist style with a penchant for doing things out of the ordinary. She brings a daring eye for color and imaginative use of inspiration from nature and India's artisanal cultural heritage to inform her designs. She favors bright colors, saturating rooms entirely in shades of blue, orange, or pink, which she balances with a careful choice of high-quality traditional wooden furniture in an untreated finish. This can be seen in her work on the home of the late actor Irrfan Khan. In the actor's living room, she installed a swing and a pond made from blue stone sourced from Nepal. Much of the furniture for the project was produced by her company, Peacock Life, which she opened in Mumbai in 2010 and in Hyderabad in 2023 to promote contemporary designs that foreground traditional Indian crafts. The brand manufactures homeware products, including lighting and furniture, such as a bean-shaped sofa whose gentle curves reference the Sarayu river.

Shabnam Gupta

1974, Mumbai, India

The Khan's residence, Oshiwara, Mumbai, India, 2016

Racha Gutierrez and Dahlia Hojeij Deleuze

1994, Abidjan, Côte d'Ivoire
1993, Abidjan, Côte d'Ivoire

Private residence, Paris, France, 2024

Friends since their teenage years, Racha Gutierrez and Dahlia Hojeij Deleuze grew up together in Abidjan, Côte d'Ivoire. Both studied architecture in Paris, discovering their shared design philosophy and complementary way of working while collaborating on their diploma project. After graduation, they remained in Paris and began undertaking commercial and residential interior design commissions while launching their first twenty-piece furniture collection. They named their design studio Ebur after the Latin word for ivory, reflecting the duo's shared roots and upbringing in West Africa. Part of a Lebanese diaspora, their designs celebrate their rich cultural history, evoking forms and patterns widely used in furniture and lighting from across the Middle East as well as decorative elements drawn from twentieth-century Italian design. Racha and Dahlia collaborated with local craftspeople in France, Italy, and Lebanon to fabricate their furniture designs, which they incorporate into their interiors, including an apartment in Paris. They modernized the apartment's existing materials, using lime plaster on the walls and polished concrete for the floor, and enlarging the door openings to make them taller to create a feeling of openness. Custom wood millwork, including built-in shelving, give the rooms a functional yet materially rich feel.

Victoria Hagan

1961, New York, NY, USA

Kips Bay Decorator Show House, New York, NY, USA, 1990

Described by *The New York Times* as "cerebral," New York-based designer Victoria Hagan redefined interior decorating in the twenty-first century with a style that defies easy classification.[62] Victoria's dislike for how her parents decorated her childhood home made her an opinionated designer from an early age. She often rode her bike past the famed interior decorator Albert Hadley's home in Pocantico Hills, New York, just to catch a glimpse inside. Trained at Parsons School of Design, Victoria interned with renowned interior designer Simone Feldman, eventually becoming a partner in Feldman's firm in the late 1980s. Together, they created rooms they described as being "about ideas, not about decoration."[63] This philosophy was most evident in their 1990 Kips Bay Show House project, which embodied their interest in composition and symbolism. It features an antique toy plane and quotes lifted from Antoine de Saint-Exupéry's French novella *Le Petit Prince*. As a result it was celebrated in the press for its inclusion of narrative as a "salon of social consciousness."[64] Drawing connections between past and present, Victoria and Simone paired a mid-century Harry Bertoia metal chair with a Louis XVI settee, dotting objects invoking childhood around the room. After Feldman's passing, Victoria launched her own eponymous firm. She maintains a strong connection with Parsons, serving on its Board of Governors, and endowing an interior design scholarship in its Master of Fine Arts program.

Marion Hall Best

1905, Dubbo, NSW, Australia
1988, Darling Point, Sydney, NSW, Australia

A room for Mary Quant, Society of Interior Designers of Australia 'Rooms on View' exhibition, Sydney, NSW, Australia, 1967

It wasn't until her mid-thirties that Marion Hall Best began her career as a decorator, quickly becoming Australia's most daring designer, renowned for her confident use of color. Initially encouraged by her father to pursue nursing, Marion's interest in architecture led her to take private art classes with Thea Proctor and immerse herself in Arts and Crafts circles of the 1920s. She enrolled at the University of Sydney, earning her architecture degree in 1938, followed by a New York-based interior design course completed via correspondence. Marion's adventurous color schemes, tactile surfaces, and playful forms amounted to her signature style. She established a store on Queen Street in Woollahra, which rejected early twentieth-century chintz and drapery, ushering in a modern aesthetic as the world faced war. During World War II, Marion worked part-time in her store so she could also make parts for planes at the de Havilland factory, and donated all her business profits to charity. Her company, Spectrum Pty Ltd, co-directed with her son, manufactured many iconic designs under license, bringing modern style to Australian homes. She was the first to import modern designs by Eero Saarinen, Joe Colombo, and Robin Day, while exporting contemporary Australian design to the rest of the world. Co-founding the Society of Interior Designers of Australia in 1951, Marion was an industry leader with an era-defining aesthetic that resonated globally.

Rania Hamed

1969, Cairo, Egypt

Orijins café, Dubai, UAE, 2021

Now based in Dubai, interior architect Rania Hamed grew up in Cairo surrounded by fabric in her mother's fashion boutique. She moved to New York to study fashion merchandising at Parsons School of Design and after graduation relocated to Dubai, where she worked for major fashion labels, including Donna Karan and Max Mara. Disillusioned with the fashion industry, Rania retrained, enrolling as an undergraduate in an interior design program at the American University in Dubai. In 2007, she founded the design firm VSHD Design, which now has offices in Dubai and Montreal. Authenticity is important to Rania, who roots her designs in their local context through her choice of materials. She specializes in designing residential and commercial spaces, seeking to express narratives inspired by her clients. Her projects are often conceptually driven, as in her design for the coffee shop Orijins in Dubai, whose curved ceilings and creamy plaster walls are designed around a central assembly of dramatic marble and travertine counters carved to resemble boulders, which she states convey "the feeling of calm and serenity one gets when sitting on a rock by the sea."[65] The minimalist, monochrome color palette highlights what Rania describes as the "beautiful imperfections" in nature, referencing sand and shells found on the beach.[66] The relative quietude and simplicity of the color scheme allow focus to be placed on the textures and patterns inherent in the natural stone, wood, and textiles of the free-standing furniture pieces.

Olga Hanono

1975, Mexico City, Mexico

Private Residence, Upper East Side, NY, USA, 2019

Interior designer Olga Hanono views design as a medium for self-expression, inspired by her interest in fashion and art, which began at a young age. Originally trained in law, Olga shifted her focus to design, studying at Universidad Iberoamericana in Mexico City, the Nuova Accademia di Belle Arti in Milan, and Sotheby's Art Institute in New York. Based between Mexico City and Miami, her style is progressive and modern, showcased in her 2019 book *The Art of Beautiful Living* published by Assouline. For this book, Olga moved to New York for eighteen months in order to be directly involved with the editorial process. Such engagement reflects Olga's hands-on approach to making her work, which, while focused on interiors, includes designing and manufacturing her own furniture, textiles, and wallpaper collections, all of which display her imaginative vibrancy. Drawing on her Mexican home's culture and folklore, she expertly combines pattern, color, and texture together with carefully chosen art and objects. She often incorporates bold, saturated hues like purple and her signature dark teal, departing from recent minimalist trends and the predominant use of white in modern Mexican interiors.[67] She describes color as the "most important layer" in her design process, applied last to bring coherence to a space.[68] In addition to her own designs, Olga has created a range of porcelain lamps for the lighting brand, Lladró. She has recently completed a master's degree in innovation, creativity and design at the Future London Academy in London.

Elizabeth Hay

1983, Devon, UK

Private residence, Singapore, 2021

Growing up in a creative family in rural Devon, designer Elizabeth Hay relocated to Singapore in 2013, where she has led her eponymous interior design firm for over a decade. Her circuitous journey to design started with a degree in philosophy, followed by stints working in advertising and fashion. Her design career began at Colefax and Fowler, followed by a role at Veere Greeney, both experiences cementing Elizabeth's love of interior design. She has since evolved her own highly recognizable aesthetic, which is quintessentially English yet imbued with patterns and colors inspired by her travels across Asia. Elizabeth researches local textiles and craft practices in the places that she visits, meeting local fabricators off the beaten track in search of items that are unique and beautiful to use in her projects. Elizabeth's use of antique and contemporary objects and furniture creates interiors that feel like intricately layered and joyful collages. This makes for spirited designs, rich with color and pattern, often featuring illustrations of plants and animals. Her highly decorative designs manage to be multicultural yet stylistically coherent. Projects like Thimphu showcase her signature bohemian-meets-countryside aesthetic, achieved through hand-painted walls and the use of warm, pastoral colors like sunset pink and cornflower blue.

Cecil Hayes

1945, Malone, FL, USA

Oceanfront condominium, USA, 1980s

Hailing from a hardworking Floridian family, at a young age, Cecil Hayes understood the importance of academic excellence. She studied art education at Florida A&M University in Tallahassee, and embarked on a career as an art teacher for a federal education program designed to integrate schools in Georgia. However, she always had an interest in art and design, and credits the women in her family for inspiring her to go back to study at the Art Institute of Fort Lauderdale. Cecil viewed interior design as more than just decoration, seeing it as a complex puzzle and art form. As a Black designer in a community where design clients were overwhelmingly white, Cecil encountered difficulty finding work, so began her career cataloging books for the library at Santa Stevens Interior Designs.[69] In 1975, with only a $6,000 loan, she took a leap and started her own business, Cecil's Designs Unlimited. Lacking industry contacts, Cecil opened a storefront to gain visibility, and began manufacturing custom pieces, taking her entire design process in-house. Her first big break was designing the interiors of actor Wesley Snipes' Florida home which has led to many other commissions in the sports and entertainment industry. Cecil has curated a number of exhibitions and published several books to illustrate the African roots of modern design and she was the interior designer for the African-American Research Library and Cultural Center in Fort Lauderdale, Florida.

The technicolor interiors of Ana Milena Hernández Palacios highlight the Colombian-born designer's skill in suffusing a space with a specific mood. The interiors of her own home and studio in Valencia lyrically merge light blue and green rooms with accents of pink, yellow and pistachio, while her artful use of eggplant tones throughout elevate the kaleidoscopic effect. Unusual, sculptural furniture, such as her bright green egg-shaped bed frame and oversized pyramidal dining chairs, are custom-made by her sister company, the lifestyle brand Mas Creations. While her interiors would not look out of place in an art gallery, her energetic approach to staging a room invokes a sense of playfulness and comfort. Her mother, a floral designer, was an early inspiration, introducing Ana to the world of decoration. Today, she focuses on how color and texture can affect people's emotions within a space.[70] After studying interior design in Valencia, and with the support of her partner Christophe Penasse, Ana set up her own design studio, Masquespacio, in 2010. The duo transformed a traditional farmhouse in Valencia with playful chromatic interiors, using floor to ceiling curtains in powdery purples, pinks, and greens to create pleated wall surfaces. They furnished each room with bespoke objects including, notably, a green and yellow dome that engulfs their bed. The studio has since designed interiors for residential, office, and hospitality projects, including an ice cream parlor in Barcelona.

Ana Milena Hernández Palacios

1982, Bogota, Colombia

Ana's home and studio, near Valencia, Spain, 2023

Beata Heuman

1983, Skåne, Sweden

Beata's home, Sweden, 2023

Swedish interior designer Beata Heuman established her London studio in 2013 after spending nine years working with London designer Nicky Haslam. Without formal training in design, Beata credits Haslam for encouraging her to take risks and infuse eccentricity into her work. Attuned to the history and character of the spaces she transforms, Beata incorporates her own distinctive touches, using color and pattern in imaginative ways. Reflecting her belief that interiors should mirror their inhabitants, Beata emphasizes the importance of displaying objects collected over time, which to her mind add depth and meaning to a space. The result is a series of lively interiors that serve as backdrops for her custom furnishings. For Beata, interiors should be dreamlike, sparking the imagination while creating a setting for everyday rituals. In the dining room of her own farmhouse in Sweden, Beata collaborated with De Gournay to create bespoke wallpaper that captures the garden setting of her home. The design features large scale illustrations of plum, linden, apple, and elderflower trees, with birds flying gracefully among them. Her farmhouse has been described as a "portal into her childhood" reflecting her ability to embrace a building's history, while still making way for fiction and imagination.[71] She has adapted this approach with her clients, encouraging them to forget the outside world through the surreal details and objects she places in her interiors to lend a sense of the otherworldly.

Linehouse is an architecture and interior design practice founded in 2013 by Alex Mok and Briar Hickling. Alex, who is Chinese-Swedish, studied architecture at the Bartlett School of Architecture in London, while Briar, a New Zealand native, graduated with a degree in interior design from Massey University in Wellington. The pair relocated separately to China, and met working together as associates at the architecture studio of Neri&Hu. Their ambition is to create poetic responses to spaces through the incorporation of specific cultural and historical references while taking a balanced approach to function and aesthetics. Linehouse has studios in Shanghai and Hong Kong, and their work ranges from a seven-story shopping center in Bangkok and WeWork office spaces in Shanghai to the interiors of private homes. Linehouse's projects are designed to express the sacred nature of everyday rituals. One way they achieve this is by working with skilled craftspeople to root their projects in a local context and engage the vast history of craft across Asia, where many of Linehouse's projects are based. Their design for dim sum restaurant John Anthony, named for the first Chinese man to be naturalized as a British citizen in 1805, recreated a British tea hall turned Chinese canteen. The project showcased the pair's interest in sustainable building practices, deploying salvaged materials like reclaimed terracotta floor tiles, hand-dyed indigo fabrics, and woven rattan.

Briar Hickling and Alex Mok

1984, Gisborne, New Zealand
1981, Stockholm, Sweden

John Anthony, Hong Kong, 2018

Min Hogg

1938, London, UK
2019, London, UK

Min's home, London, UK, c.1995

Min Hogg, editor of *World of Interiors* for nineteen years, was a pivotal figure in interior design journalism who celebrated the beauty of ordinary, lived-in spaces. Her career began in the 1950s studying furniture and interior design at the Central School of Art and Design (now Central Saint Martins) in London under Terence Conran, whose wife, Caroline, hired her as an assistant typist at *Queen* magazine. Min was a self-confessed "snooper," whose curiosity for unrefined spaces, from flaking frescoes to run-down kitchens, set her apart.[72] Despite leading one of design's most vaunted publications, Min rejected over-designed rooms, valuing authentic, amateur interiors over professionally decorated ones. She reveled in the quirks of off-beat homes, deliberately resisting the minimalism prevalent in other magazines of the time, and often lamenting the difficulty of finding colorful, unique places to feature. Min's personal style epitomized shabby chic—a term she popularized in her magazine—and in her own home, she embraced a lived-in aesthetic, saying, "Live in a tip, it's much more fun."[73] Raised in a semi-aristocratic family in Regent's Park, Min had unique opportunities, including access to Buckingham Palace for her first feature as editor. Throughout her tenure, she showcased the homes of well-known designers like Charles Jencks and Eva Jiřičná. After retiring in the late 1990s, she ventured into interior design with wallpapers that exhibited her signature eclecticism.

Nicole Hollis

1972, Jupiter, FL, USA

Private residence, Haight-Ashbury, San Francisco, CA, USA, 2021

Growing up in a small town in Florida, Nicole Hollis found early inspiration in the architecture of Palm Beach and family road trips along the East Coast. Although she now runs a successful interior design studio in San Francisco, on the West Coast, first Nicole studied graphic design in Florida before attending the Fashion Institute of Technology in New York to study interior design. She left university without graduating to pursue her dream of living in California. Nicole gained extensive experience working in architecture studios during her studies, mainly on hospitality projects which sharpened her knowledge of the industry, describing the city of New York itself as "a great education."[74] Nicole has always had a clear vision for her studio. Noting that "architects get nervous about interior designers" she brings her love of architecture and willingness to collaborate to her projects.[75] Focused mainly on residential projects, she has developed a recognizable style distinct for its use of black and white. For Nicole, color is a strategic, high-impact tool, as can be seen in her design for a historic house in the Haight-Ashbury neighborhood of San Francisco, where the view into an entirely electric blue dining room is framed by a more traditional white interior, with period detailing and a multi-colored rug. Her eye for theatrics belie a careful editing process, making for thoughtfully composed yet visually striking spaces.

Kelly Hoppen

1959, Cape Town, South Africa

Private residence, London, UK, 2020

With projects that range from designing first-class cabins for British Airways to a suite of luxury show penthouses in one of Shenzhen, China's most sought-after waterfront towers, Kelly Hoppen is among Britain's most prominent interior designers, with a profile only more elevated by the ten books she's published and several television show appearances. Awarded a CBE (Commander of the British Empire) in 2021 for her work promoting British creativity and business overseas, Kelly's entrepreneurship started at a young age. She decided to become a designer after spending vacations visiting her grandparents' characterful home in Cape Town. Inspired by her mother, a successful businesswoman, and motivated by her father's early death, Kelly set up her own company despite having no official credentials at the age of sixteen. Her first project entailed designing a kitchen for a family friend, and a commission to design racing driver Damien Hunt's home quickly followed. Her style has since evolved through working with many high-profile clients, including Victoria Beckham and Boy George. Placing art at the center of her interiors, Kelly has become known for her pared-back color palette and clean lines. In her projects, Kelly combines trends from all over the world and has most recently expanded her practice to Southeast Asia.

Shanghai-based architect Rossana Hu's design philosophy is deeply rooted in a reverence for history. Her designs blend Eastern and Western traditions through a contemporary lens, reinterpreted for the Chinese market. In 2006, Rossana co-founded Neri&Hu Design and Research Office with her partner Lyndon Neri. Together they have developed a multifaceted approach to architecture and interiors with a global outlook. Rossana earned her undergraduate degree in architecture and music from the University of California at Berkeley, followed by her master's in Architecture and Urban Planning from Princeton University. Rossana worked at several design practices in the United States, including Michael Graves & Associates, where she met Lyndon. Rossana is widely known for her building projects and furniture designs and her interiors reflect the duo's pursuit of beauty through the rawness of materials. For their hotel project, the Artyzen NEW BUND 31 hotel in Shanghai, they punctuated the space with wood paneling, using stained wood to clad both walls and furnishings to create a unique, brutalist take on a mid-century modern aesthetic, describing the interior as "carved from a single monolithic mass."[76] Rossana also is the first woman to hold the position of chair of architecture at Tongji University in Shanghai, and the third woman and first Chinese person to lead the Department of Architecture at the University of Pennsylvania's Stuart Weitzman School of Design.

Rossana Hu

1968, Kaohsiung, China

Artyzen NEW BUND 31 hotel, Shanghai, China, 2023

Barbara Hulanicki

1936, Warsaw, Poland

The Rainbow Room, Big Biba, London, UK, 1973

Born in Poland, Barbara Hulanicki grew up in Palestine, where her father served as the Polish Consul until his assassination in 1948, on the day the family planned to move to London. Despite this loss, Barbara continued to London, where she studied at the Brighton School of Art. Her first success came when a mail-order dress she designed for the *Daily Mail* attracted 17,000 orders. In 1964, Barbara founded the boutique Biba in Kensington, where she reinvented 1930s styles for the Swinging Sixties. Biba offered affordable clothing to fashionable women who shopped alongside celebrities like Twiggy and Cher. Barbara made her dresses in her apartment before expanding into a department store, Big Biba, where she dabbled in interior design with eclectic patterns, stained glass, silk-fringed lampshades, and mahogany screens. Described as "Harrods on drugs," the store even featured a psychedelic-themed restaurant called the Rainbow Room.[77] After a dispute with corporate partners and a brief stint in Brazil, Barbara moved to Miami Beach, where she rebranded as Barbara Hulanicki Design. There, she designed a nightclub for Ron Wood of the Rolling Stones, renovated a hotel, and contributed to the revival of Miami's Art Deco Historic District. In the words of the National Post "thanks to her, Miami Beach looks like it is blissed out on LSD-spiked margaritas." She was recognized by the British government with an OBE (Officer of the Order of the British Empire) in 2012.

Malene Hvidt

1986, Copenhagen, Denmark

Malene's home, Copenhagen, Denmark, 2021

Malene Hvidt is the creative force behind Copenhagen-based studio Spacon & X, renowned for its interiors, art installations, and fashion shows. Initially, Malene began a career in fashion, however, she soon left to pursue her interest in interior design. After a stint in India working for Studio Mumbai, led by the late Bijoy Jain, she returned to Denmark and co-founded Spacon & X with Nikoline Dyrup Carlsen and Svend Jacob Pedersen in 2014. Malene is interested in how the patterns of everyday life inform design, working with a limited palette of materials such as wood, stone, and metal to create carefully crafted, tactile spaces. Architecture and design have always played a significant role in her life. Her grandfather, Peter Hvidt, was an architect and furniture designer, and her family home was designed by acclaimed architect Halldor Gunnløgsson. The Japanese and Scandinavian design influences of her childhood home are reflected in her own refurbishment of a 1980s building in Copenhagen, which she designed with her partner Nikolaj Lorentz Mentze, founder of Studio 0405. The couple created new openings to fill the interior with light, furnished the rooms with solid wood pieces built by Nikolaj, and installed a built-in bench in homage to her childhood home. With Spacon & X, Malene has designed interiors for Adidas, IKEA, and the restaurant Noma. She also runs the jewelry line Les Mains des Sœurs with her sister, and has taught architecture at the Aarhus School of Architecture and the Royal Danish Academy of Fine Arts.

Kathryn M. Ireland

1961, London, UK

Private residence, Santa Monica, CA, USA, 2015

Kathryn M. Ireland is a renowned London-born interior designer who established her design firm in Los Angeles in the 1990s. Her background as an actress, clothing maker, film director, and work in music video production formed the basis for her switch to interior design, and she decided to turn the editing suite that she co-owned with her husband, Gary Weis, on Santa Monica's Main Street into a small shop selling homewares from her travels in Europe. Inspired by reading her mother's interior design magazines growing up, Kathryn's designs are eclectic, bohemian, and cozy while remaining cohesive, and evince her European roots through a mingling of traditional English silhouettes with relaxed finishes that give her spaces an inviting and homey feel. Starting with a fabric choice to set the tone, Kathryn works closely with her clients to craft spaces that reuse existing furniture, consciously restoring objects and sourcing materials locally where possible. This sustainable approach reflects her belief that homes are meant to be functional, lived in, and well-loved. Kathryn's work extends beyond interiors to include original textiles, wallpapers, and furniture. She has authored six books offering design expertise, and hosts weekend courses where she shares her favorite LA design spots and advises attendees about how to keep spaces fresh.

Polly Jessup

1899, Hartford, CT, USA
1988, Palm Beach, FL, USA

Ford House, Grosse Pointe Shores, MI, USA, c.1950s

Discretion was essential to New Englander Polly Jessup, a highly successful yet underknown interior designer who worked in Florida. Serving ultra-wealthy clients in West Palm Beach like the Fords, DuPonts, and Kennedys, Polly eschewed publicity at a time when her peers courted the media. Her eponymous practice, Jessup Inc., emanated out of designs for her own home that caught the eyes of her acquaintances. Known for tasteful, sensitive, and often floral rooms, Polly imitated classical European decadence in her creations, ranging from wallpaper to upholstery. Throughout her sixty-year career, craft remained central to Polly's practice. She believed in making what you couldn't find, often handcrafting items herself. Her studio collected and restored old furniture, focusing on woodworking, upholstery, and painting. This earned her the moniker "Grand Dame of Palm Beach Decorators," known for her "fanatical attention to detail" and for delivering high-end comfort.[78] Polly's insistence on quality and her signature use of pastel colors, in particular lilacs and roses, became familiar motifs in the homes of her famous friends who valued her eye. Profiled by *The New York Times* in the late 1980s, Polly was described as "influential if unsung."[79] Despite employing fifty-two people at one point, she received little acclaim for her work, which was distinguished by its understated simplicity and extremely high cost.

Eva Jiřičná

1939, Zlín, Czechoslovakia (now Czech Republic)

Hotel Josef, Prague, Czech Republic, 2002

In 1968, Eva Jiřičná was in London for a work placement with the Greater London Council Architects Department as Russia invaded Czechoslovakia, in the process stranding her there. Unable to return to Prague, where she had studied architecture, Eva made London her home. She was inspired by the city's freedom, which allowed her to participate in high-profile competitions that launched her career. Her work with Louis de Soissons on Brighton Marina sparked an interest for her in integrating engineering with interior design, while her store designs for retailer Joseph caught the attention of architect Richard Rogers. He hired her to design the millwork for the Lloyd's of London headquarters. After a successful collaboration over the course of a decade with her partner, architect Jan Kaplický, Eva founded Eva Jiřičná Architects in 1982. She was renowned for using glass as a structural material, transforming ordinary store units into elegant displays. In particular, her glass staircases gained acclaim, including from Steve Jobs, who sought her expertise for Apple store designs. In 1989, she returned to Prague and worked on the interiors of Frank Gehry's Fred and Ginger building after which she set up a new design studio, Architecture Interior Design (AI) with Petr Vágner. Her technology-forward approach was challenging for Czech tradespeople to replicate due to the erasure of a skilled workforce under Communism, so she trained local workers on-site, notably for Hotel Josef, one of Prague's first design hotels. Eva has been awarded a CBE (Commander of the British Empire), and the Jane Drew Prize.

Born in Hong Kong and educated in England, Betty Joel (née Mary Stewart Lockhart) met and married David Joel in Sri Lanka. The couple moved back to the United Kingdom and her career in furniture design and decoration flourished in Southsea, inspired by David's passion for carpentry. Together, they created furniture from Betty's designs, leading to the establishment of their furniture manufacturing company, Betty Joel Ltd. The company's first design series, "Token," was celebrated for its simplicity. In 1928, a chance conversation with HRH Duchess of York at the Ideal Home Exhibition introduced Betty to species of wood exported from the British Empire, and she began incorporating the likes of honey-colored sycamore into her interiors. In 1931, Betty was invited to design the "Living Room," a show apartment on Park Lane featuring wood paneling. She advocated for color, adorning walls with silver paper and installing a coral carpet with blue mohair-covered chairs in one interior. Betty criticized architects for designing everything from the weathervane to the bath faucet, believing consumers should integrate their possessions into a design-led interior. Later, she set up a company lending furniture for film and theater. However, her prominence waned after 1937 when she separated from her husband, who took over the business. Betty never rebuilt her career, reflecting on her success by saying, "I was simply a woman doing business."[80]

Betty Joel

1894, Hong Kong
1985, Hampshire, UK

Show apartment, Park Lane, London, UK, 1932

Tamsin Johnson

1985, Melbourne, VIC, Australia

Potts Point Residence, Sydney, NSW, Australia, 2023

While Tamsin Johnson's interiors have a distinctly modern appearance, they are rooted in a reverence for history influenced by her upbringing. Her father, an antiques dealer, instilled in Tamsin a love for historical furniture, which shows in her work's dialogue between old and new. After gaining a degree in fashion from the Royal Melbourne Institute of Technology, Tamsin first worked for Stella McCartney in London before training in interior design at the Inchbald School of Design. Returning to Sydney in 2005, she worked with Don McQualter at Meacham Nockles McQualter before founding her own practice in 2013. Her work embraces the specifics of the Australian climate, attentive to the unique way light in the southern hemisphere changes the perception of color in space. Her ornate Potts Point Residence project is light and playful, engaging with the details of the Victorian building and using marble as a motif throughout, notably to clad the dramatic architrave between the living room and kitchen, and on the stairs. As in much of her work, Tamsin's interiors for the house have a feeling of ease, fostering a balance between large gestures and smaller details, an approach captured in her 2021 book *Tamsin Johnson: Spaces for Living*. In Sydney's Paddington, she opened a space that serves as both an interior design office and a showroom for her custom pieces and antiques furnishings, reflecting her playful yet sophisticated style.

Melanie Kahane was known for her surprising and sometimes daring design ideas. She transformed her library into a dining room, surrounding the dining table with books, and in 1946, she created the first colored kitchen appliance, a shiny bright red stove. A multidisciplinary designer, Melanie designed hotels, theaters, and apartments, working across scales and spectrums, from designing light bulbs to furnishing entire homes. She expressed her love of color through a refined, glamorous aesthetic, as in her design for a Royal York Apartment with a red screen and red club chairs. Melanie studied at Parsons School of Design, starting her career as an illustrator of women's clothing for an advertising company. In 1935, she founded her firm, Melanie Kahane Association, undertaking interior decorating projects for department stores, beauty salons, and restaurants. In addition to designing a children's museum, in 1968, she published a children's book called *There's a Decorator in Your Doll House*. Melanie later formed part of the team for the 1958 World's Fair in Brussels and worked for the television network NBC in the Soviet Union. From designing for celebrities to working for corporate clients, Melanie was known for her energetic personality. In the year of her passing, Parsons established a scholarship in her name.

Melanie Kahane

1910, New York, NY, USA
1988, New York, NY, USA

Royal York Apartment, New York, NY
USA, c.1950s

Annabel Karim Kassar

Neuilly sur Seine, France

Ella Funt, New York, NY, USA, 2023

Annabel Karim Kassar, a French-Lebanese architect and designer with offices in London, Dubai, and Beirut, combines a modernist vocabulary with influences from across the world. She cites Le Corbusier and the Bauhaus school as key forefigures, not for their modernist pursuits of functionality, but for the emotion and spirit of each's architecture. She trained at the École des Beaux-Arts in Paris before moving to Beirut where she worked for twenty years before settling in London. Annabel believes that design should not be reduced to styling following the latest trends, but rather should draw from a rich vocabulary of painting, sculpture, and craft. In her design for the interiors of Ella Funt, a restaurant in New York, Annabel's concept was to create what she describes as "unashamed sensuality" by working with an existing mural, amplifying the use of color in the interiors, and inserting rich fabrics inspired by her time in North Africa and the Eastern Mediterranean.[81] She draws inspiration from the intimate atmosphere of vernacular, non-Western homes, where spaces flow rather than being divided. As a result, she views design not as individual objects placed within a space but as a unified whole, where form, color, light, and texture seamlessly blend. Annabel's confident use of color creates drama with her expert selection of textured fabrics, including velvet and embossed leather, heightening the sumptuous tactility of her interiors.

Mimi Maddock McMakin, a Palm Beach native, founded Kemble Interiors in 1982. Her distinctive style celebrates the beauty in the faded, worn, and well-loved, creating spaces that evoke a sense of nostalgia and warmth. Mimi's approach honors the charm of family heirlooms and the stories they carry, a reflection of her deep appreciation for history. Mimi's influence extends to her daughter, Celerie Kemble, who is now her partner in the New York office of Kemble Interiors. A Harvard graduate, Celerie initially pursued a career in film production before making the switch to interior design. Her design philosophy builds on her mother's legacy—unsurprising given that her childhood was an unofficial tutorial in interior design experienced on construction sites, browsing antique stores, and living in the unique homes designed by her mother—celebrating the sentimental and storied aspects of spaces. Mimi renovated a Palm Beach church into their family home, with cavernous interiors adorned with special objects including large vases, hanging mobiles, and even a nearly life-sized zebra. Together, Mimi and Celerie have cultivated a distinctive style blending traditional and modern influences to create interiors that are both aesthetically pleasing and rich in history and character.

Celerie Kemble and Mimi Maddock McMakin

1973, USA
1947, Palm Beach, FL, USA

Mimi's home, Palm Beach, FL, USA, 1974

Kit Kemp

"A Dining Room of One's Own," Kips Bay Decorator Show House, New York, NY, USA, 2024

Kit Kemp, one of the UK's foremost interior designers and business leaders, is renowned for her modern interpretation of the English country home. Kit began her career working for an auctioneer before joining architect Leszek Nowicki's studio, whose approach galvanized her interest in craft-based practices, particularly weaving. Together with her husband, Tim Kemp, Kit founded Firmdale Hotels. Kit is the creative force of the design for the company's eleven properties, including the latest, the Warren Street Hotel in TriBeCa. She is celebrated for her layering of patterns and surprising color combinations, especially through the use of textiles and decorative wallpapers that feature ornamental geometric prints, whimsical landscapes, or lush florals. Storytelling is central to Kit's design philosophy and she believes each room is "like a painted canvas, it has to tell a story." Accordingly, her design for the Kips Bay Decorator Show House artfully interprets author Virginia Woolf's *A Room of One's Own*, creating a whimsical English country house atmosphere through hand-painted murals and warm green and peach tones. Kit expanded into homewares through her brand Kit Kemp Design Studio, collaborating with leading design companies such as Wedgwood. She has published four books. Alongside her daughters Willow and Minnie, Kit has built a design empire, earning her an MBE (Member of the Most Excellent Order of the British Empire) in 2012.

HRH Anoud Khalid Mishaal bin Saud

Saudi Arabia

Villa in Laban, Riyadh, Saudi Arabia, 2018

Her Royal Highness Anoud Khalid Mishaal bin Saud is the founder of A Interiors and a member of the Saudi royal family. A childhood filled with visits to furniture shops and flea markets fueled Anoud's early ambition of becoming an interior designer. She studied interior design at the Prince Sultan University, and earned an MBA from Alfaisal University before finishing her first freelance project, which allowed her to establish her own independent studio in Riyadh. Over the last decade, Anoud has cultivated a distinctly modern, minimalist style marked by thoughtful juxtapositions of vintage and contemporary furnishings and artworks, and geometric motifs that echo traditional Islamic calligraphy. Anoud has undertaken projects across the world, including many private residences in Saudi Arabia, as well as her own apartment within her family's palace. In this luxurious minimalist villa in Laban, Anoud combines modern clean lines with traditional Islamic influences to create a comfortable space with a calm ambiance. The handcrafted ceilings are both elegant and accentuate the height of the rooms, while carefully chosen splashes of color draw the eye around the interior. Vintage pieces and playful accessories add a personal touch that makes this house feel like a home.

Gertrud Kleinhempel

1875, Schönefeld, Germany
1948, Althagen, Ahrenshoop, Germany

Show bedroom, Prima Esposizione Internazionale d'Arte Decorativa Moderna, Turin, Italy, 1902

One of the first female professional furniture designers in Germany, Johanna Gertrud Kleinhempel was born near Leipzig, and began her career as a drawing teacher. At age fourteen, she studied drawing at the Trades' Draughting School in Dresden, where she also trained as a teacher. She received a scholarship to study in Munich, and worked for *Jugend* magazine. Returning to Dresden in 1898, Gertrud became involved with the Dresden Workshops for Arts and Crafts, later the German Workshops Hellerau, for whom she designed the interiors of the women's pavilion, "Haus der Frau," in Cologne in 1914. Gertrud also created furniture, jewelry, and graphics, making her a respected figure in the German Arts and Crafts movement. Her playful, abstract forms caught the eye of textile manufacturer Gustav Windel, who commissioned her to design showroom interiors. Founding an art school in Bielefeld with her brothers, Gertrud proselytized the importance of practical experience over drawing, and as head of the textile class at the Bielefeld School of Crafts and Applied Arts, she became the first female professor in what was then Prussia. Despite her success, she faced gender-based obstacles, including lower pay and a contract forbidding marriage. After nearly thirty years, she left her teaching post due to her opposition to Nazi occupation. After a successful career pioneering new pedagogies and making practices, Geturd spent her final years living in relative obscurity in Althagen.

Florence Knoll

1917, Saginaw, MI, USA
2019, Coral Gables, FL, USA

Cowles Publications Office, New York, NY, USA, 1962

Florence Knoll was a pioneer of mid-century modern design, fundamentally transforming the perception of interior design as a professional endeavor. Initially crafting sofas and other pieces of furniture to fill redundant space in offices and reception areas, her creations quickly became iconic. Orphaned at a young age, Florence grew up in Michigan and studied at Cranbrook Academy of Art with design icons Eero Saarinen and Charles Eames. Her friendship with Eero led her to travel to Finland and study at the Architectural Association in London and Columbia University in New York. She later completed a degree in architecture at the Illinois Institute of Technology under Mies van der Rohe and worked for Walter Gropius and Marcel Breuer in Cambridge, Massachusetts. Positioned at the epicenter of North American modernism, her work introduced sleek silhouettes and clean lines to interior settings, reflecting her architectural training. Florence felt societal expectations steered her toward interior projects, which she embraced and transformed, defining a new era of commercial design. She co-ran the furniture company Knoll Associates and the Knoll Planning Unit, which provided bespoke design services, including space planning and furniture selection, during the postwar office building boom. While designed for corporate settings, Florence's designs are renowned for their warm materiality and human-scaled ergonomics.

Sunita Kohli

1946, Lahore, India

Private residence in Lutyens Bungalow Zone, New Delhi, India, 2004

After studying English literature at both the University of Delhi and the University of Lucknow, Sunita Kohli began her career as a teacher. She continued to harbor an interest in design, seeded in childhood when she would accompany her father to furniture auctions, and frequented *kabadi* or thrift stores to source original Edwardian furniture and artifacts from all over India for her own personal collection. Working with local craftspeople in Lucknow, she learned how to restore antique furniture, and opened Sunita Kohli Interior Designs in 1971, becoming a leader in historical interior architectural conservation before interior design was fully established as a profession in India. Within the year, she also set up Sunita Kohli and Company to manufacture classical Anglo-Indian furniture and Art Deco reproductions. In New Delhi, Sunita has restored, furnished, and decorated many British period buildings. Notable among these are Rashtrapati Bhavan, the presidential residence, and the office of the Prime Minister. In partnership with her daughter, Kohelika Kohli, Sunita founded K2India in 2010, a multidisciplinary umbrella organization that undertakes architecture and design projects, along with project management, interiors, and furniture design. Sunita and Kohelika offer sleek interiors that blend neutral colors with bright, contemporary furnishings. Sunita's philanthropy focuses on supporting women in the arts, and in 2005 she played a key role in the establishment of the Museum of Women in the Arts, India, which houses an organization aiming to empower rural master craftswomen. Sunita has written a collection of essays about craft and design, *Kala*, and in 1992, she was the first interior designer to be awarded the Padma Shri award for her services to design.

A columnist for *The Telegraph* and *House & Garden*, among many others, Rita Konig embarked on a writing career before following her passion for interior design. She credits her mother, renowned designer Nina Campbell, for introducing her to the world of interiors through time spent in her mother's store and accompanying her to building sites. Rita's career in decorating took off when she designed an apartment with television personality George Clarke for a client in Holland Park in London. After completing her second solo project, she moved to the United States to work for *Domino* magazine. While in the United States, Rita wrote a lifestyle book, *Domestic Bliss*, focused on how to live well in comfort. In 2012, she returned to London to set up her own decorating business. Rita sees herself as a decorator rather than a designer, believing that it is the embellishment of a room that completes its design. Admitting to her own love of "clutter and pattern," Rita worked on an apartment in New York for a client who claimed to be a committed minimalist.[82] Rita capitalized on the high ceilings and light-filled interiors of the apartment by using a cream palette as a backdrop. She complemented this with a tonal variety of untreated wooden floors and furniture, adding touches of color through carefully chosen upholstery and rugs. Beyond her book, she has shared her expertise through two online courses for Create Academy, and has a furniture and fabric collection.

Rita Konig

1974, London, UK

Private residence, New York, NY, USA, 2016

Agata Kurzela

1979, Gdańsk, Poland

UAE government offices, Abu Dhabi, UAE, 2023

Having trained in architecture and urban design, Agata Kurzela gained experience at some of Europe's most prominent architecture offices, working for Zaha Hadid in London and Christian de Portzamparc in Paris. She continued her work on large-scale masterplans and high-rise buildings in the Middle East where she has been practicing for almost two decades, working across scales and disciplines. In 2020 she founded her own studio, Agata Kurzela Studio, and recently undertook the retrofit of an administrative building in Abu Dhabi for the U.A.E. government. The project includes offices, meeting rooms, and a prayer room, and features a large steel staircase and mezzanine backdropped by a neutral and warm sand color palette. Red chairs add a bright, contrasting pop of color, creating a space that feels both earthy and contemporary. Agata describes her design process as "almost scientific," involving "extensive research, documentation, and experimentation" to explore a space's inherent conditions.[83] She looks for sculptural qualities in her projects' sites, drawing on history while being attentive to how light and shadow change the sites throughout the day. With an approach that is both research-driven and intuitive, Agata has no fixed style; rather her projects oscillate between minimal and maximal, from richly layered interiors to those stripped to the bone. For Agata, the joy in a project comes from what she refers to as "glitches"—happy accidents that emerge during the design process.[84] She embraces these moments as opportunities to avoid the formulaic in favor of work that is truly original.

Joanna Laajisto

1977, Helsinki, Finland

Noli Katajanokka II, Helsinki, Finland, 2023

Joanna Laajisto had a creative upbringing, studying music and performing arts before embarking on a career in the United States as a professional snowboarder in her teenage years. Keen to stay in the United States and further her education, she studied at the Interior Design Institute of Southern California and joined the architectural firm Gensler as an intern in Los Angeles. Upon graduation, she continued working with the company, contributing to the workplace team to design large-scale commercial interiors. After five years, she returned to Finland, and founded her eponymous studio in Helsinki in 2010. Joanna's work spans multiple typologies, including nightclubs, restaurants, and hotels. As a member of the Green Building Council of Finland, Joanna advocates for the sustainability of well-designed spaces, emphasizing their longevity as a key factor in environmental responsibility. Her design for the Noli Katajanokka II hotel in Helsinki showcases her characteristic quest for modern luxury pairing chunky, beautifully crafted wood furniture with rougher, natural woven textiles, wicker, and large scale moody paintings. For Joanna, luxury is a reflection of skilled craft. She favors natural materials that convey purity and authenticity, prioritizing organic shapes, raw wood, and muted earth tones, in designs that highlight the rustic side of Finnish design. In addition to her interior design projects, Joanna manufactures her own range of lighting and furniture, dubbed "New Nordic" for its contemporary take on Finnish modernism.

Róisín Lafferty

1986, Dublin, Ireland

Lovers Walk House, Cork, Republic of Ireland, c.2021

Dublin-based designer Róisín Lafferty is known for her richly layered interiors that pair confident colors with bespoke furnishings. She graduated with a degree in Interior Architecture and Furniture Design from the Dublin Institute of Technology (now the Technological University Dublin), and earned a master's degree in Product and Spatial Design from Kingston University in London, before founding her eponymous studio. Specializing in residential, retail, and hospitality, Róisín likes to subvert tradition in her designs by creating dynamic, exciting spaces that mix and deploy materials in unexpected ways. Working with stainless steel, terrazzo, natural stone, resin, and high gloss lacquer, she is interested in how architectural interiors can enhance human behavior and induce, as she states, "mind-bending experiences."[85] Daring and playful elements in her designs conjure unique, personalized atmospheres, made evident in residential interiors like Kaleidoscope and Lovers Walk. At Lovers Walk, a 1970s home in Cork, Róisín's maximalist design features a dusty pink quartzite kitchen countertop artfully contrasted with assertively clashing colored wood, creating what she describes as "a vibrant haven with an unexpected air of serenity."[86] She has shared her design perspectives through articles written for publications such as *The Irish Times*, *The Independent*, *The Gloss*, and *Image Interiors*, among others.

Nancy Lancaster

1897, Greenwood, VA, USA
1994, Little Haseley, Oxfordshire, UK

Nancy's home, London, UK, 1957

Nancy Lancaster, an American socialite born into a wealthy Virginia family, became renowned for her quintessentially English style. Educated in France, Nancy spent time in England with her famous aunt, Nancy Astor. Her youth was marked by tragedy; her parents separated in 1912, she was orphaned by age seventeen, and widowed by age nineteen. These experiences shaped her design sensibility, inspired by her summers in Virginia, her mother's taste for soft colors, and her grandfather's house, Mirador, which she later refurbished. Nancy's second marriage to Ronald Tree brought her to England, where she decorated her stately North Oxfordshire home to great acclaim, with special attention paid to the yellow room in her library. The home, known for its relaxed country style, was known to have hosted Winston Churchill on weekends during World War II. Nancy was interested in atmosphere, introducing log fires and blending American comfort with English countryside charm in her interiors. She repeated her love of yellow in her apartment in Mayfair, using as many shades as possible. Her decorating combined aristocratic shabby chic with mismatched fabrics, aiming for a well-worn, welcoming look. She often left sofas in the sun and soaked chintz in tea to soften its brightness. In the early 1940s Nancy became the co-owner of the well-known interior decorating company Colefax and Fowler, sourcing antique furniture for the brand. Her partnership with business partner John Fowler made the firm synonymous with an ageless, comfortable style despite the pair's famed bickering. Nancy's unconventional approach included ordering a decorator to "paint it the colour of Elephant's Breath," a now-famous paint color by English paint manufacturer Farrow & Ball.

Ruth Lane Poole

1885, Limerick, Republic of Ireland
1974, Sydney, NSW, Australia

The Lodge at Yarralumla, Canberra, ACT, Australia, 1927

Irish by birth, Ruth Lane Poole grew up in the household of poet W. B. Yeats, a distant relative, after her parents separated. She joined Yeats's sisters, Mary and Lily, in their decorative embroidery business based in Dublin, Dun Emer Industrie. Ruth moved to Western Australia with her husband, Charles Poole, eventually settling in Canberra. Ruth's career as a designer began with small interior projects, alongside work as a design writer for *The Australian Home Builder* and later, *Australian Home Beautiful* magazine. Influenced by her husband, who was the Commonwealth Inspector-General of Forests, Ruth developed an interest in working with native Australian materials, such as Queensland maple, which she employed to great effect in her 1927 refurbishment of the Yarralumla residence for Governor General Lord Stonehaven. She noted that her designs for the wood-paneled dining room and study had a distinctly "masculine" feel, while she aimed for a more "feminine" atmosphere in the drawing room, which was reportedly left unpaneled. Ruth had strong opinions on interior details, insisting that center lights best suited clubs and hotels, and installing furniture designs of her own that she had made by Melbourne cabinetmakers. In her later years, Ruth organized events for the Australian Forestry School community and ran her daughter's flower shop before eventually retiring in Sydney.

Jeanne Lanvin, founder of the haute couture house Lanvin, is synonymous with romanticism, complexity, and a signature color: Lanvin Blue. Despite her fame, Jeanne's beginnings were humble. She grew up in a large family and trained as a milliner at age thirteen. Early success enabled her to open a series of eponymous stores in the 1920s that offered fashion and home decor. Collaborating with Armand-Albert Rateau, who managed Lanvin Décoration, the interior design arm of the enterprise, they designed Jeanne's lavish apartment with a purple and gold color scheme replete with animal motifs, along with a striking cream and black bathroom suite made from marble, stucco, and patinated bronze. Rateau's preference for French Classicism, mixing Louis IX theatrics with Art Nouveau elements, identified a sweet spot where interiors and fashion could merge, appealing to aspirational upper middle class Parisians. Jeanne's creative approach was marked by curiosity and inventiveness, using her apartments to present couture and intertwining her life with the Lanvin brand. Her daughter, Marguerite, inspired Jeanne's first clothing line, appealing to fashionable Parisians who sought her creations for their own children. Inspiration also came from her travels, particularly through China and India, during which she kept detailed diaries chronicling found objects and observations. These journeys fueled her passion for color, leading her to establish a dye factory later in life.

Jeanne Lanvin

1867, Paris, France
1946, Le Vésinet, France

Jeanne's home, Paris, France, c.1925

146

Amy Lau

1968, AZ, USA
2025, Scottsdale, AZ, USA

Bridgehampton Getaway,
Bridgehampton, NY, USA, 2018

With an early career beginning in some of New York's most prestigious art galleries, interior designer Amy Lau always aspired to fuse art and architecture in her clients' homes. Her deep appreciation for history was rooted in her academic training, which began with her earning an art history degree from the University of Arizona, followed by a master's degree in classical and decorative arts from Sotheby's Institute of Art in New York. Amy honed her curatorial eye during her time working as a director at Thomas O'Brien's Aero Studio, and as the design director at the Lin-Weinberg Gallery, where she specialized in mid-century and contemporary furniture. In 2001, Amy launched her own interior design studio, and in 2005 she co-founded Design.05, which evolved to become the Design Miami art fair, a platform dedicated to showcasing the most important voices in vintage and modern furnishings that runs parallel to Art Basel Miami. Amy believed that a space should be curated—rather than merely decorated—to reflect her clients' tastes and interests. This philosophy is evident in her design for the home of an art collector in Bridgehampton, in which sculptures and paintings inspire the overall design scheme. Known for her use of mirrors and metallic finishes, Amy was attentive to a space's architecture and setting, striving to create a contemporary *gesamtkunstwerk*—a total work of art blending vintage and contemporary pieces with site-specific art commissions including wall sculptures by Clara Graziolino and Jennifer Pritchard.

Joanna Lavén

1982, Stockholm, Sweden

Apartment ST, Stockholm, Sweden, 2020

For Stockholm-based interior designer Joanna Lavén, the home should provide "warmth and inspiration," enhancing the lives of its inhabitants.[87] Initially discouraged from studying interior design, as those around her deemed it superficial, Joanna pursued a degree in media and communication from Stockholm University. She began her career as an interior stylist, assisting other stylists and set designers before taking on her own commissions. As an independent stylist, she continued to design commercial photoshoots for fashion and interior brands before turning her hand to interiors, which occurred in a serendipitous way. Together with her partner David Wahlgren, Joanna renovated several of their own apartments, drawing significant interest from friends and acquaintances. This led the couple to found Studio Lawahl, a portmanteau of their surnames, offering interior design and architectural services. Having built a portfolio of serene residential interiors, Joanna describes her aesthetic as "eclectic, layered, and elegant."[88] This can be seen in her design for an apartment in Stockholm, where cool light blue and green tones create a calm backdrop for a comfortable, airy sitting area. Joanna reintroduced nineteenth century architectural details such as oiled solid wood floors and ceiling stucco resonant with the building's history while furnishing the spaces with custom modern pieces. Layered textiles like soft blue velvet upholstery, a high-pile wool rug, and a lush cashmere throw add tactility and warmth, complemented by an eye-catching etched brass coffee table juxtaposed with stark black leather upholstered furniture.

Eleanor Le Maire

1897, Berkeley, CA, USA
1970, New York, NY, USA

Bullocks Wilshire store, Los Angeles, CA, USA, 1929

Eleanor Le Maire grew up in California in a creatively stimulating household. Her father, an engineer, frequently hosted architect friends who inspired Eleanor to pursue a career in architecture. She studied at the University of California, Berkeley, and later at Parsons School of Design and Columbia University in New York City. Despite earning a degree in architecture, Eleanor initially applied her skills as a stylist for Bullocks home furnishing store on Los Angeles's Wilshire Boulevard before being entrusted to lead a five million dollar refurbishment of the entire store, the success of which led to further commissions and sparked nationwide trends for retail design. In the 1930s, Eleanor launched her own interior decorating business and eventually moved to New York, where she redecorated The New Yorker Hotel and undertook international projects as far afield as Helsinki and Stockholm. By the early 1960s, she managed more than fifty employees, overseeing diverse projects ranging from transport ships and sports stadiums to automobile and office interiors. She approached her work holistically, considering all aspects of a space, explaining that she "paints with color and designs with light."[89] A pathbreaking unconventional project involved swathing the interior of Studebaker cars with confident washes of color, for which newspapers dubbed her an "industrial colorist," bringing "youth and freshness" that appealed to female clients.[90]

Little Wing Lee

1973, Boston, MA, USA

Bar Bête, New York, NY, USA, 2019

Little Wing Lee is an interior designer whose approach is informed by her professional experience with prominent architecture and design firms, including Skidmore Owings and Merrill, Rockwell Group, Ralph Appelbaum Associates, and Ace Hotel Group's Atelier Ace. Raised in an artistic family, Little Wing was significantly influenced by her mother, a modern dancer and prominent figure during the Black Arts Movement, who nurtured her appreciation for beauty and spatial awareness. Little Wing pursued her undergraduate education at Oberlin College, before embarking on a career in documentary television for over a decade. Seeking a break from working on hard hitting television shows, she undertook a program in landscape architecture at Harvard University, going on to earn a Master of Fine Arts from Pratt Institute. Her career is as diverse as her educational background. In 2010, she served as an exhibition designer for the Smithsonian's National Museum of African American History and Culture, where her interest in narrative design deepened. In 2019, she designed Bar Bête in Brooklyn's Cobble Hill neighborhood, creating a distinctive atmosphere with dark wood seating alcoves in cognac leather upholstery and textured tiles. This led to her to establish her own design studio, Studio & Projects, which focuses on cultural, residential, and hospitality spaces, and develops products, such as a rug and lighting collections. In addition to her practice, Little Wing founded Black Folks in Design, an organization and network dedicated to celebrating the contributions of Black designers and fostering solidarity and creating opportunities within the industry.

Na Li knew she wanted to pursue a career in design from a young age. She studied architecture at The Bartlett School of Architecture in London, completing her professional training at Westminster University. During her time working for architect Michaelis Boyd designing Soho Farmhouse in Oxfordshire, she met Alexander Holloway. This collaboration led to the formation of Holloway Li, where Na oversees business development. With projects spanning hospitality, retail, and the residential sector, her design approach embraces stripped-back interiors that play with proportion, often featuring theatrical moments such as color-blocked ceilings and dramatic lighting schemes. The London-based studio artfully mixes historical references with cultural typologies, from nightlife to digital making processes. While many of their projects are local, their influences draw on global themes, including a trip to Joshua Tree in California, which informed the material palette for Bermonds Locke, an apartment hotel concept in South London. Recalling the Mojave desert, rooms were finished in a rough wall texture with orange hues used throughout to unify the spaces, while an iridescent zinc passivated wall cladding lines the entrance lobby. The duo was inspired by the "ad hoc qualities of the cabin structures" at Joshua Tree, developing ways that they could repurpose construction materials.[91] This approach underpins their work, with each project starting with a sustainability brief, reflecting their commitment to working in an ecologically considerate way.

Na Li

1986, Nanjing, China

Bermonds Locke, London, UK, 2020

Xiang Li

1986, China

Loong Swim Club, Suzhou, China, 2019

In 2011, Xiang Li founded her studio, X+LIVING, in Shanghai where she creates immersive environments featuring architectural-scale objects that blur the boundary between furniture and sculpture. Her fantastical spaces come to life through bold use of color, adding a sense of whimsy and imagination. She attended high school in Malaysia, followed by studies in Shanghai at Birmingham City University in the United Kingdom, where she trained in architecture. Known for creating dreamy experiential spaces that critics frequently describe as otherworldly, Xiang has brought her whimsical touch to a diverse array of projects, ranging from family parks, cultural spaces and hotels to retail stores, and commercial renovation. Her work, positioned at the intersection of art, fashion, and architecture, coalesced around her bubblegum-infused color palette and playful pop aesthetic. Her design for Loong Swim Club in Suzhou creates an immersive space by drawing inspiration from the water, capturing its essence—which she describes as light and soft. She creates a joyfully surreal environment, contrasting calming dusty pinks with graphic black-and-white stripes and polka dots, which for Xiang introduces a rhythmic, avant-garde fashion to the space. In the dining area, several fragmented eggshells are orderly arranged in a vertical space. The gorgeous colors and fairy-tale shapes are reflected in the mirror, making people feel like they are in the wonderland. Like many of her projects, the swim club offers a mystical environment that is in equal measures fun and educational. In her interiors, the distinctive soft furnishings are all originally designed and crafted by Xiang and her team.

Born in Taiwan, Angela Lindahl, co-founder of the interior design studio Yatofu, grew up in Canada before moving to New York to study industrial design at the Pratt Institute. She went on to earn her master's degree in Interior Architecture from Aalto University in Helsinki. It was there that Angela met her business partner, Yihan Xiang. Sharing a cultural background and finding that they worked well together, the duo founded Yatofu in 2017 as students after receiving a significant commission in China. The name Yatofu reflects their playful approach to design, combining the first letters of their own names with "tofu," a mutual favorite food. Yatofu's main office is in Helsinki, with a satellite space in Shanghai. The duo's designs are characterized by their ability to blend classic Nordic design with Chinese tradition. They approached their design for a city-center apartment in Shanghai as if it were a gallery, emphasizing the display of art pieces and custom furniture made in collaboration with local artists and craftspeople, taking special care with the rarity of the home's garden in the urban center. A dazzling display wall clad entirely in Brazilian pinta verde blue marble creates a vibrant focal point. Despite the high-end, spare quality of the apartment, Yatofu inject their signature playful approach by including a custom geometric terrazzo floor, adding large areas of color and visual interest.

Angela Lindahl

1990, Taiwan

Garden Gallery Residence, Shanghai, China, 2022

Katie Lockhart

1977, Auckland, New Zealand

Franklin Road House, Ponsonby, Auckland, New Zealand, 2021

Formally trained as a designer at the Te Herenga Waka, Victoria University of Wellington, Katie Lockhart credits her well-traveled upbringing and years spent living and working abroad for her unique eye for design. Her parents collected and restored furniture, leading to many weekend antiquing trips in Katie's childhood. While a university student, Katie approached fashion designer Karen Walker, and later became her design assistant, an opportunity that exposed Katie to broader design references. Katie moved to Milan to deepen her design knowledge, and freelanced for several design magazines. She also assisted interior designer Suzy Hoodless in London. After gaining experience across several design communities, Katie returned to New Zealand to found her own studio and her work elegantly references many different design traditions ranging from Japanese craft to modernist Italian. Color is integral to Katie's work, and is often the starting point for projects. She collects scraps of paint remnants she finds on buildings to create a color library from which to draw inspiration. At Franklin Road House, a period home in Auckland, Katie collaborated with the architect Jack McKinney to create interiors that reference Sri Lankan architecture, in particular the work of Geoffrey Bawa. The interiors feature walnut cabinetry, natural fiber textiles, and upholstery redolent of tropical foliage. These elements bring warmth and liveliness to an otherwise spare space.

Hilary Loh's interior design studio, 2nd Edition, specializes in residential projects, primarily creating condominium model apartment interiors for property developers across Singapore. Hilary spent a decade working as an architectural assistant before transitioning to interior design, drawn to its detail-oriented scale. Growing up in Ipoh in northwestern Malaysia, Hilary states that from a young age she has been fascinated by the composition of objects in space, particularly their "color and texture," and at eighteen she moved to Singapore to study architecture at the Singapore Polytechnic.[92] After graduating, Hilary worked with the architecture firm Hyla Architects, where she developed her interest in interior design and had her first experience designing model apartments. She founded 2nd Edition in 2005 with the intention of focusing on refined, minimal interiors that merge simplicity with luxury, often expressed through her use of dark wood finishes. In her interiors for 3 Orchard By-The-Park apartments, Hilary devised an imaginary client to enliven her design. Organized over two floors, the apartment is designed for an urban, well-traveled couple with "discerning tastes" reflected in the sophisticated material used including mahogany and gun metal.[93] Its sleek interiors feature built-in furniture grounded in a palette of neutral tones, along with off-white and caramel-colored objects including everyday items that adorn the tables and shelves and lend a sense of cohesion to the spaces.

Hilary Loh

1974, Ipoh, Malaysia

3 Orchard By-The-Park, Singapore, 2023

Isabel López-Quesada

1962, Madrid, Spain

Isabel's home, Madrid, Spain, 2020

Isabel López-Quesada opened her first studio in Madrid at the young age of twenty. Her passion for interior design was precocious and self-taught. For Isabel it is a vocation, the strength of which continues undiminished forty years later. While maintaining her base in Madrid, over this time, she has executed projects worldwide, showcasing her ability to comprehend and enhance spaces of all kinds, imparting them with a unique character. Beyond Spain, her projects extend across the globe to places such as the United States, the United Kingdom, France, Switzerland, Japan, and the Dominican Republic. A significant project for Isabel was creating her own home, which involved joining two small residences together, completely rebuilding them in the process. The sash windows in the dining room have a London townhouse feel with French and Italian touches. The sophisticated 1960s chocolate-colored lacquered goatskin panels by Italian designer Aldo Tura were bought from a Parisian antiques dealer and create spectacular plays of light with a color and finish reminiscent of one of Isabel's obsessions, tortoise shells. Her designs display a love of texture, celebrating materials in their raw state and exuberantly patterned textiles. She extends this ethos to her home furnishings company, ISITA, founded with her daughter, Isabel Llanza. Together, they work with craftspeople from across France and Spain to reuse and recycle existing furniture pieces. Isabel primarily works on private residences, but has also designed corporate spaces and the interiors for Spanish embassies in Doha, Dakar, and Tokyo.

Margaret studied design at Swinburne University in Australia and continued her education at the Central School of Art and Design (now Central Saint Martin's) in London in 1936. After graduating, she worked at an interior design firm and taught at the Arnold School of Interior Decoration. Returning to Australia during World War II, Margaret continued work as an interior designer and color consultant, and authored three books on design. Her first book, *Interior Decoration: A Guide to Furnishing the Australian Home* (1944), was reportedly air-dropped to prisoners behind Japanese enemy lines. It advised servicewomen how to maximize their resources while embracing modern interiors. Margaret was known for her strong opinions on color and Australian design, calling Sydney "shabby" and criticizing the indiscriminate counterfeiting of imported styles. Through her roles in media as a radio personality and as a regular contributor to *Australian Home Beautiful*, she defined interior design as "the art of designing rooms which comfort the body, please the eye, and interest the mind."[94] She frequently offered advice, suggesting that "pink makes a good background for even a male room" and extolling the virtues of grey.[95] From ship designs to office interiors, Margaret believed that individuals could cultivate their design sensibilities by being attuned to their surroundings until "your head is full of color and you are aware of color all the time."[96]

Margaret Lord

1908, Warrnambool, VIC, Australia
1976, Potts Point, Sydney, NSW, Australia

Monowai ship, c.1951

Fiona Lynch

Melbourne, Australia

Fitzroy House, Fitzroy, VIC, Australia, 2016

Fiona Lynch is celebrated for her "spirited minimalism,"[97] characterized by a sophisticated, nuanced marriage of tone and texture. Having studied at the Royal Melbourne Institute of Technology, her background in fine art and interior design informs her balanced compositions. After graduating, Fiona moved to Canberra, where she gained valuable experience working for several architecture firms including John Wardle Architects. During this time, she designed retail and corporate interiors, as well as the State Library of South Australia, and took on residential projects in Hong Kong and Beijing. In 2013, she founded Fiona Lynch Office to extend her collaborations with local craftspeople and pursue her interest in sustainability. Her studio explores materials with a keen awareness of how and where they are produced, harnessing inherent qualities like the patina they acquire with age. This can be seen in projects like Fitzroy House, a residential conversion of an old boot factory where Fiona installed blackened timber joinery, creating a refined, monochromatic interior. In addition to her design practice, Fiona founded Work Shop, an extension of her studio that exhibits artworks and objects by other makers. This initiative emphasizes the "creative dualism between myriad artistic disciplines."[98] Fiona's first furniture collection was designed for the interiors for Kiln, a restaurant at the Ace Hotel in Sydney.

Once a meadow of willow trees, Sauchiehall Street in Glasgow hosts one of Margaret Macdonald Mackintosh's most notable works, the decorative panel "O Ye, All Ye, That Walk in Willowwood," which originally formed part of the interior she made for the Salon de Luxe tearoom in the city's center. Margaret's design was her visual interpretation of Dante Gabriel Rossetti's sonnet *Willowwood* using Celtic revival motifs, and featured a palette of purples and pinks, immersing them in an ethereal, forest-like ambiance. Deploying various media, including metalwork, embroidery, and textiles, Margaret often incorporated folklore, Celtic art, and poetry into her work. She studied at the Glasgow School of Art with her sister Frances, with whom she later opened the Macdonald Sisters Studio. Margaret and Frances, along with Charles Rennie Mackintosh and Herbert MacNair, formed "The Glasgow Four,"[99] and were celebrated for their radically inventive explorations of decorative and industrial art, as pioneers of Art Nouveau. Their collaborative work blurred lines of authorship, with Charles himself saying, "Margaret has genius; I have only talent."[100] This mutual admiration and wealth of skills between them led to an approach striving toward the *gesamtkunstwerk*, where the interior was treated as a total work of art, heavily reliant on highly stylized motifs that were both psychologically and metaphysically resonant, and depended on a range of artistic forms to reach their expression.

Margaret Macdonald Mackintosh

1864, Tipton, UK
1933, London, UK

The Salon de Luxe, Glasgow, UK, 1903

Elsie Mackay

1893, Shimla, India
1928, Unknown, Atlantic Ocean

Viceroy of India, 1929

For Elsie Mackay, interior decorating was just one of many pursuits that marked an adventurous life cut tragically short. Born in India to a prominent family, she had a tumultuous relationship with her father, the First Earl of Inchcape, who disowned her after she eloped with film actor Dennis Wyndham. Their marriage was annulled within two years, during which time Elsie took to the silver screen as Poppy Wyndham. After their marriage ended, she reconciled with her family, and pursued various professional activities. She became England's first woman jockey and designed luxury interiors for her father's company, the Peninsular and Oriental Steam Navigation Company (P&O). She collaborated with her mother and decorated rooms on four ocean liners, drawing inspiration from Britain's stately palaces and royal homes. She added drama to the smoking room on the *Viceroy of India* by lining the room in dark wood panels and adorning the walls with crossed swords, borrowing from the interiors of the Old Palace in Bromley-by-Bow, built for James I in 1606. Uninterested in a conventional life, she trained as a pilot while working as a decorator, and announced her ambition to become the first woman to fly across the Atlantic Ocean. In 1928, a crowd of 5,000 waited at Mitchel Field, Long Island, for Elsie and her co-pilot Captain Walter G. R. Hinchcliffe, who had set out from the Royal Air Force Cranwell station in Lincolnshire to make the crossing. The pair never arrived in their single-engine airplane, the *Endeavour*.

Natalie Mahakian

1992, Jordan

Terra Eatery, Dubai, UAE, 2020

In 2018, Natalie Mahakian co-founded an architecture and interior design practice Bone with Achraf Mzily in Dubai's Jumeirah district. While intending to work only on a one-off project together, the success of their collaboration led them to sustain it. Bone's design philosophy is rooted in stripping away excess to focus on essential form—creating spaces that evoke a quiet dialogue through architectural gestures, sensorial materials, and thoughtful detailing. Inspired by Mediterranean cultures, Bone has completed various commercial interior projects, including Bageri Form, an artisanal bakery in the Dubai Design District, and Terra Eatery, which showcases Natalie's distinct aesthetic. Like many of Bone's projects, Terra is characterized by its nod to brutalist aesthetics, blending monolithic dark surfaces with a utilitarian approach to space. Natalie and Achraf modernize their unique take on brutalism with warm, tactile surfaces, reimagining the architectural style in an inviting way. They work with earth to create sculptural forms, with natural clay finishes left in their raw state in shades of chocolate brown, deep red, and charcoal gray. Natalie is drawn to traditional building methods and materials, selecting terracotta tiles to add an element of the handmade to each of Terra's surfaces, ensuring that her spaces retain a high level of craft.

India Mahdavi

1962, Tehran, Iran

The Gallery at Sketch, London, UK, 2022

India Mahdavi's cosmopolitan childhood, coupled with her Iranian-Egyptian heritage, informs her design sensibility, which is rich in color, texture, and pattern. Born in Tehran, she was raised across America, Germany, and France before choosing to study architecture in Paris at the École des Beaux-Arts, and later graphic design and furniture design in New York at the School of Visual Arts and Parsons School of Design. Her multidisciplinary training led her to join the multifaceted studio of French interior architect and designer Christian Liaigre, where she served as artistic director for seven years. She launched her own studio in 1999, and soon after opened a showroom and homewares store in Paris. Early studio projects established India in the world of hospitality through distinctive interiors for small boutique restaurants and hotels. These activities continued to grow, and found form in the development of her own furniture line, perhaps best exemplified in her now iconic dusty pink interior for the Gallery at Sketch in London, whose extravagant, plush furnishings became an instant social media sensation. She built on this success a decade later for the restaurant's 2022 redesign, trading golden, mustard yellow for pink in the new interior's color scheme that imparts India's signature warmth alongside whimsical fixtures chosen to correspond with the new art on view by British artist Yinka Shonibare, culminating in a design that is both cozy and pop. She likens her design approach to creating customized couture garments, with each of her interiors embodying a highly tailored combination of pattern, color play, and graphic elements. India's 2021 eponymous monograph encapsulates her way of working.

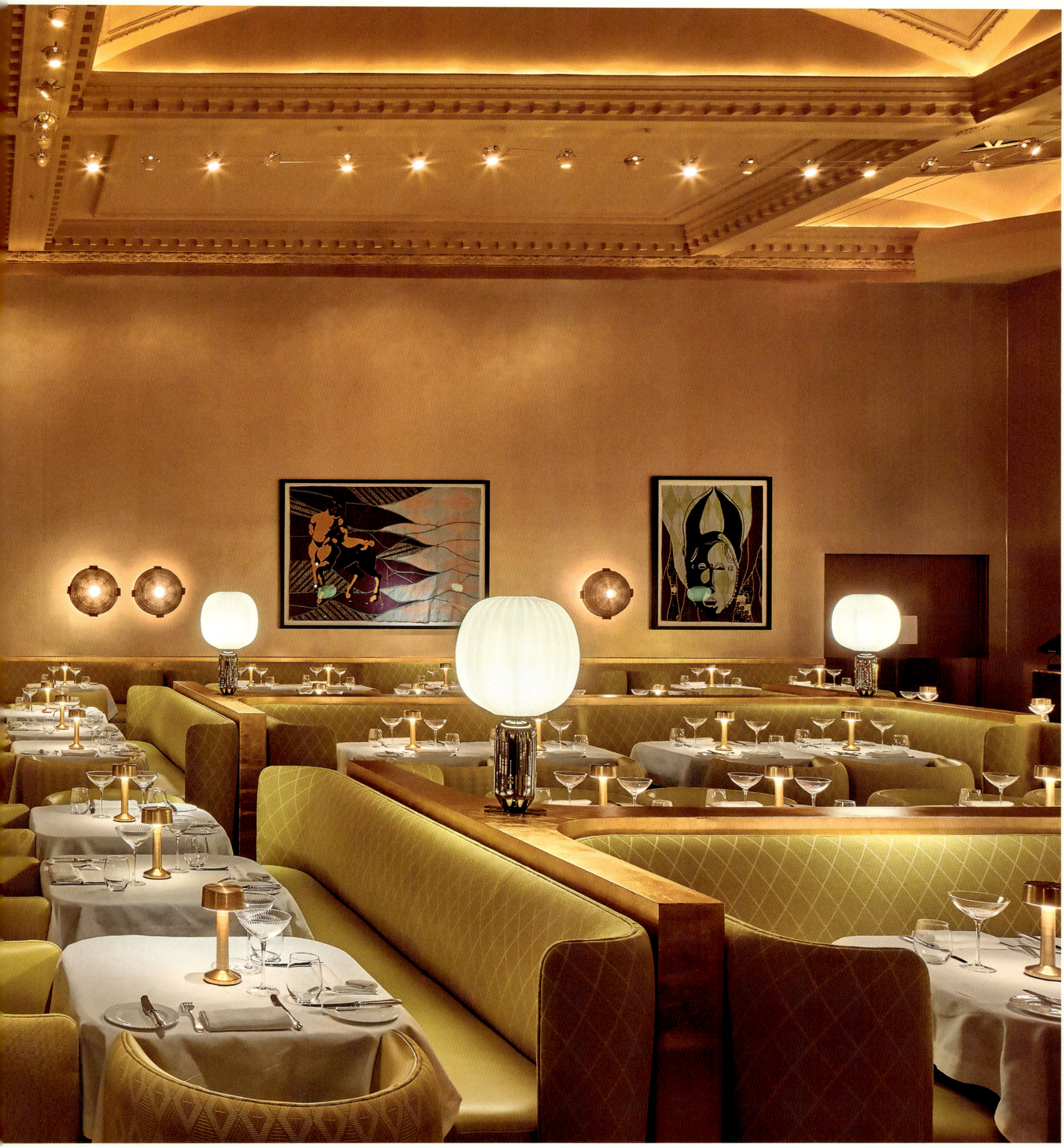

Yasmina Makram

1983, Cairo, Egypt

Palmette, Zamalek, Cairo, Egypt, 2021

Yasmina Makram "developed an appreciation for the small details" from a young age, growing up in a home filled with design magazines that nourished her passion and creativity.[101] After initially enrolling in business school, she soon realized that the corporate world held little appeal. Encouraged by her husband, she attended design school at Instituto Marangoni in Milan, where she immersed herself in the country's rich design culture. Returning to Egypt, she gained experience working in architecture studios before setting up her own firm in 2016. Yasmina's designs bridge the gap between history and modernity, weaving regional inspiration into her architectural storytelling. Her designs draw from the rich heritage of Ancient Egypt and the natural beauty of its desert landscape. Many of her projects, based in Egypt, incorporate local elements and materials in an effort to design sustainably. Her design for the interiors of the Palmette apartment in the historic Zamalek district of Cairo features an original fireplace and oversized herringbone parquet floors along with a custom made, sculptural marble bar designed so that the homeowners can sit while admiring views over the facing Aquarium Grotto Garden. The green of the garden's palm trees is echoed in the interior with modern artwork adding character to this elegant home, which is furnished with traditional pieces that reference downtown Cairo in the early twentieth century. The deep orange walls in the dining room are inspired by colors found in Egypt's landscape, and the dining table, designed by Yasmina, is paired with red leather chairs designed by Mario Bellini in 1977 for Cassina, showing her ability to pair designs from different locales and eras.

Eva Marguerre

1983, Neuenbürg, Germany

Eclectic Patio, Cologne, Germany, 2021

Eva Marguerre's interest in interior design grew out of youthful sessions spent poring over her mother's design magazines, cutting out pictures of her favorite projects and cataloging them by color.[102] She studied at the Karlsruhe University of Art and Design, where her interdisciplinary degree allowed her to experiment with a range of design applications, including for products, interiors, sets, graphics, and exhibitions. There, she met Marcel Besau, and together they founded Studio Besau-Marguerre in Hamburg in 2011. The pair are heavily guided by their process, relying on dialogue with each other to create the initial concept for a project. In addition to interior design and styling, Besau-Marguerre offers a range of services, including art direction, product design, and visual communication. They always inject surprising twists in their work, with Eva recalling a moniker—"playful purists"—a journalist once used to aptly capture their joint aesthetic evident in their use of simple geometrical forms that create a graphic two dimensional quality in their work, often softened by their extensive use of floor to ceiling curtains.[103] The duo embrace color, and are known for their inspired use of contrasting hues. In their project Eclectic Patio, a coworking café in Cologne, Eva created a series of spaces separated by semi-transparent full-height curtains each with their own color gradient blending together luminous shades of indigo, violet, pink, yellow, brown, green, and orange into dramatic colorscapes. The saturated, chromatic interior is filled with funky yet clean furniture and lighting, creating a graphic, layered effect that filters daylight through the colorful space, as if animating it in real time.

Michèle Maria Chaya and Claudia Skaff

1973, Beirut, Lebanon
1976, Tripoli, Lebanon

Harley House, London, UK, 2021

Michèle Maria Chaya is a Lebanese architect and co-leader of MARIAGROUP, a design studio she runs with her brother, Georges Maria and London based partner, Lebanese interior designer, Claudia Skaff. Known for their refined approach, Michèle and Claudia seamlessly merge traditional Middle Eastern motifs with a contemporary design sensibility, creating personally and culturally resonant spaces that are filled with artisanal craft. Together, Michèle and Claudia celebrate the art and culture of Lebanon through their signature design style that is marked by their use of rich textures and materials often sourced from Lebanese artisans, including hand carved wood, intricate metalwork, and traditional textiles. This approach endows their spaces with both luxury and cultural intimacy. MARIAGROUP's projects range from private residences to boutique hotels and restaurants in both Beirut and around the world. Recently, for a London townhouse project, Michèle and Claudia transformed the lower ground and cellar floors to enhance natural light, incorporating skylights, light wells, and conservatories. Their attention to detail and use of natural materials preserve historic elements while conjuring contemporary elegance. Their work has earned a reputation for its comfort, sophistication, and deep sense of place.

Syrie Maugham

1879, London, UK
1955, London, UK

Syrie's home, London, UK, 1932

Known as "The White Queen,"[104] Syrie Maugham was a trendsetter for modern glamour among early twentieth-century London decorators, establishing her career at the age of forty-two. Her defining project—an all-white room in her King's Road townhouse (Sibyl Colefax was a neighbor)—marked a turning point in interwar decorating. *Harper's Bazaar* remarked on the white interior, stating that it gave "that modern feeling, which in conjunction with old furniture, is so attractive."[105] Syrie's Regency style blended modern themes with a decadent past, reflecting her desire to escape her dreary Victorian upbringing. Syrie faced criticism, notably from her ex-husband, William Somerset Maugham, who accused her of business malpractice. After their separation, to maintain peace while raising their daughter, she had two separate entrances installed in their house. Her relationship with Harry Gordon Selfridge, founder of the Regent Street department store, introduced her to the synergy between creativity and commerce, leading to the opening of her first interior design shop, Syrie Ltd., on Baker Street, which later expanded to Chicago and New York. As her business evolved, so did her aesthetic, expanding her signature monochromatic palettes to include luxurious colors and patterns. Notable projects included a white rendition of Salvador Dalí's *Lobster Telephone* and, along with collector Edward James, commissioning *Dalí's Mae West Lip Sofa*. While she wasn't an artist herself, Syrie was an opulent trendsetter among the London elite, operating with a surrealist flair, popularizing practices such as gifting live animals to guests at social events.

Ellen Lehman McCluskey

1914, New York, NY, USA
1984, New York, NY, USA

Ellen's home, Southampton, Long Island, NY, USA, 1970s

Ellen Lehman McCluskey, daughter of Allan S. Lehman of Lehman Brothers, grew up wealthy, enjoying an early exposure to the arts. Her European travels with her mother ignited a lifelong appreciation for museums, palaces, and hotels, shaping her design sensibilities. She studied at the New York School of Interior Design, and later earned a master's degree in history from Columbia University. In 1946, Ellen launched her own company, quickly becoming a prominent figure in the design industry. She undertook major hospitality projects, including the grand lobby and luxury suites at the Waldorf Astoria Hotel, as well as the lobby and grand ballroom of the Plaza Hotel. Her portfolio also included corporate offices and private residences for high-profile private clients including actors Zsa Zsa Gabor and Arlene Francis. As a founder and past president of the American Institute of Interior Designers, Ellen championed the professionalization of the field. She advocated for state legislation to license interior designers, establish fee structures, and set educational requirements. Beyond her design career, Ellen was deeply involved in philanthropy, founding Just One Break, a nonprofit dedicated to vocational training and job placement for individuals living with physical disabilities. During World War II, she trained pilots and was among the first women to obtain a commercial pilot license. Additionally, she was an accomplished ice dancer, and served as a director of the New York Skating Club.

Former editor-in-chief of *Elle Decor* and *House Beautiful*, Marian McEvoy got hooked on journalism while working at the *Los Angeles Herald Examiner* during a summer break from studying at the University of Southern California. She soon dropped out of school to work in the newspaper's fashion department and, within a year, relocated to Paris at the invitation of *Women's Wear Daily*. As their European fashion editor, Marian also freelanced for numerous other outlets with by-lines in French *Vogue, Harpers & Queen, The International Herald Tribune* and *The Sunday Times* of London. In the late 1980s she settled in New York to run *Elle Decor*, where she became a familiar presence at the magazine's photoshoots, taking a hands-on approach to styling the sets and interiors. She believes in bringing a similar artistry to her own living spaces, and is as adept at directing others to execute her ideas as she is with a glue gun in hand. She became so enamored by the craft tool that she published a book, *Glue Gun Decor*, in 2005, offering fifty home decorating and craft projects showing readers how to embellish everything from walls to furniture and flower pots using unusual items such as wine bottle corks. Retiring in 2002 to her home in upstate New York, she has become a Hudson Valley artisan, decorating her eighteenth-century farmhouse and designing custom dinnerware and textiles.

Marian McEvoy

1949, Los Angeles, CA, USA

Marian's Home, Wappingers Falls, Hudson Valley, NY, USA, c.2004

Courtney McLeod

1974, New Orleans, LA, USA

Courtney's home, Harlem, NY, USA, 2019

Courtney McLeod is a New York City-based interior designer and the founder of Right Meets Left Interior Design. With a business degree from the Wharton School at the University of Pennsylvania, Courtney previously led portfolio management for a real estate investment fund before turning her hand to interior design. To gain practical skills and ground her knowledge of design history, styles, and architecture, Courtney took classes at the Parsons School of Design, the Pratt Institute, and the New York School of Interior Design, where she currently serves as a trustee. The name of her firm, Right Meets Left, reflects her philosophy of balancing innovation with logic—pairing the creative right brain with the analytical left brain. However, Courtney's interiors are anything but balanced in the conventional sense. Her designs are joyful and maximalist, as in her design for an apartment living room, where she used electric blue as a "neutral" base, complemented by orange and pink tones, to create a color-drenched jewel box-like room. Influenced by her Creole background and extensive travels throughout Europe and Asia, her work is culturally rich. Courtney's design process is client-centered, building trust with her clients, recognizing that, for many, good interior design represents a substantial investment.

Eleanor McMillen Brown was among the first interior decorators to receive professional training. She attended business and secretarial school before spending a decade traveling which sparked her interest in design, and inspired her to begin selling imported French furniture from her home. She studied for three years at the New York School of Fine and Applied Arts (now Parsons School of Design), later serving on its board and hiring only Parsons graduates at her company, McMillen Inc. Sensing how women were undermined in business and to avoid being seen as a "Lady Decorator," she named the company McMillen Inc. rather than using her full name.[106] Eleanor skillfully blended pieces from different periods—including Directoire and eighteenth-century Italian and French furniture—with modern pieces, believing good taste "must respect the past, accept the present and look forward with enthusiasm to the future."[107] Her apartment remained unchanged for over fifty years, demonstrating her belief that a well-designed interior needs no alteration. Her use of yellow, which she called "a good city color—it's cheerful," and her restrained use of patterns became hallmarks of her style.[108] Eleanor received commissions from various clients, including the White House, and was asked to decorate Sister Parish's first marital home. She maintained an active presence at her office well into her nineties.

Eleanor McMillen Brown

1890, Saint Louis, MO, USA
1991, New York, NY, USA

Eleanor's home, New York, NY, USA, c.1928

Dorothée Meilichzon

1982, Paris, France

Henrietta Experimental Hotel, London, UK, 2021

Dorothée Meilichzon, founder of the design studio CHZON, was inspired to become a designer by the French designer Philippe Starck. Dorothée initially started her career as a product designer, studying industrial design in France and the United States. Frustrated by the focus on function when designing products, in 2009, she transitioned into interior design establishing CHZON with the aim of creating unique hotel and bar interiors. Her first project was the Prescription Cocktail Club, which set the tone for her signature approach of interpreting the immediate surrounding environment and history of each place in which she designs. She conducts extensive research on the building, neighborhood, and era to ensure her interiors reflect the spirits of the cities they inhabit. She states that her designs emphasize surprise and comfort, allowing guests to "feel the vibes of the city they are in" with the aim of making them feel at home through custom furniture made by local artisans.[109] This philosophy communicates itself through her moodily lit, cozy, and colorful spaces, such as the Grand Pigalle hotel in Paris, a collaboration with the Experimental hotel group. In her iteration in Venice, Dorothée borrows from the brick tones of the surrounding buildings, which inspire the interior's color palette, and bespoke furniture, in particular oversized upholstered headboards, integrating textiles, hand-painted patterns, and mirrors.

Frances Merrill

1978, New York, NY, USA

Private residence, West Hollywood, CA, USA, 2022

Frances Merrill, the creative force behind Reath Design, grew up in New York City but developed her narrative approach to design in Los Angeles. She conveys the unique story of the people who live in her spaces through intricately layering pattern and color, showcased in projects like the remodeling of celebrated composer Igor Stravinsky's former Los Angeles home. Bold lavender kitchen cabinets and a dining room dressed in dark floral wallpaper inspired by the composer's *Fantasia* create a fantasy-inducing, immersive domestic setting that is as joyful and surprising as it is comforting. After studying creative writing and textile design, Frances began her career working at Commune Design, where she contributed to the Ace Hotel project in Palm Springs. In 2009, she founded Reath Design, developing a reputation for her uncanny and unexpected pairings of colors and textiles, mixing florals with graphic elements like her beloved stripes. Frances prefers spaces that feel worn and lived-in, and avoids adherence to any specific design era, citing Arts and Crafts designer William Morris and modernists Charles and Ray Eames as inspiration. Keen to emphasize character and story, she works with local craftspeople to make bespoke furnishings customized to each of her projects. This thoughtful approach ensures that her interiors are inimitable, age well, and are livable for their inhabitants. Frances welcomes the messiness of life with pattern and color to celebrate how people actually live.

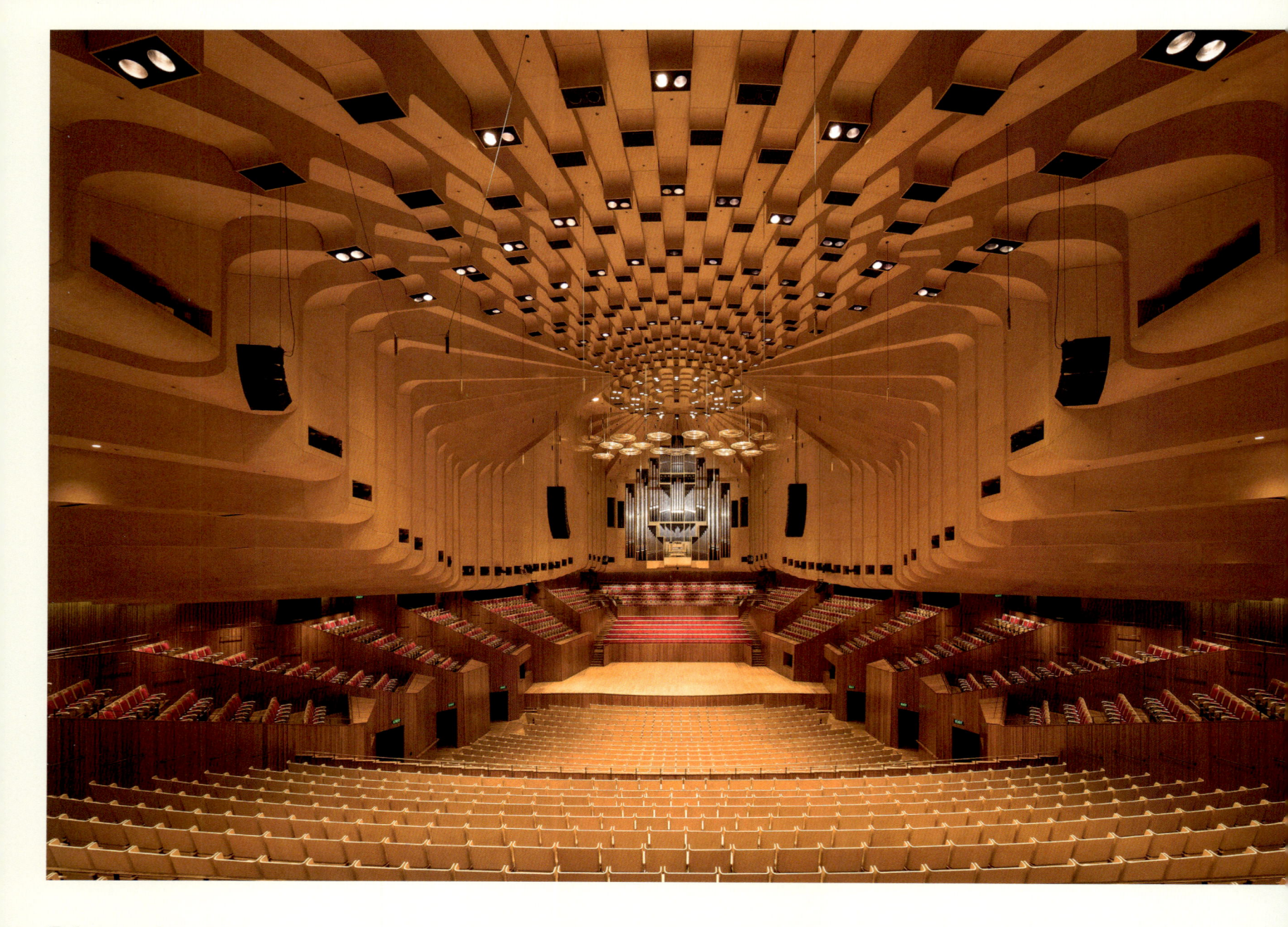

Diana Luxton Messara

Sydney, NSW, Australia

Sydney Opera House, Sydney, NSW, Australia, 1973

Diana Luxton Messara describes arriving in Sydney to work as an interior designer at the Sydney Opera House as an overwhelming, but exciting, challenge stating that it was "one of the most inspiring, wonderful experiences of my life."[110] Having grown up in the city's sleepy suburb of Cremorne in New South Wales, the Sydney Opera House was Diana's first major project. Diana built her experience at Shell Corporation and Caterpillar during an era when the industry was predominantly male. She was also one of the few women to work as a designer for the opera house. After Danish architect Jørn Utzon resigned from the project, responsibility for the delivery of the building was assumed by architect Peter Hall, whose team Diana joined in 1967. Hall's team was tasked with translating Utzon's multi-shell design into a new vernacular using Australian materials crafted by local manufacturers. In charge of the auditorium's interiors, Diana played a key role in selecting color schemes, fabrics, and finishes. A primary challenge was designing the seating. Utzon's original design could not accommodate the necessary number of seats, so Diana collaborated with a local company to develop a new mechanism to resolve the issue. The result was a functional and modern-looking chair, made in bent plywood with ample padding that adhered to the curves and upholstery of Utzon's original design. She worked on the opera house for four years, going on to practice as a painter and educator.

Elizabeth Metcalfe studied graphic design and began a career as an artist for an advertising firm, but her real love and passion was for interior design. After attending college, she opened her interior design firm, Elizabeth Metcalfe Interiors, in 1999. As a young child she was greatly influenced by her British father who passed on his love of Henry Moore sculptures, and a primary school visit to The Royal Ontario Museum in Toronto where she was introduced to the beauty of the Ancient Greeks. These influences resonate in the fluid lines and clean silhouettes of Elizabeth's interiors where she applies the time-honored principles of design that inform her work. Elizabeth has established herself as a leading interior designer in Canada with projects focused on luxury private residences. She credits her success to a commitment to designing homes that are truly original, undeniably beautiful, and deeply personal. Her design for House on the Hill, a family home in Toronto, showcases Elizabeth's ability to pair classical design elements with modern furnishings, lighting fixtures and postmodern art. A muted color palette of soft blush, oyster, and pale greens is combined with terracotta and black for contrast. Custom furniture, used throughout, is a hallmark of Elizabeth's style, and she works closely with craftspeople and embraces the handmade quality of bespoke objects.

Elizabeth Metcalfe

Canada

House on the Hill, Toronto, ON, Canada, 2024

Jeannette Meunier Biéler

1900, Sainte-Anne-de-Sabrevois, QC, Canada
1990, Kingston, ON, Canada

Jeannette's home, Montréal, QC, Canada, c.1933

Jeannette Meunier, a prize-winning student at the École des Beaux-Arts de Montréal, excelled in interior decoration and ornamental design. Before completing her studies, her talent caught the eye of Emile Lemieux, head of design at the T. Eaton Company store, who hired her as an assistant. This was a dynamic time for the company as it expanded westward across Canada, aiming to attract sophisticated urban clientele. Jeannette drew inspiration from French interiors, particularly the geometric shapes and bold patterns associated with the Art Deco period. She brought this influence to her work for Eaton's, infusing the store's studio named "l'Interieur Moderne" with a palette of silvers, beiges, and greens, which at the time was thought more suitable for swimming pools and hair salons than homes.[111] Jeannette described in her article, "La decoration, interieure moderne," published in *La Revue Moderne* in 1929, her notion of the emerging professional decorator as an "ensembleur," someone who could compose every element of a design, including creating and manufacturing each piece of furniture themselves. Married to Swiss artist André Biéler, Jeannette was deeply knowledgeable about design history and contemporary trends, further informed by their European travels. Inspired by German modern design and tubular metal furniture, she incorporated these elements into her work, and eventually left Eaton's to establish her interior design company, using her apartment as a showroom. After moving to Kingston in 1936, Jeannette scaled back her design work to raise her four children. However, she still completed several projects, including designing a nightclub interior and converting a Victorian house into a residence for women.

Ukrainian designer Yana Molodykh studied at the Kyiv National University of Construction and Architecture, followed by studies in interior design at Details Design School. Yana began her career as a draftsperson producing technical drawings, which gave her insight into the minutiae of how spaces are assembled. As a result, her interiors are all beautifully crafted, consistent in their aesthetic, and unified by her eye for detail. Yana describes her style as "eclectic" due to her love of mixing elements from different design genres, drawing on influences discovered from art, music, and travel.[112] She has designed several residences in Ukraine, as well as an apartment for friends on the shore of Lake Lugano, Campiobe d'Italia. There, an all-white color palette is softened by a bulbous, fluffy sofa, designed by Fernando and Humberto Campana, anchoring the living space. Its inclusion is a play on the many clouds floating past the room's windows, part of Yana's concept to bring the home's Alpine natural scenery indoors, which can also be seen in the monochromatic dark green bathroom. The modern interiors are complemented by objects from Ukraine such as ceramic vases and a duck egg blue painted antique wooden chest placed at the foot of a striking gray terrazzo staircase, which she included to remind her friends of their home country. The result is a cozy, tactile space that feels lived-in, yet symbolic of a fresh start.

Yana Molodykh

1972, Kyiv region, Ukraine

Private residence, Lugano Lake, Campione d'Italia, Italy, 2022

Julia Morgan

1872, San Francisco, CA, USA
1957, San Francisco, CA, USA

Hearst Castle, San Simeon, CA, USA, 1947

Julia Morgan studied engineering at the University of California, Berkeley before moving to Paris to become the first woman to attend the prestigious École des Beaux-Arts. Determined to train as an architect, Julia gained admission on her third attempt after being rejected twice, explicitly because of her gender. Defying stereotypes of her time, she completed hundreds of building projects, many featuring intricate, flamboyant, and highly decorative interiors. Her most famous work is Hearst Castle in San Simeon, California, where she employed a Spanish Colonial Revival style with Gothic elements. Commissioned by publishing magnate William Hearst to build "a little something," the project ballooned to 165 rooms.[113] It even included a zoo, which Julia designed along with the interiors and landscape. Julia's ability to construct her clients' fantasies captivated many, leading author Joan Didion to lament her eclecticism. Always in demand, Julia designed numerous homes across California and beyond. She resisted traditional gender roles and insisted on a hands-on approach, often climbing ladders to inspect work. Despite being so present in her work, her career had been historically overlooked until in 2014, at the urging of Californian architectural historians, she was posthumously recognized with the American Institute of Architects' Gold Medal, becoming the first woman to receive the accolade in the award's 107-year history.

Born in Virginia where she was instilled with a love for the outdoors, Charlotte Moss pursued an English major at Virginia Commonwealth University. A friend's encouragement led her to move to New York, where she took a position at a brokerage firm on Wall Street. However, in 1985, she chose to focus on her passion for interior design, realizing her dream by launching Charlotte Moss & Co. on the lower level of her Greenwich Village townhouse. To better serve Manhattan's wealthy clientele, she later relocated her business to the Upper East Side. Charlotte draws inspiration from her travels and infuses them into her interiors, blending French, English, and American influences with a touch of Southern warmth and hospitality. For her 2008 Kips Bay Decorator Show House, she envisioned a couple recently returned from their own world tour, desiring to surround themselves with mementos. She united disparate items—a Chinese screen with a Dutch lantern, Bonacina chairs from Lake Como, and a silk carpet from India—by using a lilac color palette. In addition to her design work, Charlotte has created products and home accessories for various manufacturers, and has authored eleven books on interior design. She was bestowed with an honorary doctorate from the New York School of Interior Design, which also awarded her its Centennial Medal of Honor in 2017.

Charlotte Moss

1951, Richmond, VA, USA

Kips Bay Decorator Show House, New York, NY, USA, 2008

Joy Moyler

1960, New York, NY, USA

Old Barn, Stanmore, Harrow, UK, 2021

Growing up in New York's Harlem, Joy Moyler always had an eye for style, and initially planned to pursue fashion, inspired by the pages of *Vogue*. However, a visit to Spain, and in particular to architect Antoni Gaudí's Sagrada Família at age fourteen, awakened a passion for architecture. Joy began her career at prestigious firms like Skidmore, Owings & Merrill and Kohn Pedersen Fox. As Head of Interior Design for Armani/Casa, Joy designed homes for celebrities such as Adrien Brody, Leonardo DiCaprio, and John Mayer. She credits her adaptability and depth of experience to having worked with lots of different companies before starting her own. Her resulting facility and versatility with a variety of styles have allowed her to take on wide-ranging commissions, including while working in fashion for Ralph Lauren, designing stores and showrooms for the brand. A fan of classical architecture, she embraces historical features in her designs, as seen in her work on an English country house known as the Old Barn, where she adorned the interior walls with Lee Jofa florals and installed bespoke chairs and loungers. Beyond her design work, Joy has served as the Design Editor for *Veranda* magazine, launched a capsule dinnerware collection, and hosted the pandemic lockdown Instagram series "High Tea with Joy," where she interviewed various creative talents.

Kim Mupangilaï

1989, Antwerp, Belgium

Kim's home, Brooklyn, NY, USA, 2022

Kim Mupangilaï, a Belgium-born, New York-based interior architect and designer, brings a unique fusion of cultures to her work, exploring the intersection of her Congolese heritage and Belgian upbringing. She studied graphic design at LUCA School of Arts and interior architecture at KU Leuven in Belgium. Taking a sabbatical to travel, she visited Australia, where a chance encounter with some New Yorkers intrigued her enough to contemplate moving to the city. Relocating to New York in 2018, Kim began working for Crème/Jun Aizaki Architecture & Design while landing her first interior project, the design of a restaurant in Brooklyn called Ponyboy Bar. However, it is the interior of her own home in New York City that showcases her interest in exploring her cross-cultural identity. Drawing on a palette of natural materials like wood, stone, raffia, and banana leaf fiber, she perceives each surface as an opportunity to display objects that reference ancestral stories. Influenced by Belgian Art Nouveau—a movement that flourished during Belgium's colonization of Congo—Kim connects modernist European design with her own Congolese heritage. In addition to interior design, her meticulous, sleek work is evident in her furniture collection, Hue, which evokes the beauty of traditional Congolese currency tools, balancing functionality with an aesthetic narrative.

Elsie Nanji

1956, Chennai, India

Private residence, Malabar Hill, Mumbai, India, 2022

Elsie Nanji left her hometown of Chennai to study applied art at Sophia Polytechnic in Mumbai, graduating in 1979. She then joined the advertising world, where she cultivated a network of writers, film directors, photographers, architects, and fine artists. Elsie was invited to be a founding partner of the Ambience advertising agency, which was later acquired by Publicis. She then became managing partner for Red Lion, Publicis's specialized design department. Elsie's journey into interior design began when she styled her own villa in Kashid, which was designed by architect Nozer Wadia. The villa's entirely white design featured painted peacock blue door frames and a spiral staircase. Nozer then invited Elsie to style and design a few other projects. Elsie describes her design style as "eccentric," blending objects, colors, and textures to craft a narrative for her spaces.[114] Despite having no formal education in interior design, she excels in balancing practicality with unexpected visual elements, echoing her personal mantra: "dream with the child within." Her current practice specializes in residential as well as commercial and hospitality projects, including the Mahindra Museum of Living History in Mumbai. For a penthouse in Malabar Hill, Elsie transformed a luxury pied-a-terre by adding a glass ceiling, large windows, and retractable blinds to maximize natural light. She installed a large painting depicting a seaside city to complement a mix of vintage and contemporary furniture.

Founder of the design studio OTTO, Paola Navone is one of Italy's most successful designers. After studying architecture in her hometown of Turin, Paola underwent a period of exploration before fully committing to a career in design; she worked for the Italian design magazine *Casabella*, and tried her hand at a range of media, participating in avant-garde groups and traveling across Africa and Southeast Asia. After groundbreaking work with Studio Alchimia and the Memphis Group, Paola went on to win the inaugural Osaka International Design Award in 1983. In the early 80s she began living between Europe and Asia, which profoundly influenced her approach to design and connected her with diverse cultures, inspiring her vibrant use of color. However, she finds the local supermarket or rummaging around a friend's attic just as inspiring. Her interiors are known for blending local handicrafts with her extensive knowledge of industrial design and manufacturing. Unlike product design, Paola believes that interior design offers more opportunities for creativity and experimentation. She primarily focuses on hospitality projects, including restaurants, hotels, and offices. Her maximal design for the 25hours Hotel Piazza San Paolino in Florence was inspired by Dante's *Divine Comedy*. Each room evokes a scene from heaven and hell, animated by monochromatic color palettes, textured materials, and surrealist touches, introduced through large sculptures and ornaments.

Paola Navone

1950, Turin, Italy

25hours Hotel Piazza San Paolino, Florence, Italy, 2021

Tanwa Newbold

1980, Lagos, Nigeria

Abstract Home, Lagos, Nigeria, 2021

Tanwa Newbold grew up in a creative household in Lagos where her father, an architect, nurtured her early interest in design. Moving to the United States at age fourteen, she later studied business for her undergraduate degree in Tennessee, before pursuing her master's degree in investment banking in the United Kingdom. After working in financial services in Memphis, London, and Lagos, Tanwa shifted her focus to interiors. Her journey into design began with producing and selling furniture in the United States and United Kingdom, where she explored blending traditional African aesthetics with contemporary forms. Recognizing the potential of the Nigerian market, she returned home and founded Nu Mi Design House, an interior design and furniture studio. Tanwa's residential projects are known for their serene, neutral-toned backgrounds that highlight sculptural furniture pieces, often upholstered in bright, primary colors. Her designs not only showcase her talent, but also champion local artisans, providing a platform for emerging African designers. She is committed to transforming Nigeria's design landscape by highlighting the quality of the country's raw materials. She also advocates for the value of locally made products, which can compete with internationally favored brands. In addition to her design work, Tanwa hosts the annual NU MI Design Luxury Exhibition that features Nigerian-made furniture and art, celebrating and promoting local craftwork.

Anna Maria Niemeyer

1929, Rio de Janeiro, Brazil
2012, Rio de Janeiro, Brazil

Palácio da Alvorada, Brasilia, Brazil, 1958

As a young architect and designer, Anna Maria Niemeyer moved to Brasília with her father, renowned modernist architect Oscar Niemeyer, to design the interiors of the government buildings for Brazil's new capital. Brasília's architecture symbolized the country's progressive social and economic politics, fostering an expanding middle class eager to furnish their homes with modern furniture. Anna Maria transformed these spaces into gallery-like settings, incorporating furniture from designers like Mies van der Rohe and fellow Brazilian architect Lina Bo Bardi. Anna Maria's interiors seamlessly blended Persian rugs and antiques with modern designs, and featured walls adorned with tapestries and Jacaranda wood paneling. Any furniture she couldn't source, she designed herself. The company responsible for building the city, Companhia Urbanizadora da Nova Capital do Brasil (NOVACAP), employed Anna Maria for an additional thirteen years. During this time, she worked on prestigious projects including for the Palácio da Alvorada, where she famously covered an entire wall in gold tiles. In 1973, Anna Maria returned to her hometown of Rio de Janeiro and opened her own art gallery, Galeria Anna Maria Niemeyer. She later founded the Museum of Contemporary Art in Niterói, a project also designed in collaboration with her father. Anna Maria's work was a vital and singular contribution to the coherence and elegance of modern Brazilian architecture.

Michelle Nussbaumer

1958, Abilene, TX, USA

Michelle's home, Dallas, TX, USA, 2019

Michelle Nussbaumer, the founder of the lifestyle brand and showroom Ceylon et Cie, is an interior designer renowned for infusing modern designs with old-world elements. With a passion for creating spaces influenced by global cultures, Michelle has built an impressive career, recently capturing her work in her book *Wanderlust: Interiors That Bring the World Home*. Based in Dallas, and having lived prior in Rome, Michelle has designed a diverse array of projects, ranging from a hacienda in San Antonio to a Georgian house in England's Cotswolds, as well as a neo-Mayan residence in her home city. Growing up in a family deeply rooted in the arts—her father was a poet, her aunt a decorator, and her grandmother a potter—Michelle's creative pursuits began early; she could often be found painting alongside her mother in her mother's studio. Michelle also spent time acting and studying the lighting, makeup, and set design that go into theatrical productions, all of which also shaped her passion for creating emotionally evocative spaces. Her own Dallas home displays the full range of her creativity, with a dense layering of furniture, objects, and fabrics enveloping each space. The result is a unique interior that mixes high-end pieces with found objects to affect a sumptuous mid-century glamour still rooted in the American South.

Georgia O'Keeffe, a Wisconsin native, left her hometown to study at the Art Institute of Chicago and the Art Students League in New York, where she was influenced by her professor, the painter Arthur Wesley Dow. She embraced abstraction under his tutelage, but initially worked as a commercial artist while teaching in West Texas. She found support for her work in collector Alfred Stieglitz, who later became her husband. After his death, Georgia moved to New Mexico, building her iconic home—known for its unique combination of traditional adobe construction with modernist architecture—in Abiquiú with companion Maria Chabot. Known for her large-scale abstract paintings of flowers, Georgia rebelled against the popular aesthetic standards of the time. In New Mexico she could explore the stark landscape and pay homage to the visual cultures of the nearby Indigenous Tewa people alongside her own modernist aesthetic. Georgia purchased the bare but materially rich, dilapidated eighteenth-century hacienda from the Catholic Church. The exterior of the building was finished with cement stucco, while the interior surfaces were finished in adobe plaster by an all-woman labor force because it was thought that they had a smoother hand with application. Georgia blended mid-century modern furniture with items built by herself or local craftspeople. She added shells, bones, flowers, and rocks from her collection, creating a medley of texture, color, and pattern that expressed, in her words, "the wideness and wonder of the world."[115]

Georgia O'Keeffe

1887, Sun Prairie, WI, USA
1986, Santa Fe, NM, USA

Georgia's Home, Abiquiú, NM, USA, 1949

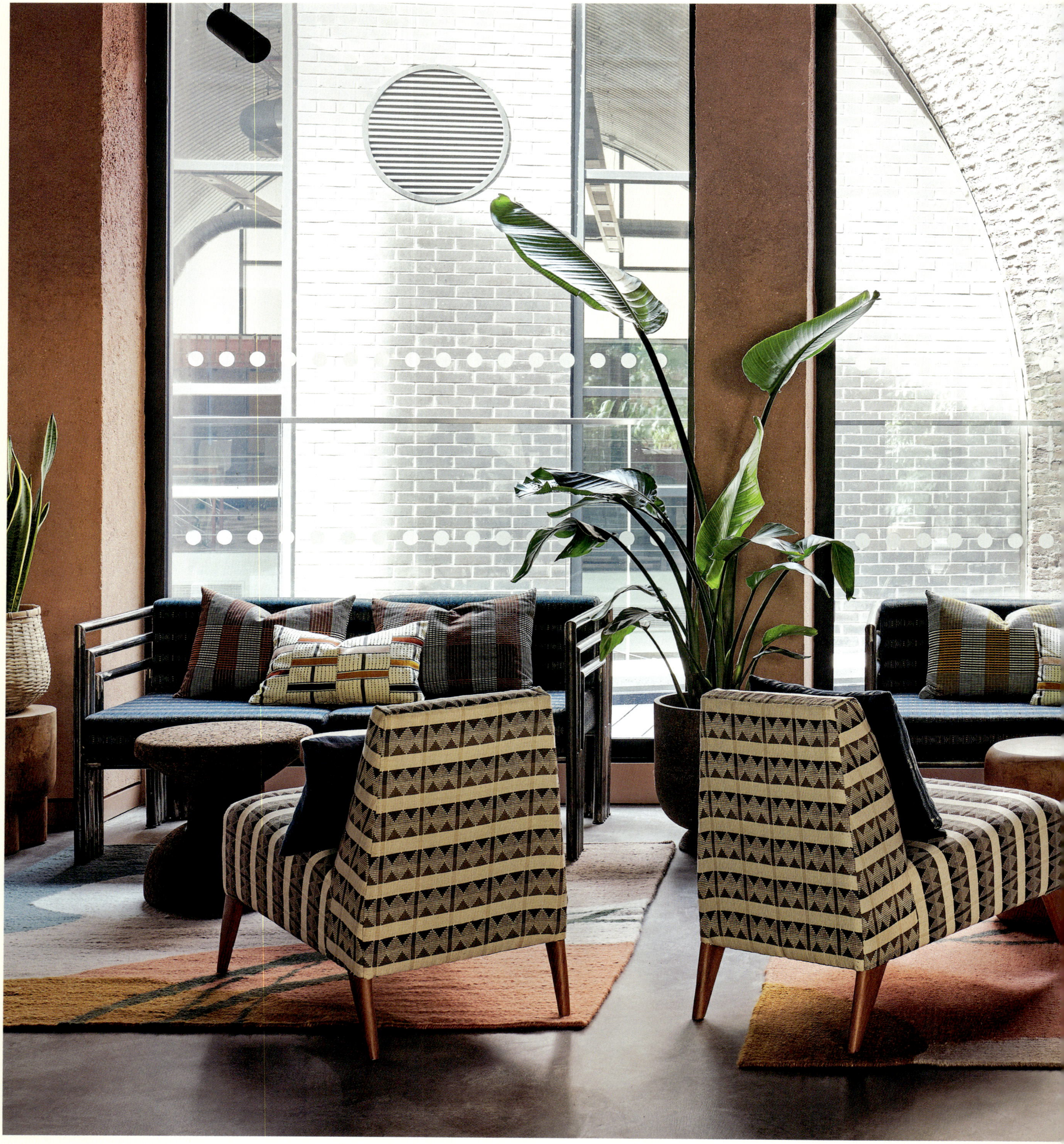

Tola Ojuolape

The Africa Centre, London, 2022

Nigerian by birth, but raised in Ennis, County Clare, Ireland, Tola Ojuolape studied interior architecture in Sligo, followed by a year at the Politecnico di Milano in Italy. An early university project designing a lamp sparked Tola's interest in handmade objects. She crafted the piece using handmade batik fabric, introducing color through the use of locally sourced natural dyes. Tola's in-depth, research-driven approach informs her interior design projects, which come together through a careful consideration of location, architecture, and heritage.[116] Finding inspiration in local landscapes and cultures, she deftly blends her African heritage with contemporary forms inspired by global art and fashion. Despite varied influences, her style remains understated, focusing on careful material pairings that underscore tactility. Based in London since 2012, Tola has completed numerous projects, including the interiors for The Africa Centre in Southwark, South London, a dedicated space to celebrate and promote African culture. Tola's designs draw on her experiences traveling across Africa, admiring the diverse design cultures such as the zigzag patters found in Ghanaian kente cloth and super mastery of craft including metal work, beading and woven materials, which she observed in places like Morocco, Rwanda, and Senegal. At The Africa Centre, she juxtaposes earthy terracotta colors with indigo clay plaster, referencing artisan cloth making in Mozambique and South Africa.

Tosin Oshinowo

1980, Ibadan, Nigeria

FG private residence, Ilashe Beach, Lagos, Nigeria, 2018

Growing up in Lagos, Nigeria, Tosin Oshinowo was an imaginative child, sketching floor plans for the family house that her father was building. She moved to Yorkshire in the U.K. to complete her secondary education, and remained in the country to gain her degree in architecture from Kingston University. Interested in learning more about the urbanism of her hometown of Lagos, Tosin undertook a master's degree in development at University College London, going on to study at the Architectural Association in London and the IE University in Madrid. She also worked at architecture firms Skidmore Owings & Merrill in London and the Office of Metropolitan Architecture in Rotterdam. In 2009, Tosin returned to Nigeria to found her own studio, cmDesign Atelier, in 2013 (now Oshinówò Studio). Her design philosophy, which she refers to as "Afro Minimalism,"[117] melds Yoruban design traditions with global modernist aesthetics, reflected in projects like FG private residence, where an all-white color scheme creates a clean and fresh look. In 2022 Tosin realized her masterplan design for rebuilding the Ngarannam village in Borno state in northwest Nigeria, consisting of new buildings to replace a settlement destroyed by the Boko Haram terrorist group. Further extending her practice, Tosin created furniture brand Ilé-Ilà, meaning "House of Lines" in Yoruba, that uses West African hardwoods and traditional textiles. She also curated the second Sharjah Architecture Triennial, and joined the cohort of Loeb Fellows at Harvard University in 2025.

Tosin Oshinowo

Maria Osminina

1984, Saint Petersburg, Russia

Maria's home, Saint Petersburg, Russia
2019

Saint Petersburg-based designer Maria Osminina creates stark interiors that celebrate pure lines and crisp geometries. Using a palette of off-white tones punctuated by sculptural furniture, Maria's design philosophy is underpinned by a fine arts background. She studied at the Saint Petersburg University of Technology and Design, then began working first as an art dealer and furniture designer, and co-founded the gallery Inner Voice in 2016 with her partner, Pavel Osminin. Working as a curator and art director, Maria's first interior design project came about when she purchased an apartment, built at the beginning of the twentieth century. In renovating it, she accentuated its historic features, maintaining the ornate plaster ceiling molds and applying a unfinished plaster to the walls. Blurring the boundaries between art and design, Maria enjoys contrasting luxury with sparseness, often using rough, imperfect, natural textures and materials like marble, limestone, and wood to delineate her elegant, clean forms. She references the long history of these materials as building products to emphasize her interest in fusing ancient and modern design technologies to arrive at her distinct notion of the contemporary. Air and light are key elements in her aesthetic that foreground sparsely placed artworks and unfinished and uneven surfaces placed in sharp contrast to monolithic, often freestanding furniture, celebrating, "the wonderful imperfection" of materials.[118]

Elisa Ossino

Lentini, Sicily, Italy

Perfect Darkness, Milan Design Week, Milan, Italy, 2019

Sicilian by birth, Milan-based designer Elisa Ossino trained in the city as an architect at the Politecnico di Milano. She followed her interest in research, undertaking a collaboration with artists and architects focused on the relationship between linguistics and computer-aided design. She credits this experience as central to her design thinking when starting a project. Elisa built her portfolio as a stylist for design magazines, quickly becoming known for her unique use of color and abstraction. Her interiors are characterized by her daring use of geometric forms, which she layers to create illusory spaces that feel like inhabiting an abstract painting. Combining such geometric forms with bright colors gives Elisa's spaces a timeless quality. Alongside her own design studio, founded in 2006 and which focuses on residential and retail interiors, Elisa set up the multidisciplinary company H+O with Danish designer Josephine Akvama Hoffmeyer, specializing in surface design. Their first project, Perfect Darkness, was staged at Milan Design Week in 2019. It used handmade ceramic tiles as a feature in every room of an apartment to highlight the duality between dark and light spaces through the use of brown and blue walls contrasted with bright red and yellow modern furniture. Elisa has initiated other organizations alongside collaborators, including Nume, a design brand for children's furniture, and Officina Temporanea, which focuses on the connection between design and social issues.

Dutch-born designer Marie-Anne Oudejans founded the successful New York fashion label, Tocca, before she took a break to live abroad in Rome and Madrid. The second chapter of her design career emerged unexpectedly. A fateful plane journey to Japan altered her path when a fellow passenger suggested she travel to India. She relocated to the country and eventually settled in Jaipur, in the northwestern state of Rajasthan, known for its vibrant dusty pink buildings. As an interior designer, Marie-Anne has embraced a similar monochromatic color palette in her projects. She drenched Hotel Narain Niwas Palace's Bar Palladio in a teal blue and bright ruby red adorned with stenciled white patterning, evoking traditional Indian decorative motifs and local wood block printing. Despite having no formal design training, Marie-Anne has completed projects around the world, including a boutique in London inspired by India's tropical fauna, which blends light green walls with black and white striped display cases. Working closely with Indian artisans, Marie-Anne's designs, regardless of their location, are imbued with a sense of the country's cultural heritage. She seamlessly blends these influences with architectural forms from her childhood, such as tents and canopies designed and crafted by her grandmother. These structures have become a recurring theme in her interiors. As she puts it, "Everything I do has tents."[119]

Marie-Anne Oudejans

1964, The Hague, The Netherlands

Bar Palladio, Jaipur, Rajasthan, India, 2013

Laura Panebianco

1984, Cali, Colombia

Private residence, Amsterdam,
The Netherlands, 2022

Based in Mexico City, Laura Panebianco creates bright, uplifting interiors worldwide. A Colombian native, Laura moved to the U.S. as a teenager. Inspired to pursue a career in architecture after watching her parents design and build their family home, she studied architecture at Wellesley College in Massachusetts and interior design at the Pratt Institute in New York, developing a design sensibility inspired by her Italian, Mexican, and American heritage. This global perspective was deepened through an internship with former Memphis Group member Matteo Thun in Milan, and time spent working in New York and Miami, where she relocated after graduation to found her own studio, Studio Panebianco, in 2016. Seeking a new adventure with her family, she moved to Mexico City in 2018. Inspired by the location and context of her projects, Laura works closely with architects to create interiors, believing in the power of design to impact well-being. In Amsterdam, Laura transformed a family home by introducing a limited palette of light browns and creamy whites as a backdrop to her client's art collection. For Laura, the quality of timelessness is captured by a space that authentically represents the personality of her clients. She extends this belief through her commitment to ecological design, often reusing materials, sourcing furniture locally, and refurbishing furniture already owned by her clients, stating that sustainability is "a major responsibility in an industry that produces so much waste."[120]

Sister Parish

1910, Morristown, NJ, USA
1994, Dark Harbor, ME, USA

The White House, Washington, D.C., USA, c.1960

Dorothy May Kinnicutt, affectionately called "Sister" by her brother, tried to trade under her husband's name, Mrs. Henry Parish II, but remained known as Sister all her life. Inspired by her time in Paris as a teenager, Sister brought a love of French furniture back to the United States, where she designed the interiors for her first home on a budget, painting the floors raspberry red with white stencilled diamonds. While decorating ran in the family (her cousin was acclaimed decorator Dorothy Draper), Sister had no professional experience of her own. She opened her decorating business in New Jersey at age twenty-three, with friends and family among her first clients, and within ten years, she had expanded to Manhattan. Sister believed design talent was innate, famously saying, "You either have it or you don't." Her confidence and unique vision persuaded wealthy New York elites to incorporate handicrafts into their upscale rooms. She became known for draping traditional patchwork quilts across beds and sofas, placing value in the history and local industry behind objects. She often drove to rural Alabama to visit the women of the Freedom Quilting Bee who made her quilts, accompanied by her Pekinese, Yummy. Her interiors caught the attention of First Lady Jacqueline Kennedy, who invited Sister to participate in the redecoration of the White House in the early 1960s. Sister nurtured talent, discovering the acclaimed designer, Albert Hadley, whose first job was to assist her at the White House, modestly claiming he "only did the curtains."[121] Her unstudied and accessible American Country style became particularly chic in the 1970s and 1980s, allowing women to give the impression that they had decorated themselves rather than invited Sister into their homes.

Luisa Parisi

1914, Cantù, Italy
1990, Como, Italy

Apartment Nessi, Bergamo, Italy, 1955

Luisa Parisi, an icon of mid-century Italian design, worked alongside her husband, Ico Parisi, for nearly fifty years. Despite her significant contributions, she has only recently been recognized as participating in the creation of their interior designs, in charge of the business, styling the interiors, and contributing textile elements. The couple's modernist style, infused with a characteristic Italian flair, became commercially successful. Luisa, who first trained as a nurse, studied under Gio Ponti at the Politecnico di Milano, and began her design career with her first husband, Giovanni Galfetti, who was killed in World War II. She later connected with Ico through the group Studio Tecnico Artistico Alto Quota, finding solace and a shared interest in integrating the fine arts, especially painters and sculptors, into their design work. This approach sought to merge culture and crafts, elevating domestic settings beyond mere functionality. In 1948 the couple launched their design firm and gallery, La Ruota (The Wheel), in Como. They worked locally, undertaking numerous interior projects, including apartment Nessi in Bergamo, where the couple used Ico's furniture designs for Cassina to create a modern, mid-century interior. Luisa added the finishing touches, introducing decorative objects including a lamp, curtains, and a painting by Mario Radice. During their joint career, Luisa and Ico designed over 150 interiors, blending art with everyday life.

Born in Turkey, Sevil Peach persuaded her Father to allow her to come to London at age sixteen to study design, ultimately studying interior architecture at the University of Brighton. After a successful career at several large architectural practices in London and Istanbul, she co-founded her own studio with Gary Turnbull in 1994. The duo aimed to maintain a personal, hands-on, and design-led approach in their work. Quickly specializing in workplace design, Sevil built a roster of high-profile clients such as Deloitte, Microsoft, Novartis, Swiss Re, Kvadrat, and Artek. Working globally, their longest-standing partnership is with the design giant Vitra, for whom they have designed office interiors in multiple locations, including the Vitra "Citizen Office" in Weil am Rhein. Sevil's design challenges the compartmentalized nature of the traditional office with a series of variable, interactive spaces that encourage communication and collaboration. Sevil's interiors are often described as dynamic and non-territorial, emphasizing communality. This approach anticipated trends like co-working, in which Sevil has also been a pioneer. She believes in human-centered design that can function as a tool for social change, and in highly digitized times she focuses on tactile comfort as a way to nurture creativity. Sevil's interiors use natural materials and timeless furniture, which she believes is crucial to a design that is as sustainable as it is comfortable.

Sevil Peach

1949, Istanbul, Turkey

Vitra "Citizen Office," Weil am Rhein, Germany, 2000, updated 2010

Mónica Penaguião

1966, Lisbon, Portugal

Lóios apartment, Lisbon, Portugal, 2021

Mónica Penaguião is a Portuguese interior designer and founder of Poeira Interior Design, with studios in Portugal and Brazil. Mónica was only fifteen when she turned her uncle's home into a makeshift shop. It proved to be an early prototype for her successful POEIRA brand, which eventually opened stores in Lisbon, Rio de Janeiro, São Paulo, and Maputo in Mozambique. Mónica studied at the António Arroio Art School in Lisbon before traveling abroad and living in Belgium for five years. When she returned to Portugal, she made the switch to interior design, led by a pluralistic design philosophy drawing inspiration from art, architecture, music, literature, and travel. She embraces an ad hoc aesthetic, preferring atmospheres that are personal, lived-in, and organic rather than pristine. Mónica often integrates the surrounding natural landscape into her projects, and her design practice extends beyond interiors to the creation of bespoke furniture and decorative objects, including sofas, ceramics, and craft items, which she manufactures in partnership with well-known brands including Bela Silva, Capellini, and Ingo Maurer. Her design for a home in the Alfama neighborhood of Lisbon showcases her eye for color and composition. She painted walls light blue and dusty pink, infusing a traditional apartment with freshness and a sense of rhythm through colorful furnishings punctuating the large spaces.

One of the twentieth century's most accomplished architects, Charlotte Perriand is most well known for her furniture design, which she never conceived of in isolation, but as part of a larger interior setting. Le Corbusier hired Charlotte in 1927 after seeing her Le Bar sous le toit apartment design at the Salon d'Automne that year. Initially rejected for a position at his Paris studio with the remark, "We don't embroider cushions here," she soon became a driving force in his workshop.[122] During her ten years with Le Corbusier, she explored unusual materials, shapes, and colors in her furniture and interior design, reflecting her indomitable, cosmopolitan, and fun-loving personality. Charlotte proposed new ways of living, evident in her ingenious designs for moveable, multifunctional furniture that enabled small-space living, such as her 150-square-foot (14-square-meter) apartment concept, emphasizing spatial efficiency. After living in Tokyo consulting for the Japanese Ministry of Commerce from 1941–1942, she spent time in Vietnam and Brazil, continuing to develop her growing design vocabulary. In this period she created designs such as offices for Air France in London. In her later years, Charlotte was the architect of Les Arcs, a ski resort in the French Alps. There she created a porous relationship between domestic activities, opening kitchens to living areas, and integrating Alpine air into the interior through balcony openings that embraced the mountain landscape.

Charlotte Perriand

1903, Paris, France
1999, Paris, France

Arc 1600, Savoie, France, c.1968

Brigitte Peterhans

1928, Sulz, Germany
2021, Chicago, IL, USA

Baxter International Inc., Chicago, IL, USA, 1975

Brigitte Peterhans, a meticulous modernist, charted an unconventional path to interior design. Her father, a Lutheran pastor and architecture enthusiast, insisted she study architecture to become an interior designer. The University of Stuttgart required that she first take woodworking classes and spend six months participating in the reconstruction of its buildings before she could enroll in classes. During a summer in Switzerland, she met Myron Goldsmith, who showed her slides of Mies van der Rohe's recently completed Farnsworth House, and encouraged her to study with him at the Illinois Institute of Technology in Chicago. Traveling to America on a Fulbright Scholarship, she followed Goldsmith's advice, studying under van der Rohe while working part-time for the architecture firm Skidmore, Owings & Merrill (SOM). After completing her studies, she returned to Germany, and worked independently for five years. Her carpentry experience proved invaluable when designer Jane Graham called, asking if Brigitte had experience with cabinetmaking. She went on to work exclusively with Bruce and Jane Graham at SOM, focusing on interior design and joined the company's Chicago office in 1968. Over her thirty-three year career at SOM, she contributed to iconic projects like the Willis Tower and the Broadgate Exchange House. At Baxter International Inc. in Chicago she used a bright color scheme for planters containing large trees in a glazed winter garden.

Kerry Phelan grew up in a creative family in Eltham, a suburb of Melbourne known for its anti-establishment history as the site of a counter-cultural movement in the late 1960s and early 1970s. Kerry studied art, sculpture, graphic design, and photography. While she never formally trained in interior design, she learned valuable design skills working in her father's interior design studio and joinery factory. This hands-on experience was balanced by an appreciation of the structured and meticulous methods for producing furniture and architectural elements.[123] She applied this design sensibility to her first job as a window dresser for a bookshop, but only lasted six months in the role, due to the outlandish nature of her compositions. Without formal training in design, Kerry continued to develop an intuitive approach, founding the interior design firm Hecker Phelan in 1999, which became Hecker Phelan Guthrie in 2003. Her projects are recognizable for their attention to detail; she works across a range of scales, from holistic planning to smaller elements such as the quality of light in a space. In 2010, she left Hecker Phelan Guthrie to initiate her eponymous design office K.P.D.O. with Stephen Javens. Working collaboratively within the studio, Kerry designs bespoke interiors in Australia and Hong Kong. Inspired by music and fashion, her style has been described as hard-edged and glamorous. This is conveyed in the sculptural furniture of residential projects like Penthouse II.

Kerry Phelan

1965, Melbourne, VIC, Australia

Penthouse II, Melbourne, VIC, Australia, 2018

Clodagh

County Mayo, Republic of Ireland

Private residence, Santa Monica, CA, USA, 2019

Irish-born, award-winning designer Clodagh (Phipps) has, since the 1980s, made New York her home. Having grown up in the country in a house that was once the summer home of nineteenth-century Irish poet and playwright, Oscar Wilde, Clodagh's interest in design was sparked during her recovery from a horseback injury. A newspaper ad led her to fashion design, and after studying pattern making in Dublin, she launched her eponymous brand at age seventeen, igniting an entrepreneurial streak that she maintains to this day. In the early 1970s, a move to Spain shifted her focus to interior design, where she worked on residential, landscape, and hospitality projects. Arriving in New York in 1983, Clodagh opened a small design store in the East Village with Ivy Ross and Sherry Williams, catching the attention of magazines like *Vogue* for her emphasis on well-being and feng shui, calling it "the design store of the decade."[124] Consulting a feng shui master for each project, she follows four principles: Contemplate, Cleanse, Clarify, and Create Your Own Spaces which she details in her book, *Total Design*.[125] Clodagh's designs, now spanning thirty-five countries and which include hotels, spas, private residences, restaurants, retail stores, and showrooms, are known for their artisanal details and use of natural materials, often inspired by objects she encounters in her travels. A long time advocate for sustainability, she promotes sustainable cleaning with lemon, vinegar, and pine to refresh spaces, a signature hallmark of her sensual, modern interiors.

Louisa Pierce and Emily Ward described themselves as nomads before starting their eponymous interior design firm, Pierce & Ward. Having met by chance in a bar in New York, the duo are now based between Los Angeles, New York, and Birmingham. Despite having no formal training in design, the pair quickly built a roster of high-profile clients, drawing on shared influences derived from travel, art, fashion, and film that coalesce in interiors that reflect each designer's diverse background. Louisa draws on more traditional themes and vintage design whereas Emily is influenced by visual culture from art and film. Their approaches overlap when creating organic interiors, mixing opulent patterns, subdued colors, and vintage objects to achieve a whimsical aesthetic. The romance of a Pierce & Ward interior is often punctuated by black and white stripes. Famous clients include Dakota Johnson and Josh Brolin. For the latter they designed a home in Malibu in which they used a palette of coral, ochre, and forest green, layering material textures to achieve their signature aesthetic. They paired a rattan lantern with red velvet 1980s Jay Spectre steamer lounge chairs, and adorned the walls with paintings to conjure a feeling of anything-goes ease punched up with a healthy dose of old-world glamour. Louisa and Emily are careful to avoid over-designing, to ensure their spaces feel naturally and effortlessly stylish.

Louisa Pierce and Emily Ward

1980, Birmingham, AL, USA
1985, Laguna Beach, CA, USA

Josh Brolin's residence, Malibu, CA, USA, 2024

Sarah Poniatowski

1973, Neuilly, France

Sarah's home, Paris, France, 2024

Sarah Poniatowski was immersed in the world of design from an early age—her father was an editor at French *Vogue*, and her mother was a decorator. Born a Polish princess, after initial studies in theater, philosophy, and communications, Sarah founded Maison Sarah Lavoine, an interior design studio, in 2002. She later debuted her first furniture and home decor collection in 2012. The studio's trademark style is to use color enthusiastically through a daring mix-and-match of patterns and materials. She has even named a signature color after herself, a deep blue-green called "Bleu Sarah." Careful furniture choices temper her wanton colors; she sources and designs pieces with clean-lined, contemporary silhouettes that are made by master craftspeople using traditional European methods. Sarah's intuitive design ethic and love for fine detail have evolved over the two decades of her studio's life to result in ever stronger, more sophisticated projects that embrace the unexpected. She believes interiors should be warm, colorful, and livable, prioritizing the enjoyment of the space over mere aesthetic appeal. This ethos is captured in multiple publications including *Couleurs Sarah* (2019). Among her notable projects is the Café de Paris hotel in Biarritz, where she created chic spaces inspired by beach huts, using Bleu Sarah on the ceiling and shades of marine blues and greens for carpets and furnishings alongside materials like linen, woven rope, and woven wicker to evoke the sea.

Cuban-born Clara Porset is renowned as a modern furniture designer in Mexico, where she collaborated with prominent modernist architects, including Mario Pani and Luis Barragán. After studying and traveling abroad in her youth, Clara returned to Cuba in 1932 to serve as artistic director for the Technical School for Women. Due to political persecution, she fled Cuba for New York, where she lived as a self-described "exile" before settling in Mexico by 1935.[126] While teaching at the School of Industrial Design at the National Autonomous University of Mexico (UNAM), she introduced industrial design to the public through lectures, promoting the lexicon "interior designer" over "decorator" to elevate the profession. Clara designed low-cost furniture for government housing projects in Mexico City, integrating modern technology into functional, vernacular furniture, most notably for the low-sitting *Butaque* chair, which she reinvented for mass production. Clara tested her designs in her own home before production, striving for simplicity and functionality. She advocated for the value of designers' skills in the face of rapid industrial growth, believing design could be both practical and socially transformative. Her work was praised for its foregrounding of Mexican craft alongside its industrial prowess. Her designs extended beyond the domestic sphere, including furniture for the executive suites of the Chrysler Building in New York.

Clara Porset

1895, Matanzas, Cuba
1981, Chimalistac, Mexico

Clara's home, Chimalistac, Mexico City, Mexico, c.1950s

Andrée Putman

1925, Paris, France
2013, Paris, France

Morgans Hotel, New York, NY, USA, 1984

Andrée Putman believed overt displays of wealth could confuse the simplicity and character of a space. A style icon herself, Andrée wore designer clothing and costume jewelry alike. She persuaded her clients that mixing styles best expressed individuality, asserting that "eclecticism, when it works, shows who a person is."[127] Insisting on modesty as a key ingredient to style, she was seen as a sensible designer even though she thought of herself as a rebel. Her high/low mix and match sensibility made her work accessible and easy to replicate for consumers. In 1977 she opened her store, Ecart International, which specialized in late-century modernism and showcased and sold her designs. Andrée's stark, contemporary aesthetic combined historical and classical styles with modern silhouettes. She applied this combination as a consultant for the Palladium nightclub in New York, and the interiors of the Paramount and the Morgans Hotel in Manhattan. Known as the first boutique hotel, her designs for Morgans put her name on the map. Over a six-decade career, she became a sought-after designer on both sides of the Atlantic, working on everything from apartments to Air France's Concorde interiors. She created, in her own words, "sweet and clean envelopes for exceptional human beings,"[128] with clients including Karl Lagerfeld, Thierry Mugler, Yves Saint Laurent, and Azzedine Alaïa.

Diana Radomysler

1960, São Paulo, Brazil

Sentosa House, Singapore, 2020

Diana Radomysler's comeback to architecture began with a chance encounter while on vacation; friends introduced her to Brazilian architect Marcio Kogan, who persuaded her to leave her job running her father's metalworking factory and join his firm, Studio MK27. Over thirty years, she has become a partner, as well as director of the interiors and design departments, leading a team emphasizing key principles of attention to detail and designing from the eye of a craftsperson. Radomysler describes her style as "contemporary with roots in modernism," citing Lina Bo Bardi, Charlotte Perriand, and Gio Ponti's holistic design approach as inspiration.[129] She layers her modern designs with antique finds to add depth and personality to each project, incorporating organic materials such as different species of wood as a nod to her Brazilian heritage. For Diana every element within a space should tell a story, creating environments that are "not only beautiful but also warm and characterful."[130] While she values clean lines, she experiments with asymmetry, color, and light to add dynamism, often achieved through bespoke furnishings. For Sentosa House, she "embraced excess," and created bold juxtapositions for an elegant composition.[131] Large sheer curtains allow dappled light to filter in, creating a soft atmosphere, while an entire wall is covered by dark walnut shelving, adding warmth and serving as a backdrop for artworks, including a gold sculpture by Brazilian artist Artur Lescher.

Chessy Rayner

1931, Perrysburg, OH, USA
1998, New York, NY, USA

Bill Blass's apartment, New York, NY, USA, c.1972

Chessy Rayner was an influential interior decorator and former fashion icon, celebrated for her refined but playful approach to design. Born into New York's high society, Chessy was a fixture on the city's social scene, and was frequently photographed and featured in *Women's Wear Daily* for her striking looks and couture fashions. She began her career as a fashion editor, working at *Ladies' Home Journal*, *Glamour*, and *Vogue*, before leaving the fashion industry to pursue her desire for greater creative freedom. In search of a lasting creative outlet, Chessy co-founded the design firm MAC II with her close friend, Mica Ertegun, where she exhibited her flair for color and knack for blending styles. Known for spare yet luxurious interiors, MAC II created effortlessly elegant spaces whose comfortable seating, soft finishes, and vivid artworks melded seamlessly into the rooms that held them, rather than standing out as focal points. Chessy's talent for recontextualizing unconventional items into high-end decor distinguished her designs; for example, she often bought furniture at department stores for use in luxury settings, stating that "not everything has to be refined."[132] Her style was a heady mix of the minimal and whimsical, displaying her love for what she called "offbeat things," unique touches that brought joy and character to her spaces.[133] This can be seen in the penthouse apartment she designed for Bill Blass in New York in the 1970s. In contrast, her later understated redesign of the same apartment demonstrated her talent for creating elegant interiors. She arranged period furniture—such as chaise longues and classical wood pieces—against a backdrop of brilliant white walls, with dark wood flooring enhancing the sophisticated look.

Interior design was one of the few creative industries accessible to women during the interwar period. Talented across multiple disciplines, Lilly Reich found commercial success in furnishings and textiles. Initially a fashion designer, Lilly collaborated with the Wiener Werkstätte and was appointed to the board of directors of the Deutscher Werkbund. Both organizations promoted the industrialization of interior design as a means of modernizing the country, which shaped Lilly's formative project, the *Haus der Frau* at the Deutscher Werkbund's 1914 exhibition in Cologne. Lilly embraced modern utilitarian forms and luxurious materials like leather, marble, mirrored chrome, glass, and onyx. Working primarily in Berlin, Lilly met architect Ludwig Mies van der Rohe, with whom she co-authored notable works, including the *Barcelona Chair* for The Barcelona Pavilion in 1929. While Mies often receives sole credit, Lilly's role as Director for the German contribution to the Barcelona International Exhibition was invaluable. Recognizing her exceptional skills, Mies invited Lilly to the Bauhaus design school in Dessau, where she became one of the few women to lead a department. The Nazis closed the school in 1933, coinciding with the pair's completion of the Villa Tugendhat in Brno, a significant modernist project in what is now the Czech Republic. In the late 1930s, Mies emigrated to the United States, while Lilly remained in Germany to continue teaching.

Lilly Reich

1885, Berlin, Germany
1947, Berlin, Germany

Villa Tugendhat, Brno, Czech Republic, 1930

Suzanne Rheinstein

1946, New Orleans, LA, USA
2023, Los Angeles, CA, USA

Private residence, Northern California, USA, c.2019

New Orleans native Suzanne Rheinstein was celebrated for infusing her interiors with a Southern flair. Although her mother was a decorator and owned an antiques store, Suzanne initially pursued a career in journalism. Studying English literature at Tulane University, she worked as a freelance television producer and as a researcher for Pulitzer Prize-winning journalist Hodding Carter. In 1977 she married Fred Rheinstein, a television producer based on the West Coast and the couple moved to Los Angeles. Her passion for design led her to follow in her mother's footsteps, and in 1988, she opened Hollyhock, an antiques and decorative arts store. A gateway into interior design for Suzanne, Hollyhock offered upholstered furniture, William Yeoward glasses, and eighteenth-century prints. Suzanne's style—East Coast sophistication married with the relaxed lifestyle of California and the American South—was captured in her mantra, "Fewer things, but better ones."[134] Her interiors often mixed Regency and nineteenth-century French antiques with anachronistic objects, such as cowboy-style chairs and seventeenth-century Japanese chests found in her clients' homes. In one notable project, a Northern California residential library, Suzanne incorporated a lacquered green ceiling to match the wall color, adding depth and elegance to the space. She earned many accolades over the years, including the Albert Hadley Lifetime Achievement Award from the New York School of Interior Design.

Katie Ridder

1961, Ann Arbor, MI, USA

Katie's home, Millbrook, NY, USA, 2012

Katie Ridder grew up in California and discovered her passion for interior design at a young age sewing quilts and entering them into craft fairs. She was inspired by a local decorator who painted trompe l'oeil carpets onto floors and was influenced by her uncle's collection of European antiques. Katie's journey into the design world began with a five-year stint as an assistant at the magazine *House & Garden* in New York where she mastered the smaller details and practical aspects of design as she staged photoshoots. A transformative trip to Turkey exposed her to luxurious fabrics and accessories, prompting her to open a homewares store in New York City. In the six years she ran her store, she attracted her first interior design clients, deepening her knowledge of the materials and textiles that have come to shape her painterly yet unfussy interiors. Katie designs with a photographer's eye, borrowed from her editorial background, which enables her to fearlessly compose color and volume to arrive at eclectic yet harmonious spaces. She has authored several books, including *Rooms* and *A House in the Country* (co-authored with her husband, architect Peter Pennoyer), the latter showcasing the home they built in Millbrook, New York. There, Katie has employed sophisticated color blocking, patterned upholstery, and antique furniture, infusing each room with vibrant reds, pinks, oranges, and yellows that both contrast with, and complement, the home's Greek Revival architecture.

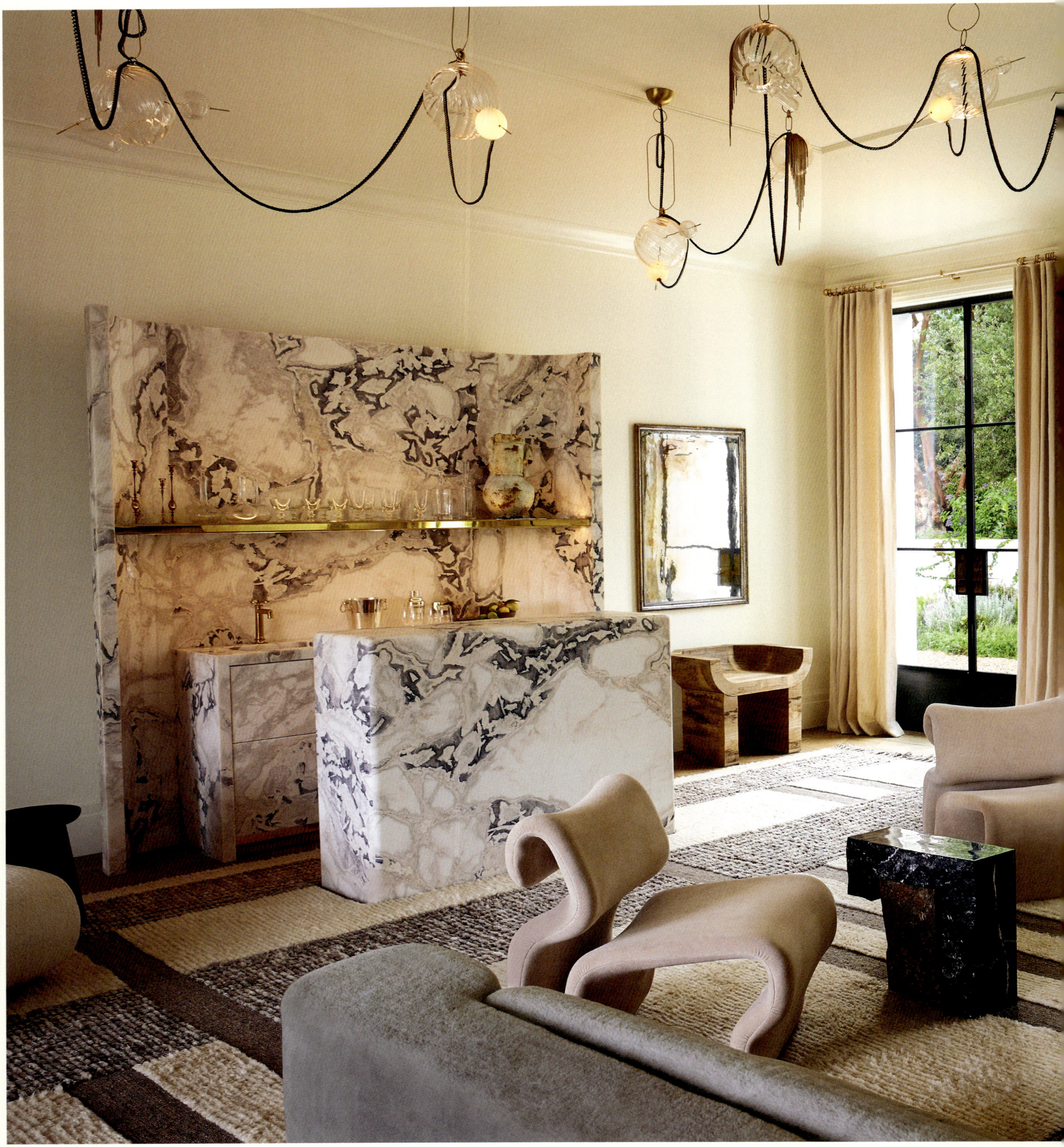

Brigette Romanek

1974, Chicago, IL, USA

Gwyneth Paltrow's home, Montecito, CA, USA, 2023

Brigette Romanek is a self-taught interior designer based in Los Angeles. Her youth was spent between the South Side of Chicago and traveling with her mother, who was a professional singer, and this exposure to different places and styles encouraged Brigette's creativity. After a short stint in London, she moved to Los Angeles, where she began to help her friends design their homes. What started as a passion project quickly became a full-blown career. She founded her eponymous studio in 2018, designing for high-profile clients including Beyoncé, Demi Moore, and Gwyneth Paltrow, who wrote the foreword to Brigette's monograph, *Livable Luxe*. A leader in the recent wave of talented, female-led interior design firms in Los Angeles, Brigette distinguishes her interiors through her love of mixing classical pieces with quirky and contemporary foils. She channels the personality of each of her clients in the creation of her interiors, as in her design for Gwyneth's home, which married strong, simple forms with organic textures and understated colors. For the dining room, Brigette chose a romantic, hand-painted scenic wallpaper to contrast with a starkly contemporary table and chairs. The interior includes a sculpture by D'lisa Creager and many bespoke commissions from Gwyneth's favorite designers and friends, including a large-scale sculptural lighting installation by designer Lindsey Adelman.

Catarina Rosas, Catarina Soares Pereira, and Cláudia Soares Pereira

1945, Braga, Portugal
1970, Braga, Portugal
1973, Braga, Portugal

Showroom, Lisbon, Portugal, 2019

Catarina and Cláudia Soares Pereira have a rich legacy rooted in their family's history and love for furniture and interior design. In the 1980s, their grandfather purchased a dilapidated eighteenth-century manor house in Braga, north of Lisbon, for their mother, interior designer Catarina Rosas. She spent two years restoring the property before founding her interior design business, Casa do Passadiço, in 1993. Cláudia and Catarina Soares Pereira soon joined the firm, motivated by the lifelong passion for design they inherited from their family, who surrounded them with art from an early age. Casa do Passadiço operates out of the restored manor house, showcasing the family's elegant style of discreet luxury, where antiques blend with contemporary pieces, creating a sophisticated and timeless aesthetic. Catarina, Cláudia, and Catarina specialize in bespoke furniture and plan to launch their own line, produced by local artisans in Braga. Their portfolio includes both residential and commercial projects, such as several stores for the fashion house Aquazzura. In 2019, the trio opened a second showroom in Lisbon and in 2024 they opened a third in Porto. The lobby of the Lisbon showroom makes a statement with its glossy, red paneled wall and striking marble reception desk, while the sitting room is painted and furnished entirely in white, offering a serene ambiance. Elegant curved sofas introduce a sense of movement which is echoed by the large abstract artwork on the wall.

Ruby Ross Wood stood out among the early "Lady Decorators"[135] due to her lack of upper-class background.[136] At the turn of the twentieth century, she was a journalist for Vogue when she was enlisted by famous decorator Elsie de Wolfe to ghostwrite articles for The Delineator magazine, which were later reworked into Elsie's successful book, The House in Good Taste. Ruby's initial projects, including her publication The Honest House and her company, a decorating store and interiors firm called Modernist Studio, failed to find success. Undeterred, Ruby joined the department store Wanamaker's heading their decorating department Belmaison, and worked with Nancy McClelland in the famed fourth floor antiques division Au Quatrième, building her profile before establishing Ruby Ross Wood Inc. Ruby decorated her apartment as a showroom, supposedly moving annually to redecorate. Known for her skill in pairing antique and modern furniture with a vibrant use of color, she built a customer base among her clients from Au Quatrième. Notable projects included a monochromatic red drawing room and a green bedroom accented with purple and black. Her most famous design was the Swan House in Atlanta, featuring antique Chinese wallpaper, English furniture, and her signature plaid taffeta curtains. Ruby's design talent was revered, especially by her protégé, the renowned designer Billy Baldwin.

Ruby Ross Wood

1881, Monticello, GA, USA
1950, Syosset, NY, USA

The Swan House, Atlanta, GA, USA, 1928

Maye Ruiz

1985, León, Guanajuato, Mexico

Casa Coa, San Miguel de Allende, Mexico, 2024

From residential projects to bars and hotels, designer Maye Ruiz has become a sought-after name in Mexico for her creative, joyful, and color-drenched interiors. Experimenting with interior design as a child in her grandmother's house, Maye followed her passion by studying design at La Salle Bajío university in her hometown of León. Her time there sourcing textiles broadened Maye's perspective on richer color palettes and sparked her passion for color, and in 2021, she launched her own design studio in San Miguel de Allende. The city's Spanish Baroque architecture inspires Maye's designs, where she blends Mexico's rich cultural heritage with contemporary shapes and bold, often acidic colors. Her project Casa Coa, a residential design on one of San Miguel de Allende's most beautiful streets, showcases her skillful use of dramatic tonal pairings with avocado green millwork setting off deep burgundy tiling and furnishings, with botanical wallpaper prints functioning as a bridge to weave the powerful hues together into a cohesive scheme. The result is an interior that has postmodern traits within an eclectic style that enhances the colonial character of San Miguel de Allende, with every surface painted in a contrasting hue, from ceilings to door frames. The highly chromatic rooms are unified by a checkerboard motif that repeats throughout the house and into the courtyard, bringing a sense of coherence and rhythm to the entire space.

American-Sudanese designer Rabah Saied's studio Styled Habitat, based in the Dubai Design District, is renowned for creating some of the region's most stylish interiors across residential, commercial, and hospitality projects. Her interest in design caught the attention of her boss, who encouraged her to study the subject formally. Since founding Styled Habitat in 2016, Rabah has infused her designs with her unique notion of luxury, coining the motto "Design is Luxury for All."[137] Her interiors layer neutral tones to create quiet, understated spaces. This is evident in Rabah's design for BAYN Café in Qasr Al Muwaiji, where she drew inspiration from the site's existing mudbrick building, dating back to 1897. Blurring the boundaries between interior and exterior, Rabah—who also oversaw the café's architectural design—introduced a modern structure with floor-to-ceiling windows that flood the space with natural light. Inside, a rich terracotta clay-plastered ceiling envelops the space, while a bronze coffee bar serves as the focal point. In addition to her work as an interior designer, Rabah has designed products for other companies, including sustainable architectural surfaces manufacturer Cosentino, for whom she designed a playful series of modular furniture units in a capsule collection using carbon neutral materials.

Rabah Saeid

1976, Khartoum, Sudan

Bayn Coffee, Qasr Al Muwaiji, Abu Dhabi, UAE, 2023

Tara and Tessa Sakhi

1989, Beirut, Lebanon
1991, Beirut, Lebanon

"I was Hearing Colours," Sax jazz restaurant and lounge, Beirut, Lebanon, 2017

Tara and Tessa Sakhi are Lebanese-Polish architects and designers who collaborate together in designs that deftly merge heritage with modernity, driven by a shared commitment to design innovation and sensorial experiences. Tara, based in Paris, Venice, and Beirut, leads the multidisciplinary architecture and design studio T SAKHI founded in 2016. Tessa is based between Venice, London and Beirut and runs her eponymous architectural and interiors studio. Born in Beirut, the sisters' creative journey began at the Academy Libanaise des Beaux-Arts in Beirut, where they studied together. Tara later pursued her studies at the École Supérieure d'Architecture in Paris, while Tessa continued at the American University of Beirut's Faculty of Architecture. After graduation, they decided to collaborate on their first interior design project. Their work reflects a unique blend of Arab and European cultures. Their design for a restaurant and jazz lounge in Beirut featured deep teal walls and gold furniture, an early emblem showcasing their ability to bring together disparate materials to create sumptuous experiences. For their solo exhibition during the Venice Glass Week, the sisters exhibited sculptural vessels which were the result of experimentation with glassblowers on the island of Murano in Venice. Through disrupting traditional processes they have created work that is a testament to their bold approach to materiality, experimentation, and improvised forms.

Teresa Sapey

1962, Cuneo, Italy

Palazzo dei Fiori, Venice, Italy, 2023

Teresa Sapey is an internationally renowned designer, hailing from Italy and now based in Madrid. She studied architecture at the Politecnico di Torino before pursuing a bachelor's degree in fine arts at the Parsons School of Design campus in Paris. Graduating in 1985, her first client was her father's secretary, for whom she designed a home. Finding few opportunities for architects in Italy, Teresa relocated to Spain, where the design industry was thriving. In Spain, Teresa expressed her creativity through various hospitality projects, contributing to the burgeoning tourist sector in Madrid. In 1990, she founded her design studio, Teresa Sapey + Partners, and over the years, she has collaborated with iconic design brands such as Vondom, iSiMAR, Coordonné, and Diabla, for whom she has created a range of products, including chairs, rugs, and lamps. Teresa now co-runs the studio with her daughter, Francesca Heathcote Sapey. Together, they have delivered numerous interiors, from celebrated residential designs to award-winning retail and hospitality spaces, and even a parking lot for the Hotel Puerta América in Madrid. Her design, Palazzo dei Fiori, for Room Mate Hotels in Venice, exemplifies her playful yet refined style. Inspired by the concept of a Venetian secret garden, the hotel, set within a grand palazzo, features oversized furniture pieces rendered in pastel colors and earthy hues taken from the regional flowers of northern Italy.

Laura Sartori Rimini

1964, Milan, Italy

Private residence, Italy, 2010

The decadent interiors of architect Laura Sartori Rimini evoke a bygone era, featuring highly decorative baroque details layered with rich, deep colors like burgundy, emerald, violet, and gold. Drawn to the city's history, Laura studied architecture in central Florence, going on to complete a master's degree in building restoration before forming Studio Peregalli Sartori with her business partner Roberto Peregalli in the early 90s. Their sumptuous old world style—inspired by their mentor, interior architect Renzo Mongiardino—honors historical references while maintaining a sense of play. The duo embark on annual sourcing trips to handpick the antiques they place throughout their spaces to construct the imagined narratives captured by the title of their 2011 monograph, *The Invention of the Past*. Laura's designs tend toward the dreamlike, as she explains, "it's always a re-interpretation, like a reverie."[138] Her detailed designs draw not just on the past, but also from nature, prioritizing organic shapes and motifs in wallpapers and textiles. Her project for a northern Italian Renaissance palazzo is as timeworn as it is opulent, featuring rust velvet sofas and ornate antique carpets hung on the walls, revealing behind them a fresco depicting a classical Renaissance building elevation replete with grand columns. In Laura's own apartment in London, she collages disparate styles and influences to create a distinctive heady mix, embodying her fascination with "how things get broken…and then fixed."[139]

Uruguayan native Katty Schiebeck was keen to travel the world and, at the age of nineteen, had the opportunity to move to Barcelona. Working in real estate, she developed a keen eye for interiors, advising clients on how to renovate and refurbish their homes. Katty combines the vibrancy of Latin America with a northern European-inspired neutral color palette to create a unique aesthetic that interweaves unusual furniture shapes and materials such as honey-colored wood and dramatically veined marble. A self-taught interior designer, Katty aims to uncover and highlight a building's original existing attributes, from revealing ceramic tiles to restoring historic cornicing. Her aesthetic is warm and comfortable, featuring mid-century modern pieces while respecting clean lines and emphasizing light. Without overcrowding a room, Katty uses furniture to delineate space, describing her style as museum-like minimalism. Her successful blog, Somewhere I Would Like to Live, serves as a digital archive of her design interests and influences, incorporating photography, travel, and interiors. With projects in diverse locations such as Silicon Valley and India, Katty successfully imbues her projects with a love of natural materials and sculptural volumes firmly settled in their cultural contexts.

Katty Schiebeck

1989, Colonia, Uruguay

Bilú Riviera, Montevideo, Uruguay, 2024

Gaby Schreiber

1916, Austria
1991, UK

Queen Elizabeth 2, late 1950s

Gaby Schreiber studied theater and interior design across Europe, starting her career as an interior decorator in Vienna before establishing her own business in 1935. She gained a reputation for her pottery, glassware, light fittings, and household objects, but her production was curtailed at the start of World War II, as she was forced to flee to the United Kingdom. There she worked in Lord Antrim's furniture factory and, influenced by the Bauhaus, experimented with molded melamine. She designed plastic products and plastic-encased cabinetry for pioneering manufacturer Runcolite, earning her the moniker, the "Plastics Queen of England."[140] Promoted as a housewife who could appeal to other women, Gaby was both glamorous and easily relatable. She enjoyed unusual color combinations, evident in her own home which was painted beige with apricot-colored furnishings. As an avid art collector, she credited Henri Matisse with teaching her how complementary pink and orange could be. In 1943, she returned to interior design, setting up her firm, Gaby Schreiber & Associates, in London. She won contracts for small-scale interiors, but gained real fame in the late 1950s as the designer chosen to overhaul the interiors for the British Overseas Airways Corporation's major airlines. Gaby also joined a team of many high-profile designers to work on the *Queen Elizabeth 2*. Gaby designed its theater, creating a stone white and cyclamen interior with plum and puce seats.

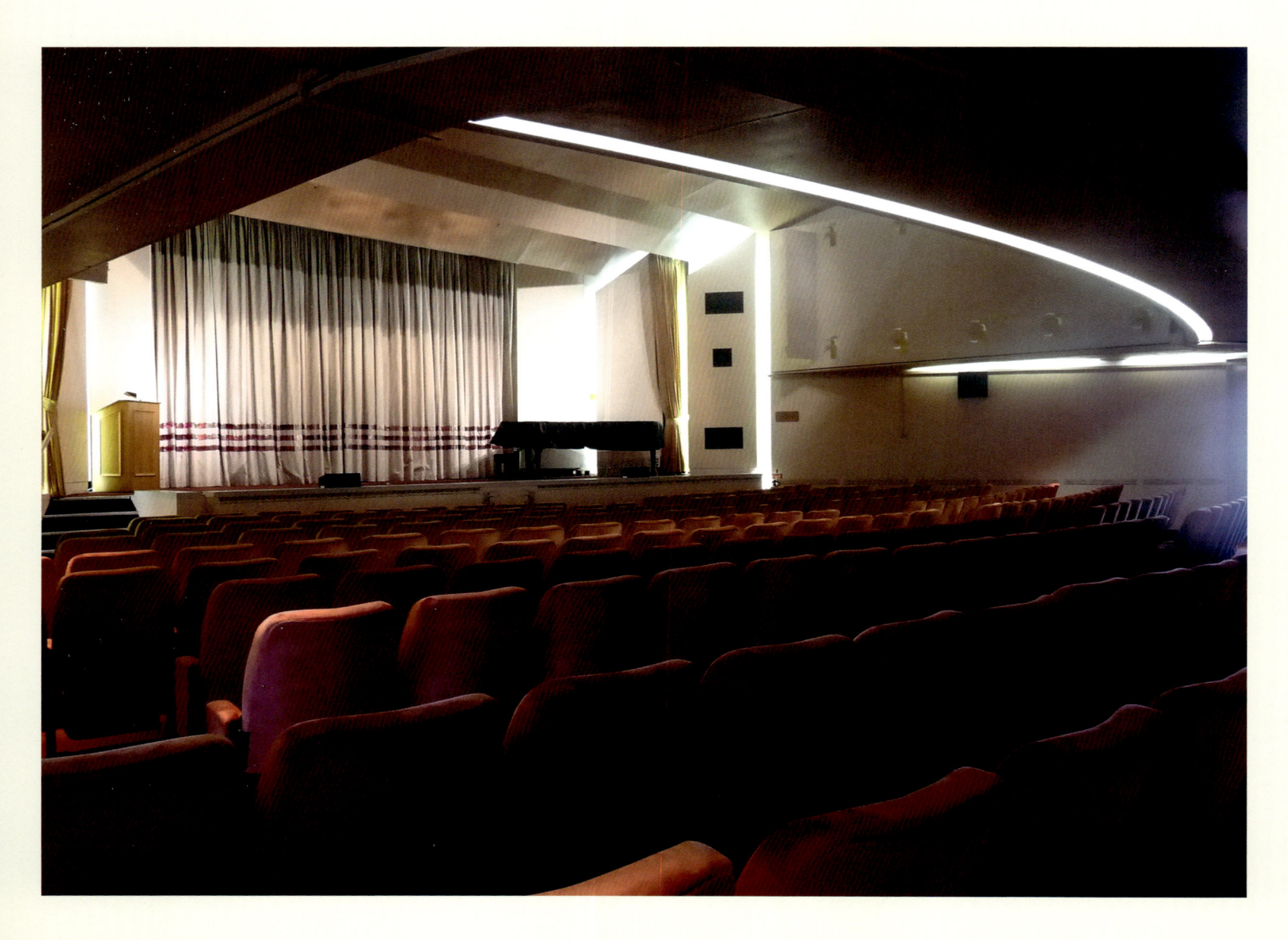

Truus Schröder played a significant role in the creation of the Rietveld Schröder House with designer Gerrit Rietveld, a contribution for which she is often overlooked. Truus met Gerrit in 1911, and they maintained a close and intimate relationship, even though both were married at the time. Truus felt trapped by her marriage and the duties of homemaking that had overtaken her original vision for her life as one of study and work. Her husband's death in 1923 allowed her to commission Rietveld to create the Rietveld Schröder House in Utrecht for her and her children. Their collaboration had already begun before this commission, when Truus had Gerrit modernize a room in her home by introducing innovative furniture and a gray painted datum. These stylistic changes resonated with her interest in Dadaism and emerging modernist art trends. An early supporter of the De Stijl movement, Truus sought a home that broke from conventional interiors. Dissatisfied with Rietveld's initial proposal, she became an integral contributor to the design process. She designed sliding walls on the first floor that could configure to create one large living area that emphasized openness and a connection to the natural landscape outside. Truus and Gerrit established a business in its ground-floor studio, designing De Stijl-inspired interiors. They only lived together after the passing of Gerrit's wife, and continued to champion principles of simple design, embodied by the house they now shared.

Truus Schröder

1889, Deventer, The Netherlands
1985, Utrecht, The Netherlands

Rietveld Schröder House, Utrecht, The Netherlands, 1924

Anastasia Schuler

1987, Magadan, Russia

Anastasia's home, Zurich, Switzerland, 2018

Anastasia Schuler grew up in eastern Russia, surrounded by Soviet-era design. Pushing against the practical decor and uniform interiors, Anastasia's imagination overflowed with new, inventive design possibilities for her family's home. She tested some of these ideas in the iconic computer game, *The Sims*, which allowed her to design entire worlds unfettered from the constraints of her everyday life, with special attention paid to the homes for her digital inhabitants. Anastasia earned a degree in business and entrepreneurship in tourism, and moved to Zurich, however, her continuing interest in design motivated her to relocate to London to further her studies at KLC School of Design. Returning to Switzerland, Anastasia worked for the furniture giant Vitra, where she gained valuable experience marketing iconic design pieces. In 2018, she established ASD Studio, undertaking a range of projects globally. Her style is modern and minimalist, accented with color and reflective surfaces, with quirky, metallic furniture in stark, concrete settings a recurring motif in her work. Inspired by art, music, film, architecture, and travel, Anastasia's work evinces a fascination with human nature, particularly the personal stories of her clients. For her own home she created a "study in contrasts" making a space that feels modern and tactile.[141] Well-worn books, mementos from her travels, and her daughter's artwork all form an integral part of her interior to capture memories, drawing out what goes unspoken to inform a sensory space that one can touch and feel.

Margarete Schütte-Lihotzky's most notable interior, the Frankfurt Kitchen, was designed while she was working for the Frankfurt building department. It became the first mass-produced fitted kitchen, and was installed in 10,000 homes in Germany in the late 1920s. Measuring 13 feet long by 7 feet wide (3.4 by 2 meters), it featured a layout based on efficiency studies embodying the era's leading scientific and technological approaches to house design. Margarete believed that transforming the home would lead to the "economic independence and self-realization of women."[142] She was the first female architecture student at the Kunstgewerbeschule (now the Vienna School of Arts and Crafts) in 1915 and was involved in the Social Democratic Workers' Party of Austria (SDAP) campaign to build social housing. It reflected her belief that poor living conditions could be as deadly as direct violence. In 1941, her political activism led to imprisonment by the Nazis on charges of acting as a courier for the Communist Party of Austria. After escaping execution, Margarete returned to Vienna in 1945, setting up "warm rooms" for the homeless, a precursor to modern social welfare kitchens. Due to her Communist Party affiliations, she struggled to find work in Austria and so pursued work in Cuba and China. She published a memoir about her political activities and took legal action against those who diminished the significance of Nazi concentration camps. Her dedication to social justice and vitality were evident even in her later years, exemplified by the waltz she danced on her one hundredth birthday.

Margarete Schütte-Lihotzky

1897, Vienna, Austria
2000, Vienna, Austria

Frankfurt Kitchen, Frankfurt, Germany, c.1926

Gillian Segal

1989, Vancouver, BC, Canada

Private Residence, West Palm Beach, FL, USA, 2020

In 2013, Gillian Segal founded her eponymous firm in Vancouver, specializing in the design of luxury residential and boutique commercial spaces. At just twenty-four years old, the Canadian designer had already built a roster of clients, allowing her to leave the design firm where she worked to set up on her own. Despite knowing from a young age that she wanted to be a designer, Gillian initially enrolled in a more general Bachelor of Arts degree, pursuing as many courses in the arts as possible. Frustrated with the limitations of her studies, she simultaneously undertook training in design at the British Columbia Institute of Technology. Her love for the decorative arts translates through her modern aesthetic, which draws on classical themes to create an elegant, clean style. Gillian is most interested in how the interior functions as a site of self-expression, conveyed by stimulating the senses through texture, color, and light to make rooms as comfortable as they are dynamic. Interiors like a residence she designed in Palm Beach showcase how she carefully tunes furniture and objects to color within a space, using a serene but saturated palette of greens in the living room employing a technique she refers to as "dunking," painting every surface, including the ceiling in Farrow & Ball's Card Room Green.[143] This effect serves as a backdrop to quirky furniture, including dramatically oversized poufs and sculptural bespoke pieces.

Tekla Evelina Severin, a Stockholm-based interior architect, colorist, designer, and photographer, graduated in 2010 from the Interior Architecture and Furniture Design program at Konstfack University of Arts, Crafts and Design. Rather than adopting a traditional minimalist Scandinavian palette of whites, beiges, and grays, Tekla's signature is her use of color, and understanding of color theory, articulating that "Color is always relative, never absolute. It's what you put next to it that defines it."[144] Early in her career, she worked at an architecture studio, where a rarely used material library filled with colors and textures ignited her passion for maximalist interiors and bold colors. In 2015, Tekla founded her own multidisciplinary studio spanning architecture, set design, and color consulting. Quickly establishing her signature style through exhibitions of her work in Milan, Bologna, and Copenhagen, she gained a following as a color expert and trend forecaster online. Her "Teklan Editions" collaborations with companies such as IKEA and Fjällräven have grown her international reputation, as has her role as artistic director for the interior materials brand Toniton, which she launched with collaborators in 2020. Her project "An Apartment of One's Own" for Spanish furniture maker Sancal at the 2022 Salone del Mobile showcases her ability to extend her daring color palettes across a range of materials, including color-dyed wood and bespoke terrazzo floor and wall surfaces.

Tekla Evelina Severin

1981, Gävle, Sweden

"An Apartment of One's Own," Escenas by Sancal, Salone del Mobile, Milan, Italy, 2022

Darshini Shah

1984, Mumbai, India

Dhvani Bhanushali residence, Mumbai, India, 2022

Darshini Shah is an interior designer whose interiors are shaped by Indian crafts, particularly through the incorporation of Pichwai, an ancient Indian art form with vibrant and intricate patterns and motifs painted on cloth. The motifs like lotuses, elephants, peacocks, and cows have symbolic significance. She frequently visits Rajasthan in northwestern India to source furniture pieces and find inspiration, as Pichwai is prevalent throughout the state. Darshini integrates motifs borrowed from Rajasthani art into her designs through colorful murals and hand-painted walls. Collaborating with Indian artisans and craftspeople skilled in traditional art forms, she sources antique and vintage furniture while customizing Pichwai artworks for her projects, emphasizing sustainability through restoration and reuse. Darshini has become Bollywood's go-to interior designer, creating spaces for filmmaker Imtiaz Ali, actress Katrina Kaif, and Saif Ali and Kareena Kapoor Khan's ancestral home, Pataudi Palace. Darshini has also extended her practice to highrise developments, such as the interiors for singer Dhvani Bhanushali's home on the seventy-sixth floor of a Mumbai skyscraper. For this project, Darshini was tasked with uniting four separate apartments to create one cohesive family home. She spent considerable time getting to know each family member, and embraced the core challenge of maximizing the extraordinary views. She opted to use white marble floors and glass doors throughout to minimize the threshold between inside and outside.

Pamela Shamshiri's love for interiors is rooted in her childhood spent playing among the furniture in her father's six-story showroom in Tehran. After the Iranian Revolution, aged nine, she moved with her family to Los Angeles, going on to study the history of art and architecture at Smith College. She then earned a master's degree in film production design at NYU. This research-driven education, particularly her work designing for period films, sparked her interest in narrative and storytelling. These have become defining features of her interior design practice and are inspired by the history of the buildings in which she works. Pamela co-founded the award-winning multidisciplinary firm Commune, which quickly gained recognition for its fusing of architecture, interiors, graphic, and product design. They are best known for their work for the Ace Hotel group. In 2016, Pamela co-founded Studio Shamshiri, focusing on residential, commercial, and hospitality projects. She is committed to supporting local craftspeople and favors working with organic materials that develop a patina with age. The studio's design for Maison de la Luz, now known as Maison Métier, in New Orleans, exemplifies Pamela's knowledge of history and attention to detail. The hotel, set in a historic early 1900s building, is layered with colors and textures drawn from various eras, unified by a signature style that makes hospitality spaces feel intimate in scale, like a private home.

Pamela Shamshiri

1970, Tehran, Iran

Maison Métier, New Orleans, LA, USA, 2019

Elodie Sire

1975, France

Private residence, Tuscany, Italy, 2014

Elodie Sire, an interior architect, discovered her passion for design after watching a TV show about interiors at the age of ten. Growing up in a family that valued a comfortable and well-furnished home, Elodie developed a deep appreciation for interiors that serve practical needs while expressing personal history and character. Founding her agency, d.Mesure, in 2007, Elodie has established herself as a designer who shuns the uniformity of trends, and instead emphasizes a unique narrative for each project. This approach quickly gained acclaim, so much so that her first solo project graced the cover of *Elle Decoration* in 2008. Elodie is known for her ability to balance timeless simplicity with playful fantasy, creating a distinctive, layered aesthetic that blends diverse styles. She carefully curates her interiors with a thoughtful but often minimal arrangement of furnishings, her spaces enlivened by punchy colors and bold patterns, adding personality and character to her designs. For the interior of an eighteenth-century stone farmhouse in a UNESCO protected area of Tuscany, she accompanied her client to flea markets to hunt for the perfect home furnishings. Sourcing architectural salvage materials, Elodie paired these finds with other vintage items, classic Italian designs by Gio Ponti and Franco Albini, and her own custom furniture, including a metal desk, finished with a leather surface to achieve a modern yet rustic atmosphere.

Halina Skibniewska was a quiet revolutionary. She was part of the Home Army, an underground resistance movement during World War II, and later became known for her sensitive, deeply socialist designs for apartment blocks across Poland. The postwar political landscape provided fertile ground for her ideas, which she developed alongside Polish modernist architects like Helena and Szymon Syrkus, members of the International Congresses of Modern Architecture. Halina incorporated humanistic, social, and technological themes, focusing on the social function of design. An early advocate for accessibility in housing, she recognized the importance of designing for people as they aged or became infirm. Her designs were so popular that peers often said they wanted to "live at Skibniewska's."[145] As a correspondent for the French magazine *L'Architecture d'Aujourd'hui*, she promoted open-plan home models and flexible apartments that could adapt to changing user needs and evolving family structures. Halina's designs featured furniture that could be rearranged to suit different living situations. She was ahead of her time in addressing environmental concerns, advocating for buildings to be adapted rather than demolished. Halina believed in responding to practical concerns, especially as economic conditions worsened and home sizes shrank. From 1958 she designed many public housing estates and her passion for public service led to her serving as a Member of Parliament.

Halina Skibniewska

1921, Warsaw, Poland
2011, Warsaw, Poland

Sady Żoliborskie Estate, Warsaw, Poland, c. 1958–72

Lena Solovyeva

1975, Moscow, Russia

Carré Blanc, Moscow, Russia, 2024

Lena Solovyeva is a multidisciplinary designer and artist from Moscow. Starting her career during the post-Perestroika period, Lena benefited from Moscow's increased connectivity to international art and design communities. This exposure to various disciplines led her to co-found Art Bureau 1/1 (Oneoverone) with Ilya Klimov in 2006 and embark on projects internationally. Their first project, a boutique jewelry store on Rue Saint-Honoré in Paris, marked the beginning of numerous private and public projects across Russia and Europe. Inspired by painting, music, nature, and architecture, Lena's projects are defined by the seamless integration of artworks within the interior. Drawing inspiration from the personalities of her clients, Lena aims to tell a story with her designs. This results in emotionally rich spaces. In her design for the apartment Carré Blanc, Lena used the local scenery surrounding Lake Baikal as inspiration, reflected in her choice of icy silver, snowy white, and berry red tones in the space. She creates a sensory experience through natural materials, including gray marble the color and veining of which evoke the look and texture of birch branches in the snow.[146] Lena is a practicing artist, and her collection of furniture, Object/Modules, was presented in 2024 at the PAD Paris design fair. She also teaches at Moscow's British Higher School of Art & Design, where she emphasizes the need for collaboration between designers and craftspeople to promote sustainability in design.

Maria Speake is an expert in the reuse of architectural salvage and reclaimed materials. In 1993, she and her partner, Adam Hills, founded their design studio Retrouvius after studying architecture together at the Glasgow School of Art. It was at university that their interest in repurposing building materials began, with Maria responsible for the interior design of their joint projects. The duo are skilled at reinventing any material, from hand-dyed reclaimed fabrics to whole sections of buildings—including wood paneling, fireplaces, and even limestone recovered from Heathrow Airport. Through her work with Retrouvius, Maria showcases the patina of a material's previous life, creating unusual furnishing combinations born out of the availability of a given material. This constraint not only prevents waste, but adds character and imbues an interior with a sense of history. In fashion designer Bella Freud's house, Maria used Iroko, a reclaimed tropical hardwood, for the worktops in the kitchen, and glass panels from Unilever House and Battersea Power Station paired with salvaged marble in the bathroom. Maria achieves a unified identity in the interior by applying a graphic color palette to the walls and floor, with a green carpet and mustard and brown paint colors used in the bedroom, creating the sense of an indoor courtyard. In every Retrouvius project, Maria modernizes worn and weary materials with her effortless sense of style.

Maria Speake

1970, London, UK

Bella Freud's Shed, London, UK, 2019

Anna Spiro

1978, Brisbane, QLD, Australia

Brisbane Cottage, Brisbane, QLD, Australia, 2020

Having left school at age seventeen, Anna Spiro received vocational training in design, working for John Black, a leading Brisbane-based interior designer. She became a partner in his firm after only six years, and they rebranded as Black & Spiro. After a number of years of collaboration, she took the reins of the business and eventually renamed it Anna Spiro Design in 2015. Her aesthetic is very much her own. For Anna, the element of surprise is key to her signature approach, be it focusing on an antique piece of furniture or an unusual work of art. Her love of richly layered fabrics, the interplay of painted colors, and the use of bold, patterned wallpapers has made her spaces instantly recognizable. Her design for a guest cottage exudes her maximalist philosophy, with vibrant turquoise blue walls in the living room complemented by a custom-designed sofa and textiles from her own hand-printed fabric collection. Her design for the cottage was based on the colors of the Australian bush from "orange and pink flowers in the garden to the brown soil."[147] In her designs, standout fabric prints often serve as the foundation for a rich narrative, with each element contributing to a cohesive composition, an approach captured in her book, *Anna Spiro: A Life in Pattern*.

Isabelle Stanislas

1970, Fontenay-sous-Bois, France

Private residence, Paris, France, 2021

Educated at the École des Beaux-Arts in Paris, French designer Isabelle Stanislas began her career working with a group of friends in a collective known as Passage du Cheval Blanc, engaging in multi-disciplinary projects across art, photography, landscape design, and architecture. A chance encounter led her to the fashion world, where she started designing boutiques for Zadig&Voltaire. Her interiors, edgy and raw, contrasted sharply with the hyper-feminine aesthetics popular in interiors of the time. This concept quickly gained international recognition, leading to collaborations with leading fashion houses such as Hermès, Schiaparelli, and Cartier. Her modern approach, infused with French and Italian craftsmanship, earned her prestigious commissions, including the Élysée Palace in Paris, the official residence of the president of France. Isabelle's expertise and eye for the interplay of contrasting materials like marble and cashmere are showcased in her book, *Isabelle Stanislas: Designing Spaces, Drawing Emotions*. The book highlights her ability to weave historical references into contemporary forms. It features projects from around the world, including numerous residential designs in Paris, where she pairs minimalist white and beige tones with warm timber furniture, accents of black paint, and flecks of gold.

Sara Story

1974, Tokyo, Japan

Gramercy Park Townhouse, New York, NY, USA, 2021

Sara Story draws inspiration from her global upbringing, particularly her time spent in Asia. Born in Japan and raised between Singapore and Texas, she experienced a diverse cultural landscape that continues to influence her work. Having been brought up traveling the world with parents who appreciated and collected art, Sara's own townhouse renovation in Gramercy Park showcases her talent for incorporating an eclectic mix of found objects collected over two decades of travel, an interior design methodology reminiscent of collage. In her home Sara created a patchwork style by drawing on different eras of design. This can be seen in the living room where she paired a 1970s Swedish caramel colored leather sofa with a Carrara marble coffee table. Her adventurous spirit is evident in her extracurricular pursuits, such as playing elephant polo in Thailand and climbing Mount Kilimanjaro. With a master's degree in interior architecture, and experience under the mentorship of Victoria Hagan, Sara founded her namesake firm in Manhattan. Her firm has designed projects in locales ranging from Aspen and the Hamptons, to Beverly Hills and Texas, as well as internationally. Known for her fresh, multi-layered, artful interiors, Sara strives to create spaces that people want to spend time in. She believes art and lighting bring "whimsy and magic" to an interior, adding depth and ambience.[148]

Madeline Stuart

Los Angeles, CA, USA

Private residence, Telluride, CO, USA, 2022

Esteemed Californian interior designer Madeline Stuart has a background as unique as her designs. As a child, she appeared in a cameo role in *Willy Wonka & the Chocolate Factory*, directed by her father. Influenced by her mother, a seasoned designer who worked with clients like Neil Diamond and Alan Alda, Madeline spent her early career as the decorator of choice for high profile clients including Larry David and Lindsey Buckingham. A friend's introduction led to Madeline's first design project, where she painted cabinets, hung drapes, and taught herself to draw to scale, designing her own custom furniture. She has a strong reverence for interior design history and emphasizes the importance of integrating furniture and objects from the past into her designs, believing that a room without such juxtaposition lacks interest, depth, and soul. From crafting the colorful and ornate interiors of a Bhutanese-inspired home in Colorado to the dark wood paneling of an Arts and Crafts home in Beverly Hills, Madeline's eye for composition allows her to create immersive environments. This is captured in her book *No Place Like Home: Interiors by Madeline Stuart* (2019) which describes how her belief in the endurance of historical trends "be it modernist or traditional" imbues her own work with a sense of timeless elegance.[149]

Ulla Tafdrup

1906, Denmark
1996, Denmark

Built version of Ulla's Søndergårdspark Kitchen design, 1940s

Ulla Tafdrup created one of the most simple yet impactful and replicated spatial interventions of the twentieth century. During the interwar period, Ulla questioned the functionality of the kitchen, which was then a closed-off space where women labored out of sight. By making a small window in the wall separating the kitchen from its adjacent dining room, Ulla connected women to their families, transforming housework into a more social activity during which everyone could spend time together without disrupting domestic tasks. In addition to creating the precursor to the open-plan kitchen and dining room, Ulla conducted extensive research into the way women use the kitchen. Through time-motion studies and investigations into how to reduce the number of steps required to navigate the space, including organizing different zones for cold and hot meals, her goal was to conceive the kitchen as the most important and central room in a house, rather than relegating it to an overlooked ancillary space. Throughout her lifetime, Ulla received extensive media attention for her work, traveling internationally and appearing on Danish television. She was one of many women who gained recognition for revolutionizing architecture for social good in Denmark. This group included Ragna Grubb, who ran her own studio, and Karen Hvistendahl and Ingeborg Schmidt, who created housing for low-income families, pioneering some of the country's first large-scale housing projects.

Naoko Takenouchi gained extensive experience as a restaurant designer in Tokyo, bringing her expertise in hospitality to her design partnership with her husband, architect Marc Webb, whom she met while working together in Thailand. The couple founded Takenouchi Webb in Singapore in 2006, and their first project involved converting the chapel that served as the couple's own wedding venue into a restaurant called The White Rabbit. Naoko's resourcefulness and design imagination stem from childhood. As a girl she made her own toys from materials her parents gifted her. She trained as an architect and interior designer in Japan and England, and worked for Shigeru Ban and Design Studio Spin on projects throughout Asia before specializing in interior design in Singapore for SCDA Architects. The growing culinary scene in Singapore coincided with the establishment of Naoko's studio, allowing her to leverage her background to secure opportunities in restaurant design. For the members' club Straits Clan, Naoko and Marc drew on their love and knowledge of iconic twentieth-century design while defining a modern Singaporean aesthetic. They integrated elements such as Shanghai plaster, a finish that replicates stone, and glazed tilework. The couple like to work with natural finishes, and Naoko in particular is attentive to detail, crafting every aspect of a space and styling each object.

Naoko Takenouchi

1974, Hamamatsu, Japan

Private dining room, Forma, Singapore, 2023

Rose Tarlow

1944, New York, NY, USA

Rose's home, Provence, France, 1991

Designer Rose Tarlow began her career as an antiques dealer and boutique owner in Los Angeles, establishing R. Tarlow Antiques in 1976. This store evolved into her flagship showroom, Rose Tarlow Melrose House, in West Hollywood, where she began creating and selling antique furniture reproductions, with up to 400 pieces concurrently in production. She is selective in her choice of projects, stating that "I never take a job unless it intrigues me" resulting in only five clients in a fifteen-year period.[150] Courting a timeless aesthetic, Rose embraces what she describes as an emotional approach to design, believing that furniture possesses individualistic traits and that "a chair has a human quality to it."[151] The uncomplicated, seemingly effortless beauty of her interiors belies a fastidious eye for detail. She once commissioned an artist to meticulously hand paint replicas of a rare eighteenth-century Chinese design as wallpaper panels for her dining room, only to carefully distress the freshly painted wallpaper herself with sandpaper and steel wool to make them appear more aged, much to the horror of her family. Her book, *The Private House*, was re-released by Rizzoli in 2024, and involved a similar duration to complete due to Rose's exceedingly careful and discerning eye. The book, positioned as her personal manifesto, encourages the reader to cultivate their own personal style with their home's interior.

Nthabi Taukobong

1973, Soweto, South Africa

Steyn City Showhouse, Johannesburg, South Africa, 2015

After twenty-one years of working as an interior designer, Nthabi Taukobong wrote a letter to herself ruminating on her career. Nthabi realized that she was writing a memoir that could serve as a template for other young designers. She published her book, *The Real Interior*, in 2019, detailing her upbringing in Soweto during apartheid, her move to Durban at the age of ten, and her father's attempts to educate his children. Nthabi's passion for decorating began at a young age, and she formally studied interior design at Durban University of Technology, followed by a year studying in Calgary, Canada as a Rotary Exchange scholar. After graduation, Nthabi found herself leading the project to redesign the interiors of the famous Blue Train, a luxury hotel on wheels in South Africa. Founding her own company, Ditau Interiors, in Johannesburg, Nthabi describes herself as a spiritual architect and storyteller. Curating spaces that reference the rich cultural heritage of African design, she sources materials and furniture from across the continent. For Nthabi, comfort is central to the harmony and balance she seeks in her designs. She specializes in residential and leisure projects, counting presidents and African royalty among her clientele. She holds influential roles as a board member of The African Institute of the Interior Design Professions (IID) and is chairperson of The Black Interior Designers Forum (BID).

Paola Trombetta

1959, Milan, Italy

Patio house, Medina of Marrakech, Morocco, 2020

Paola Trombetta has made Morocco her home since 2009, when she founded her design practice TRABDESIGN in Marrakech. She studied architecture at the Politecnico di Milano but switched to industrial design under the tutelage of Marco Zanuso. Paola continued to work with Marco after graduation, contributing to interior projects such as the Piccolo Teatro in Milan. Her career progressed as she took on architectural roles designing public buildings, including schools and sports complexes, as well as private residences. She maintained a relationship with her alma mater, returning to teach there until the late 1990s, all the while directing her own design firm, through which she expanded her practice to include furniture and interior design. Drawn to Morocco's rich material culture, Paola relocated there and established TRABDESIGN with architect Bruno Melotto. Together, they create minimal yet comfortable spaces that integrate local colors and textures. Paola's work in Morocco ranges from the renovation of riads to homes. For the riad Dar Al Dall, she used traditional tile work known as *zellige*, along with carved plaster to preserve the history of the building, while for a notable redesign for a small house in the Medina of Marrakech, she focused on conveying a contemporary architectural language still rooted in local traditions. Here, textured surfaces such as an olive green velvet sofa and geometric patterned orange rug capture the atmosphere of her adopted country.

Suzanne Tucker

Private residence, San Francisco, CA, USA, 2020

Interior designer Suzanne Tucker grew up in Montecito, California, where the bucolic landscape, along with accompanying her parents to their friends' houses for parties, impacted her early love of architecture, design, and horticulture. Suzanne initially studied interior architecture at the University of Oregon before transferring to UCLA, where she established her deft eye for scale and proportions. While spending time in London, Suzanne developed a love for English decorating, particularly the colors and decorative flourishes characteristic of the country house aesthetic. Returning to California, she became the protégée of renowned designer Michael Taylor, after which Suzanne and her husband and partner, Timothy F. Marks, founded their joint studio, Tucker & Marks, in 1986. Suzanne eschews fleeting trends by weaving together elements from different historical periods while embracing her client's personal style. She believes that good design is not about rules or trends but about creating enduring style and beauty that has the ability to enhance a person's daily life. Such versatility is evident in her work on an Italianate Renaissance-style palazzo, where she prioritized capturing natural light while framing views, creating ease of flow with seductive sight lines, and establishing the backdrop for her clients' art and antiques collection.

Virginia Tupker

1978, London, UK

Lauren Santo Domingo's home, Southampton, NY, USA, 2019

As editor for *House & Garden USA* and home editor for *Vogue*, Virginia Tupker brings a compositional and editorial eye to her own designs. She turned her hand to interior design after a colleague, the shoe designer Tabitha Simmons, invited her to decorate her Manhattan brownstone, where Virginia introduced bold, wide blue and white stripes and an oversized butterfly rug. The success of this project, which was widely published, led to more residential and commercial commissions where Virginia was able to further explore her playful, elegant aesthetic. Responsive to the personality of her clients, Virginia rejects the notion that she has a recognizable style of her own, apart from her willingness to make daring choices when it comes to color and pattern. This is evident in her use of oversized white and blue tattersall checks in the design of a bedroom in the Upper East Side apartment of fashion editor Derek Blasberg, or the rich colors and delicate layered textile prints deployed in the living room of Moda Operandi co-founder Lauren Santo Domingo's house in Southampton, New York. Having grown up in South West London, surrounded by design, Virginia is now based in Connecticut in the United States.

Rose Uniacke

1963, Oxford, UK

Rose's home, London, UK, 2012

Rose Uniacke is an acclaimed multi-disciplinary designer renowned for her refined approach to interiors and architecture. Following in her mother's footsteps, Rose worked as an antiques dealer, when she first developed her eye for quality and craft, receiving early training in furniture restoration and gilding. This background instilled a deep respect for history, which Rose skillfully weaves throughout her own interiors. Her book, *Rose Uniacke at Home*, published in 2021, documents the renovation of her personal London residence, originally built in 1860 and once the studio of artist James Rannie Swinton. Her work on the house, restoring plasterwork and moldings, showcases her signature style of harmoniously blending historical integrity with contemporary elegance to create inviting, timeless spaces. Keen to retain the stripped back, bare feel of the building before its restoration, she used a subtle material palette throughout, focusing on untreated materials, including marble, stone, wooden floorboards, and linen. Rose's minimalist approach favors simplicity over unnecessary decoration, pairing the sophisticated with the relaxed to infuse warmth in grand settings. Her thoughtful combinations of evocative textures and neutral tones allow a room to feel both restrained and full of character. Unable to source specific furniture pieces for her own home, Rose worked closely with craftspeople to design furniture and lighting, which led to the launch of her own furniture line, Rose Uniacke Editions, in 2010. She now sells antiques and a custom range of homeware; including furniture, fabrics, paint, and accessories, across three dedicated shops on London's Pimlico Road in Chelsea.

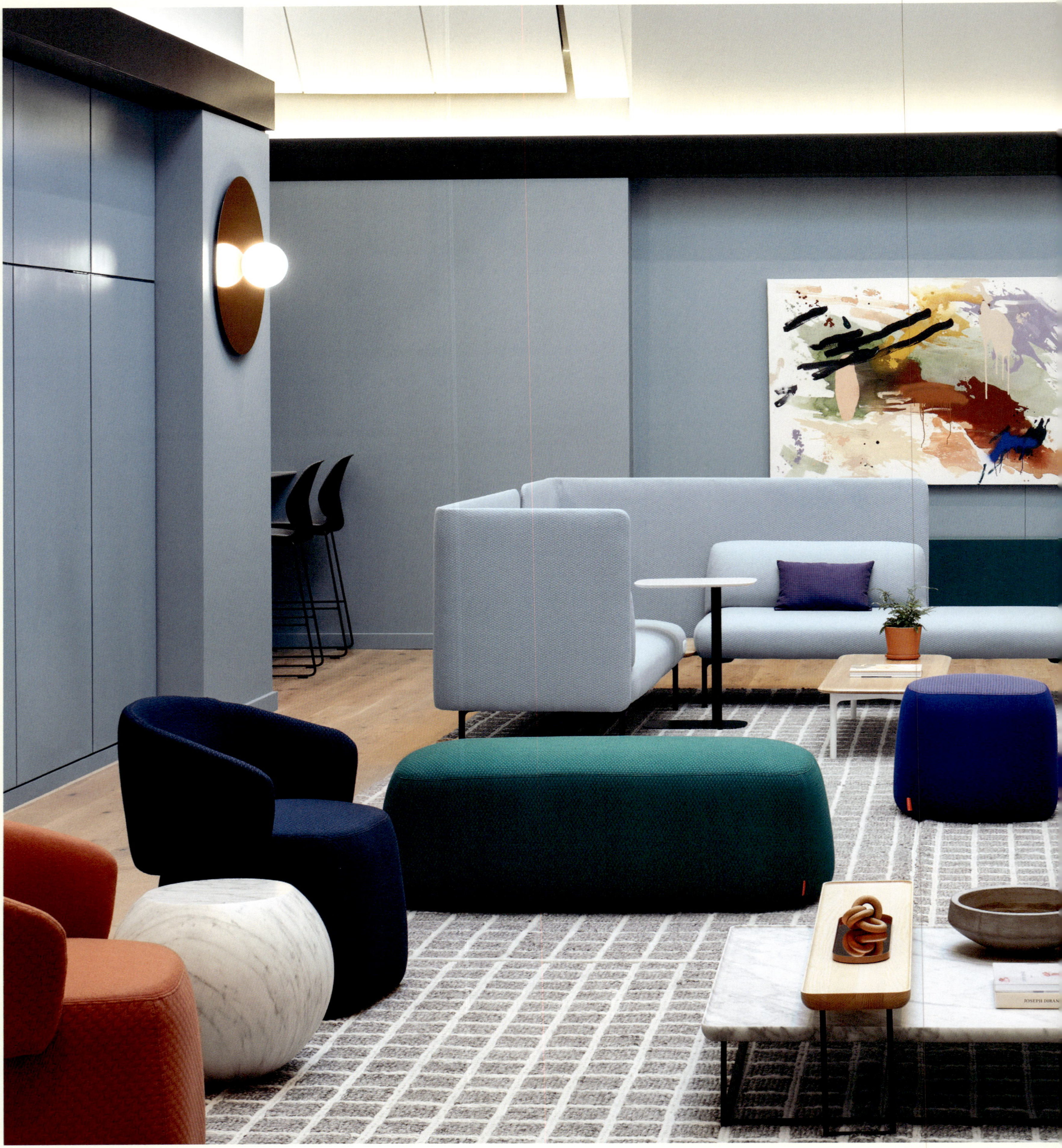

Patricia Urquiola

1961, Oviedo, Spain

Haworth Hotel at Hope College, Holland, MI, USA, 2021

Originally from Oviedo, Spain, Patricia Urquiola studied architecture and design at the Universidad Politécnica de Madrid and completed her studies at the Politecnico di Milano in Italy. She was tutored by designer Achille Castiglioni, who encouraged her to embrace all scales of design and instilled in her the importance of fun as part of a design ethos. She further developed her playful yet functional approach at De Padova, working alongside another iconic designer, Vico Magistretti. After becoming the head of product design at De Padova, Patricia moved to the Lissoni & Partners design group and, in 2001, started her eponymous design studio. Patricia is well known for her work across a broad range of disciplines, particularly in furniture and object design for brands including Alessi, Cappellini, and Moroso. Her interiors often feature her own designs, such as in her interior for a hotel for Haworth in Holland, Michigan, which features custom-made modular seating. Her first hotel interior in the U.S., Haworth's color palette developed out of Patricia's celebration of the city's famous tulip festival, conveyed through bursts of bright red, dark blue, and green in carefully arranged chairs and rugs set against washes of pastel blue for the walls and sofas. Alongside leading her own design practice, Patricia has been the Creative Director of Cassina since 2015.

Noura van Dijk

1960, São Paulo, Brazil

GAS Moema, Vila Nova Conceição, São Paulo, Brazil, 2007

Based in São Paulo, interior designer Noura van Dijk has built a substantial portfolio of residential and commercial projects over the last thirty years. She founded her eponymous company in 1999 after a circuitous route into design. Initially studying communications at Fundação Armando Alvares Penteado, she later gained postgraduate degrees in marketing with qualifications in interior design at the Panamericana School of Art and Design, and the Architecture and Urbanism College at the University of São Paulo. Noura has served as the director of the São Paulo Region and President of the Brazilian Association of Interior Designers. Her designs include apartments in São Paulo's upscale Higienópolis and Itaim Bibi neighborhoods, expressing her classic yet commercial style, featuring sleek reflective surfaces, where artworks and furniture pieces are placed throughout the interiors, accented by her signature use of the color red. At GAS Moema in Vila Nova Conceição, Noura created a stark interior with white walls and a low ceiling serving as a backdrop to wall installations placed in the room's corners. These architectural scale artworks, covered in reflective surfaces such as tile and reflective blackened glass, enclose a sitting space within an art gallery setting. Cone-shaped, dark colored armchairs, along with fluorescent strip lighting and a polished white floor, add to the overall effect.

De Stijl was an art movement that swept across Europe, propelled by its main proponents Dutch artists Theo van Doesburg and Piet Mondrian. Their paintings have become synonymous with a planar and primary-colored compositional method of organizing space, yet many notable women, including Theo's wife, Nelly, were also influential in shaping De Stijl. Nelly, who studied music at the Royal Conservatoire of The Hague, toured Europe with Theo, performing under her alias Pétro van Doesburg. The couple's Meudon home and studio, built using Nelly's inheritance following her father's death, features colored walls that act as dividing planes, embodying the couple's shared aesthetic pursuit of non-hierarchical architecture. The space is devoid of ornament, prioritizing the visual and spiritual over function. With pivoting walls, creative spaces could be closed off or opened up in dialogue with the cubic form of the house. Five tones of gray dominate the shared studio, set off by bright yellow accents that Nelly introduced. Simple yet striking furnishings—including a bright red sofa, electric blue curtains, and a concrete table—play with color, weight, and light in an otherwise sparse environment, while a stained glass skylight filters colored light into the space from above. Nelly lived in the studio for over forty years after Theo's early death and, by welcoming artists and architects, made it a pilgrimage destination for modern art.

Nelly van Doesburg

1899, The Hague, The Netherlands
1975, Meudon, France

Home and Studio, Meudon, France, c.1931

Sarah Vanrenen

1970, Johannesburg, South Africa

Notting Hill Home, London, UK, 2022

Through her eponymous company, Sarah Vanrenen Ltd. Sarah Vanrenen creates comfortable interiors, eschewing the overly polished in favor of the lived-in. Her style harmoniously blends English country charm with New York eclecticism, arrived at through layering textures, juicy colors, and evocative patterns. Vanrenen has a knack for curating spaces filled with a mix of classical and contemporary artworks, and high-end furnishings and homewares, many of which are meticulously crafted by skilled artisans. Sarah cultivated her distinctive aesthetic through influences she picked up in her early years, growing up between London and the English countryside, as well as through frequent travels to South Africa. Her mother, decorator Penny Morrison, played a significant role in shaping her design sensibility, exposing her to the world of interiors, fabrics, and antiques from a young age. Sarah's work often features dramatic gestures, conveyed through striking prints and wallpapers. Her design of a Notting Hill home showcases this strategy with an entryway adorned with an oversized floral wallpaper, setting the tone for the rest of the home, which is layered with decorative patterns and lush colors. Sarah designs her own textiles, one example of which is used for the home's curtains. Her delicate printed curtains recur throughout the apartment, fully enclosing the primary bed and even the lavish bathtub, elevating the home's small spaces and quite literally draping them in luxury.

Lella Vignelli, born in Italy and based in New York, was an icon of contemporary design, working closely with her husband, Massimo Vignelli. Born into a family of architects, Lella's career began at architects Skidmore, Owings & Merrill (SOM), where she honed her approach to design, focusing on problem-solving rather than trends. Her education at the University of Venice encompassed architecture, product, furniture, and interior design, influencing her holistic approach. She believed that "design is not an embellishment but part of the manufacturing process," emphasizing function and simplicity over decoration. Together the Vignellis created many iconic designs, including Bloomingdale's signature brown paper bag, the American Airlines logo, and the New York City subway map. Eschewing domestic projects, their portfolio included significant, mostly commercial, interior design commissions. One of their favorite commissions was for Saint Peter's Church in New York, designed in 1977. At Saint Peter's, the Vignellis handled every aspect of the interior design, including the furniture and objects within, as well as all graphic elements, showcasing their unique synthesis of industrial, graphic, and furniture design. Lella often described herself as the realist to Massimo's dreamer, a dynamic that defined their minimalist and functional style. With eleven offices worldwide, the Vignellis consciously built a joint identity, ensuring they received equal recognition for their contributions.

Lella Vignelli

1934, Milan, Italy
2016, New York, NY, USA

Saint Peter's Church, New York, NY, USA, 1977

Nanda Vigo

1936, Milan, Italy
2020, Milan, Italy

The Beetle Under the Leaf House,
Vicenza, Italy, c.1968

Milanese architect Nanda Vigo was renowned as a light artist with a diverse career that spanned architecture, interiors, and furniture design. With an instinct for form, her whimsical, maximalist yet functional designs include the Due Più Chair and Linea Floor Lamp. She trained as an architect in Lausanne, Switzerland, before traveling to the United States to study at Taliesin, the school founded by Frank Lloyd Wright. There she was disappointed by Wright's attitude toward students and the design culture she encountered, and left within a month to live in San Francisco. Returning to Italy, Nanda secured her first interior project, Casa Zero, for a young couple where she stripped the house and created an all-white interior inspired by her avant-garde art group, Gruppo Zero. Nanda later organized the first group show for Gruppo Zero, whose focus on light and motion profoundly influenced her approach to design. Her projects during this period ranged from a proposal for a cemetery in a tower in Milan's suburbs to the interior of architect Gio Ponti's Lo Scarabeo sotto la Foglia (The Beetle Under the Leaf) house in 1968. She adorned the house with white ceramic tiles, neon surfaces, and a spiral staircase covered in synthetic gray fur. Ponti's belief in the total integration of art and architecture inspired Nanda to push disciplinary boundaries, which led to her programing a series of performance events on the staircase of the Palazzo dell'Arte at the Milan Triennale in 1973.

Ana Volante

1983, Caracas, Venezuela

Project 5, Cojedes, Venezuela, 2023

Ana Volante's interest in design stems from her childhood, inspired by her grandfather's work as an artist and architect. She studied interior design at the Design Institute of Caracas, Venezuela before moving to Milan to further her education. Upon returning to Caracas, Ana gained experience in architectural firms before launching her own interior design studio in the late 1990s. Ana favors geometric motifs, with art playing a fundamental role in her work, creating a counterpoint to a construction palette of environmentally conscious natural materials, from rich woods to tropical-inspired textiles. Her prioritization of sustainable materials is echoed by her incorporation of artisanal and locally sourced decorative items, which bring warmth to her spaces. In her design for a living space in Cojedes, Ana repurposed slices from two large tree trunks, placing them in the center of the space to serve as a coffee table, and complemented their warm wood tones with a solid wood dining table, streaked gray and white marble bar, raw linen upholstery and wicker armchairs. After nearly twenty years as an interior designer, Ana launched her own furniture line in 2020, drawing inspiration from her grandfather's designs. Dubbed the Moon Collection, the pieces possess a sculptural quality, allowing them to exist not only as functional pieces, but also as art objects on their own when not in use, a concept underpinning all of her work.

Vritima Wadhwa

1988, Delhi, India

Kaméi, New Delhi, India, 2024

After gaining her degree in furniture and interior design from the National Institute of Design in Ahmedabad, India, Vritima Wadhwa worked with other designers. In 2013, she founded Project 810, a design studio based in New Delhi focused on contemporary Indian design within a global context. It produces holistic spatial experiences with interior designers, furniture designers, and architects working together across residential, retail, hospitality, and furniture projects. Vritima describes a process-driven approach of research, exploration, and iteration to create human-centered designs that incorporate local resources and crafts, stating that her "design narratives often revolve around material and form, ensuring that each space is rooted in its context."[152] She grew up in a creative family and experimented with different disciplines, including pottery. Her mother manufactured furniture, and Vritima credits her experience in the workshop with making her comfortable around materials and hands-on processes from an early age. Describing her style as "impactful minimalism,"[153] her latest project, Kaméi (meaning turtle in Japanese), is a contemporary Asian dining experience with walls adorned in warm terracotta earth tones, creating a meditative ambiance complemented by oiled solid wood tables, minimal lighting, and metal screens which add a sense of theatricality to the space.

Joyce Wang graduated with degrees in architecture and materials science from the Massachusetts Institute of Technology in Boston and later completed her master's in interior design at the Royal College of Art in London. Based between London and Hong Kong, Joyce undertakes projects internationally. Early in her career, she gained valuable experience at British architect Norman Foster's studio before establishing her own studio in Hong Kong. Her first independent project was a cake shop for a friend, where she discovered a passion for refined finishes and intricate details. Since then, her projects have grown in scope and sophistication, focusing on luxury hospitality spaces, especially hotels, members' clubs, spas, and restaurants. Although her aesthetic is defined by its opulence, Joyce defines true luxury as stemming from small, thoughtful details that enhance a space's functionality. Her strong client relationships have led to repeat collaborations, such as with the Mandarin Oriental Hotel Group and Mott 32 restaurant group, for whom she has designed projects in Las Vegas, Dubai, and Singapore. Known for her cinematic style, Joyce aims to create dramatic, memorable interiors. For Mott 32 in Singapore, Joyce created a large canopy over the main dining room, reminiscent of Chinese pagodas, encircling the space with plants and intricate hand-painted motifs, including a gold leaf pattern applied to a semi-gloss blue background.

Joyce Wang

1982, Hawaii, USA

Mott 32, Marina Bay Sands, Singapore, 2020

Ni Wang

1984, Chengdu, China

Dog House, Beijing, China, 2018

Ni Wang is the founder of Atelier About Architecture. She graduated from the University of Sydney with both a bachelor's and a master's degree in architecture. Since establishing her firm in 2013, Ni has overseen numerous architectural and interior design projects, including Dog House, a home designed for a woman and her dog in Beijing. Providing treatment and bathing facilities for the ailing dog, the interior design allowed the dog to enjoy a relaxing atmosphere alongside his owner. Ni researched how dogs perceive colors, discovering that they can only recognize blue and red wavelengths. This insight inspired her design, featuring soft pink, yellow, and blue tones, large ramps for big dogs which are covered in a special treatment to provide better grip. Ni's architectural philosophy emphasizes materiality while expressing immaterial aspects, such as memory and emotion. For example, in Dog House, each surface has been carefully considered, from tiled floors to acoustic curtains, to create a practical space, while the thoughtful application of color and lighting carefully curates a calm ambient atmosphere for her multi-species client. She views her work as a process of observation and understanding, likening it to a dance between asking questions and solving problems, rooting her designs in their sites and cultural contexts. She sees herself as a mediator between past and present, individual and collective, public and private, and rural and urban.

Originally from South Carolina, Kelly Wearstler developed a passion for collecting vintage fashion magazines as a teenager, which led her to study graphic design at the Massachusetts College of Art and Design. Initially pursuing a career in graphic design, she soon transitioned to interior design, and graduated with a degree in both fields. In the mid-1990s, she founded her eponymous firm, and began working in the hotel industry before quickly expanding to the residential, commercial, and hospitality sectors. Already a successful designer, Kelly rose to prominence in the early 2000s after completing her first major interior project, a bungalow in Venice, California, that she designed for a couple introduced to her by a friend. She filled the space with vintage furniture sourced from the Rose Bowl Flea Market in Pasadena, as well as other markets, setting the tone for her collected style. She describes her approach as "mixology," blending elements that defy easy categorization.[154] Her style, often described as maximalist, is known for finding beauty in the unconventional. Kelly aims to create a real sense of soul in her work, with designs often defined by a low-slung 1970s vibe—"It's slouchy, it's sexy, it's relaxed, and it's cool," she says.[155] Kelly is the author of six books, including *Synchronicity* (2023). Her firm now employs nearly fifty people and she is beginning to incorporate AI into her work.

Kelly Wearstler

Myrtle Beach, SC, USA

Private residence, Malibu Beach, CA, USA, 2007

Edith Wharton

1862, New York, NY, USA
1937, Saint Brice, Seine-et-Oise, France

The Mount, Lenox, MA, 1902

Acclaimed for her writing, Edith Wharton began her literary career during the Gilded Age, a period of American expansion that fueled social ambition among the newly rich. Born in America during the Civil War, Edith grew up in Europe before returning at age ten, when the family settled into life in their fashionable Manhattan brownstone. This was a formative period for Edith, who educated herself in her father's library while navigating the social expectations of young debutantes. While best known for her Pulitzer Prize-winning novel, *The Age of Innocence*, Edith's first book, *The Decoration of Houses*, pioneered elegance and simplicity in house design. She argued against separating decorating from architecture, advocating for rooms where "architecture became decoration."[156] Co-authored with Beaux-Arts architect Ogden Codman, this was her only nonfiction work, but it influenced a generation of decorators. Her aesthetic of "moderation" and "fitness" preempted minimalist fashions of the next century. Edith honed her design principles at The Mount, her home in the Berkshires, where she created an Italianate garden.[157] She continued her writing career producing over forty books, the themes of which often focused on contemporary materialism and women's liberation. Refusing to be confined by societal norms, Edith was a renowned philanthropist, supporting the Allied forces during World War I, and earning the French Legion of Honor in 1916.

Candace Wheeler

1827, Delhi, NY, USA
1923, New York, NY, USA

Mark Twain's House, Hartford, CT, USA, c.1881

Raised in a Presbyterian household on a farm in Delhi, New York, Candace Wheeler spent much of her life doing charity work until she later, at age forty-nine, became a textile designer and interior decorator. Two life-changing events sparked her interest in design: first, a visit to the Centennial International Exhibition in Philadelphia in 1876, where she was impressed by the work of the Royal School of Art Needlework; and second, the loss of her adult daughter to kidney disease, which galvanized Candace's efforts to support young women. Candace considered design a viable career for women in an era when such activities were considered hobbies. She co-founded the Society of Decorative Arts in New York City in 1877 and a year later the New York Exchange for Women's Work as a way to create infrastructure and generate support for women to earn income from art and design work after the Civil War. She worked with Louis Comfort Tiffany on high-profile commissions, including the redecoration of the White House and of author Mark Twain's house. She soon established her own firm, the Associated Artists, where she employed as many as forty "sister workers."[158] Her most notable works included the interior design for the Woman's Building at the World's Columbian Exposition in Chicago in 1893. Candace endorsed American-made products and lectured on art and commerce. She found art uplifting because it "keeps us in touch with heavenly things."[159]

Jialun Xiong

1993, Chongqing, China

19 Town Restaurant, City of Industry, CA, USA, 2022

Growing up in Chongqing, designer Jialun Xiong draws inspiration from the local landscape, shaped by winding rivers and steep hills, which she describes as filled "with a kaleidoscope of layers and high-rises that adapt to the terrain."[160] She left for the U.S. to attend business school at Indiana University Bloomington. However, after her first year, she decided to major in interior design and architecture instead. She subsequently studied for her master's degree in environmental design, with a focus on furniture, after which she joined a large firm and contributed to hospitality projects, including the Four Seasons Hotel Chicago and the Aria resort and casino in Las Vegas. Based in Los Angeles, her work expertly considers the relationship between objects and space. Retaining the reverence for the interplay between natural beauty and human-made invention she cultivated in her hometown, Jialun introduces abstract geometric furniture in earthy tones to create a distinctive balance between nature and innovation. Her thoughtful, cerebral style is evident in her design for the 19 Town restaurant in California, where she mixed minimalist silhouettes with luxurious finish materials. Brushed stainless steel features prominently, from the Formica reception desk to the banquettes, which are upholstered in green leather and vinyl. The project shows her deft handling of the relationships between structure, form, and proportion, and celebrates the inherent beauty of raw materials.

Chen Xuan

Qingdao, China

Zhang Jie's studio, outside Beijing, China, c.2020

Architect Dr. Lea Chen, known in China as Chen Xuan, grew up in the coastal city of Qingdao. She moved to Beijing and graduated with a degree in architecture from the Central Academy of Fine Arts in 1999, later earning her doctorate with a focus on the architecture of modern art museums. In 2004, Lea founded her design studio, Shishang Architecture, and has since become one of China's leading designers, working across residential, hospitality, and cultural projects. Lea's interiors are often minimal, and her style is heavily influenced by her study of the European Modern Movement, favoring the use of a restrained palette, often featuring only one color and material. She collaborates internationally, including with the Italian furniture brand VGnewtrend, with whom she created a luxury furniture collection, Oriental Treasures, in 2018. The pieces in the collection reinvent classical Chinese designs through the lens of Italian craft tradition, such as an apothecary cabinet whose many drawers—that would customarily hold herbs in traditional Chinese medicine—float atop a slim 24k gold-embellished stand. She counts many celebrities among her clients, including actor Jackie Chan and sculptor Zhang Jie, for whom she designed a studio with modern furniture artfully placed in a stark concrete interior to emphasize dramatic mountain views. In addition to her design practice, Lea nurtures many creative outlets. She hosts TV shows dedicated to design and sings in the band The Key.

Jane Yu

1937, China

Geller House III, Lawrence, NY, USA, 1969

Jane Yu worked as the head of interiors for architect Marcel Breuer from 1964 to 1980. Her journey to the United States as a political refugee led her to Chicago, where she settled before joining Breuer's team. Trained as an architect in Shanghai, the cultural differences were stark for Jane; in Communist China, nearly half of her classmates were women, and there were no barriers for women on construction sites. Despite her extensive training and expertise, Jane faced challenges in Breuer's male-dominated office, where her talents were often overlooked, not least by Breuer himself, who lamented the lack of female talent in his studio. During her career with Breuer, Jane contributed to several projects, including the design of the interiors for Avery Fisher Hall and work for Bertram and Phyllis Geller. The Gellers valued her work so much that they privately commissioned her to design their home, Geller House III, in 1978 in Lawrence, New York. The Gellers believed she could deliver a quicker, simpler design than Breuer, but asked her to be discreet about the commission to avoid offending him. Because of the secrecy surrounding the project, Jane's work was overlooked for regional awards, and over the years, many of her designs have been destroyed, with one site recently being repurposed as a tennis court.

Born in Moravia in the Austro-Hungarian Empire (now the Czech Republic), Liane Zimbler spent her childhood in Vienna, where her father worked for the railroads. She attended the Vienna Arts and Crafts School and worked as a fashion designer and illustrator for renowned designer Emilie Flöge. During World War I, Liane worked for the Bamberger furniture factory and the Rosenberger Design Studio, becoming the first woman licensed as a civil engineer in Austria in 1938. Her designs featured light-colored, functional, modern furniture, balancing comfort and Bauhaus aesthetics. She identified a need amid the economic downturn of the late 1920s for flexible interiors, as middle-class households reduced their staff, which garnered her many interior commissions and allowed her to start her own firm. Her success designing the Ephrussi Bank building, a corporate interior in Vienna, allowed her to open a second branch of her interior design company in Prague. Liane also participated in groups like the Association of Professional Women in Austria, serving as president of the Austrian board of the International Housing Society. In 1938, she escaped occupied Europe, settling in Los Angeles, where she worked for interior designer Anita Toor. Liane took over the company after Anita's death and rebuilt her own brand. She completed many residential projects and lectured frequently, often collaborating with her daughter, Eva Zimbler, who joined the company in 1958.

Liane Zimbler

1892, Přerov, Moravia, Czech Republic
1987, Los Angeles, CA, USA

Private residence, Germany, c.1935

Diana Żurek

1993, Olkusz, Poland

Private residence, Kraków, Poland, 2023

Diana Zurek trained as an architect, aspiring to work on large-scale projects due to her fascination with the challenges posed by the interplay between technical resolution and creative expression. Her interest in design began in high school, when she started working as a fashion model. Traveling internationally, Diana was exposed to the world of design, and was particularly inspired by the fantasy and magic of photoshoot sets. Her work as an architect began designing for museum exhibitions, where she learned the power of crafting narratives through space, realizing the power of smaller, more intimately scaled projects. For Diana, even the simple act of a homeowner making coffee for themselves can inspire a design. Her experiences working for Cobe in Denmark and with Kengo Kuma in Japan shaped her approach, teaching her the beauty of emptiness and lightness in traditional and modern architecture. Motivated to carve her own path, Diana founded Furora, focusing on minimalist interiors that collage small, thoughtful moments. Her modern designs often incorporate older furniture pieces reimagined in new forms and contexts, and use hidden storage and clever lighting to guide movement, blending raw materials with geometric precision. This is showcased in her redesign of an open-plan apartment in Kraków. She used custom-made furniture to define individual spaces, while a palette of dark brown wood and stone adds a sense of solidity to the light and airy interior.

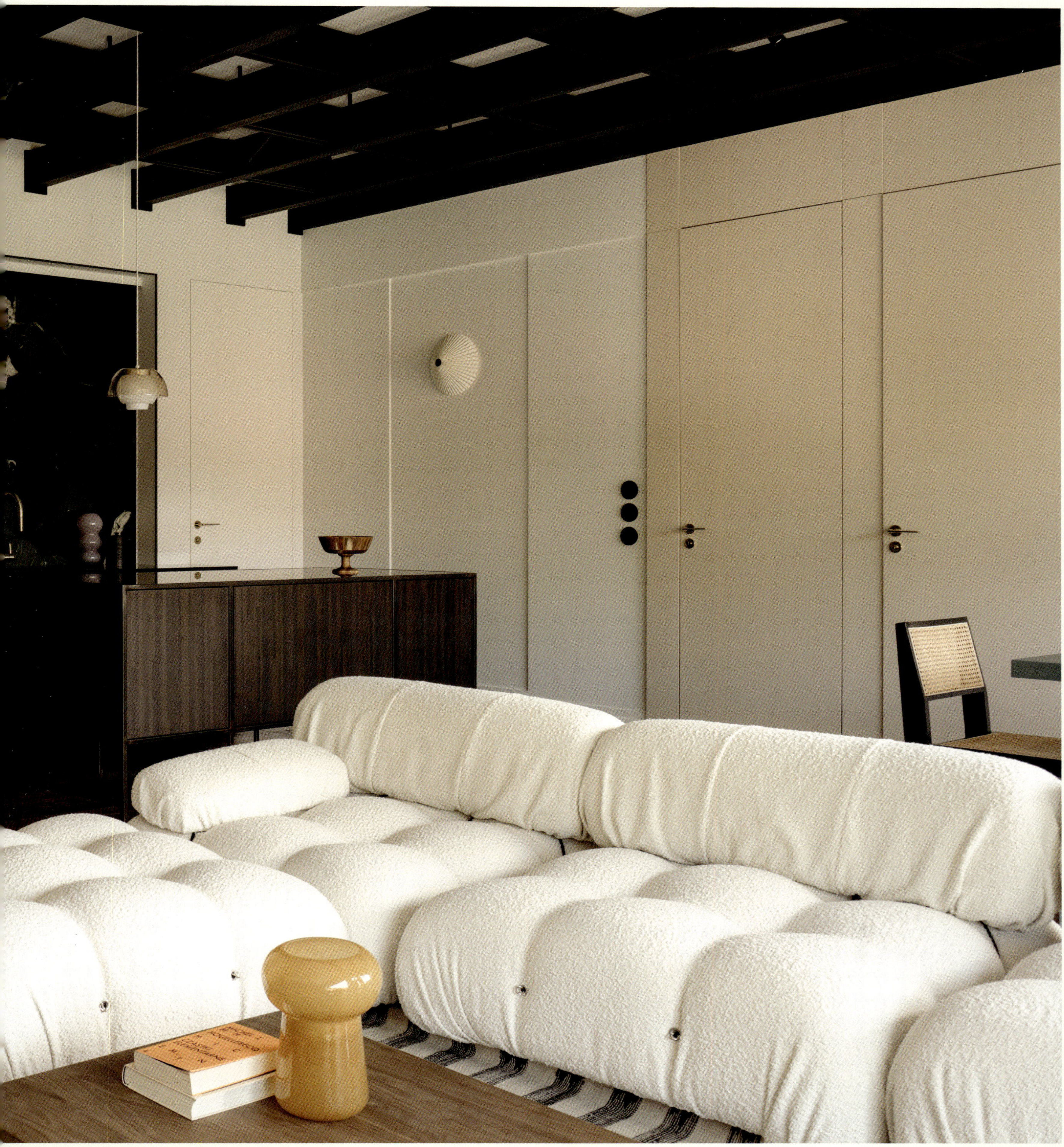

TIMELINE

1880s

Candace Wheeler, p.259

1900s

Mary Colter, p.67

Eugenia Errázuriz, p.87

Gertrud Kleinhempel, p.136

Margaret Macdonald Mackintosh, p.159

Edith Wharton, p.258

1910s

Vanessa Bell, p.38

Karin Bergöö Larsson, p.40

Elsie de Wolfe, p.76

Frances Elkins, p.86

1920s

Sibyl Colefax, p.65

Rose Cumming, p.71

Eileen Gray, p.105

Ruth Lane Poole, p.144

Jeanne Lanvin, p.145

Eleanor Le Maire, p.149

Elsie Mackay, p.160

TIMELINE

Eleanor McMillen Brown, p.171

Ruby Ross Wood, p.215

Truus Schröder, p.223

1930s

Margarete Schütte-Lihotzky, p.225

Aino Aalto, p.12

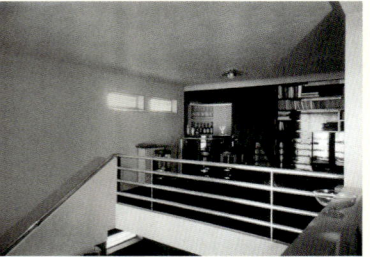

Adrienne Górska de Montaut, p.104

Betty Joel, p.129

Syrie Maugham, p.167

Jeannette Meunier Biéler, p.176

Lilly Reich, p.209

1940s

Nelly van Doesburg, p.249

Liane Zimbler, p.263

Madeleine Castaing, p.57

Dorothy Draper, p.81

Ray Eames, p.85

Greta Magnusson Grossman, p.106

Julia Morgan, p.178

1950s

Georgia O'Keeffe, p.187

Ulla Tafdrup, p.238

Elissa Aalto, p.13

Lina Bo Bardi, p.45

Polly Jessup, p.127

Melanie Kahane, p.131

Nancy Lancaster, p.143

Margaret Lord, p.157

Anna Maria Niemeyer, p.185

Luisa Parisi, p.196

Clara Porset, p.205

1960s

Halina Skibniewska, p.231

Claire Bataille, p.36

Cini Boeri, p.46

Sigrun Bülow-Hübe, p.53

Nina Campbell, p.55

Mary Featherston, p.92

Dora Gad, p.97

269

TIMELINE

Elsa Gullberg, p.108

Marion Hall Best, p.112

Florence Knoll, p.137

Sister Parish, p.195

Charlotte Perriand, p.199

Gaby Schreiber, p.222

Nanda Vigo, p.252

Jane Yu, p.262

1970s

Gae Aulenti, p.31

Sybil Connolly, p.68

Barbara D'Arcy, p.74

Mica Ertegun, p.88

Barbara Hulanicki, p.124

Celerie Kemble and Mimi Maddock McMakin, p.133

Ellen Lehman McCluskey, p.168

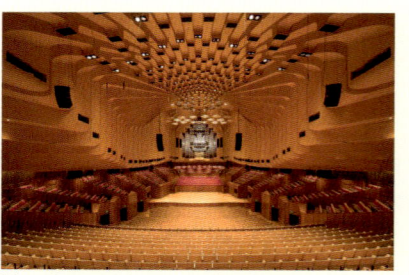

Diana Luxton Messara, p.174

Brigitte Peterhans, p.200

Chessy Rayner, p.208

Lella Vignelli, p.251

1980s

Laura Ashley, p.28

Cecil Hayes, p.116

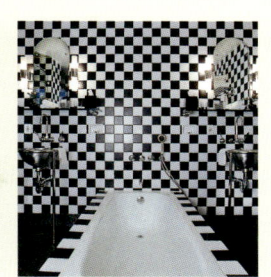

Andrée Putman, p.206

1990s

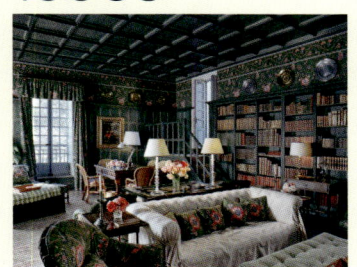

Marella Agnelli, p.16

Victoria Hagan, p.111

Min Hogg, p.120

Rose Tarlow, p.240

2000s

Zeina Aboukheir, p.14

Rie Azuma, p.32

Sabrina Bignami, p.43

Zeynep Fadıllıoğlu, p.90

Camilla Guinness, p.107

Eva Jiřičná, p.128

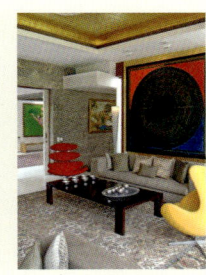

Sunita Kohli, p.138

Marian McEvoy, p.169

Charlotte Moss, p.179

Noura van Dijk, p.248

Kelly Wearstler, p.257

2010s

Paula Alvarez de Toledo and Marine Delaloy, p.22

TIMELINE

Nada Andric, p.23

Iris Apfel, p.24

Valentina Audrito, p.30

Neydine Bak, p.34

Sheila Bridges, p.50

Athena Calderone, p.54

Gloria Cortina, p.69

Ilse Crawford, p.70

Kana Cussen, p.72

Aline Asmar d'Amman, p.73

Pallavi Dean, p.77

Kesha Franklin, p.95

Emanuela Frattini Magnusson, p.96

Yasmine Ghoniem, p.101

Shabnam Gupta, p.109

Olga Hanono, p.114

Briar Hickling and Alex Mok, p.119

Kathryn M. Ireland, p.126

HRH Anoud Khalid Mishaal bin Saud, p.135

Rita Konig, p.139

Amy Lau, pp.146–147

Little Wing Lee, p.150

Xiang Li, p.152

Fiona Lynch, p.158

Courtney McLeod, p.170

Michelle Nussbaumer, p.186

Tosin Oshinowo, p.190

Maria Osminina, p.191

Elisa Ossino, p.192

Marie-Anne Oudejans, p.193

Sevil Peach, p.197

Kerry Phelan, p.201

Clodagh, p.202

Suzanne Rheinstein, p.210

Katie Ridder, p.211

Catarina Rosas, Catarina Soares Pereira, and Cláudia Soares Pereira, p.214

Tara and Tessa Sakhi, p.218

Laura Sartori Rimini, p.220

Anastasia Schuler, p.224

Pamela Shamshiri, p.229

TIMELINE

Elodie Sire, p.230

Maria Speake, p.233

Nthabi Taukobong, p.241

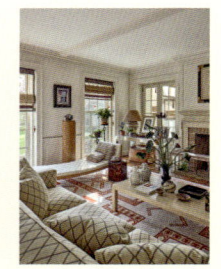

Virginia Tupker, p.244

2020s

Rose Uniacke, p.245

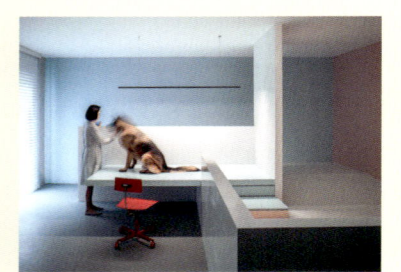

Ni Wang, p.256

Lotta Agaton, p.15

Farah Ahmed Mathias, p.17

Selma Akkari and Rawan Muqaddas, p.18

Aisha Al Sowaidi, p.19

Miriam Alía, p.20

Nebras Aljoaib, p.21

Olimpiada Arefieva, p.25

Sophie Ashby, pp.26–27

Sofía Aspe, p.29

Talitha Bainbridge, p.33

Elvira Bakubayeva and Aisulu Uali, p.35

Kelly Behun, p.37

Sandra Benhamou, p.39

Falguni Bhatia and Priyanka Itadkar, p.41

Natalia Bianchi, p.42

Justina Blakeney, p.44

Linda Boronkay, p.47

Muriel Brandolini, p.48

Sally Breer, p.49

Tiffany Brooks, p.51

Ester Bruzkus, p.52

Cristina Carulla, p.56

Cristina Celestino, p.58

Vicky Charles, p.59

Ghida Chehab, p.60

Khuan Chew, p.61

Vera Chu, p.62

Rachel Chudley, p.63

Petra Cienciálová and Kateřina Průchová, p.64

Erica Colpitts, p.66

Alex Dauley, p.75

Chiara Di Pinto and Arianna Lelli Mami, p.78

Nicole Dohmen, p.79

275

TIMELINE

Olayinka Dosekun-Adjei, p.80

Sophie Dries, p.82

Nathalie and Virginie Droulers, p.83

Marika Dru, p.84

Stefanie Everaert and Caroline Lateur, p.89

Shahira Fahmy, p.91

Claudina Flores, p.93

Olga Fradina, p.94

Charu Gandhi, p.98

Hanne Gathe, p.99

Lauren Geremia, p.100

Sandra Githinji, p.102

Laura Gonzalez, p.103

Racha Gutierrez and Dahlia Hojeij Deleuze, p.110

Rania Hamed, p.113

Elizabeth Hay, p.115

Ana Milena Hernández Palacios, p.117

Beata Heuman, p.118

Nicole Hollis, p.121

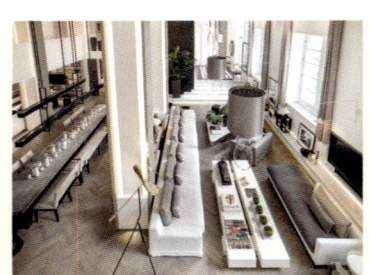

Kelly Hoppen, p.122

Rossana Hu, p.123

Malene Hvidt, p.125

Tamsin Johnson, p.130

Annabel Karim Kassar, p.132

Kit Kemp, p.134

Agata Kurzela, p.140

Joanna Laajisto, p.141

Róisín Lafferty, p.142

Joanna Lavén, p.148

Na Li, p.151

Angela Lindahl, p.153

Katie Lockhart, p.154

Hilary Loh, p.155

Isabel López-Quesada, p.156

Natalie Mahakian, p.161

India Mahdavi, pp.162–163

Yasmina Makram, p.164

Eva Marguerre, p.165

Michèle Maria Chaya and Claudia Skaff, p.166

Dorothée Meilichzon, p.172

Frances Merrill, p.173

Elizabeth Metcalfe, p.175

Yana Molodykh, p.177

TIMELINE

Joy Moyler, p.180

Kim Mupangilaï, p.181

Elsie Nanji, p.182

Paola Navone, p.183

Tanwa Newbold, p.184

Tola Ojuolape, pp.188–189

Laura Panebianco, p.194

Mónica Penaguião, p.198

Louisa Pierce and Emily Ward, p.203

Sarah Poniatowski, p.204

Diana Radomysler, p.207

Brigette Romanek, pp.212–213

Maye Ruiz, p.216

Rabah Saeid, p.217

Teresa Sapey, p.219

Katty Schiebeck, p.221

Gillian Segal, p.226

Tekla Evelina Severin, p.227

Darshini Shah, p.228

Lena Solovyeva, p.232

Anna Spiro, p.234

Isabelle Stanislas, p.235

Sara Story, p.236

Madeline Stuart, p.237

Naoko Takenouchi, p.239

Paola Trombetta, p.242

Suzanne Tucker, p.243

Patricia Urquiola, pp.246–247

Sarah Vanrenen, p.250

Ana Volante, p.253

Vritima Wadhwa, p.254

Joyce Wang, p.255

Jialun Xiong, p.260

Chen Xuan, p.261

Diana Żurek, p.264–265

ENDNOTES

Aino Aalto
1   Aino Aalto quoted in Joan Durham's "Finnish Couple is Producing Socially-Designed Furniture." *Altoona Tribune*. Thursday August 3, 1939.
2   Ibid.

Zeina Aboukheir
3   www.moudira.com/our-story

Selma Akkari and Rawan Muqaddas
4   Selma Akkari and Rawan Muqaddas quoted in Jenni Kayne's "Tour a Traditional-Turned-Timeless Home Renovation in Brooklyn's Historic Cobble Hill." Jenni Kayne. May 25, 2023. First accessed March 2, 2025.

Miriam Alía
5   Miriam Alía quoted in Adrienne Breaux's "This Renovated Madrid Apartment Mixes 70s Vibes with Modern Style." Apartment Therapy. September 4, 2023. First accessed February 20, 2025.
6   Miriam Alía quoted in Iván Meade's "In Conversation with Miriam Alía." LifeMstyle. May 10, 2018. First accessed December 2, 2024.
7   Ibid.

Nebras Aljoaib
8   Interview with Nebras Aljoib via email. January 4, 2024.
9   Nebras Aljoaib quoted in Pratyush Sarup's "AD100 Riyadh Designer Nebras AlJoaib Reimagines Italian Craft from an Arab Perspective." *Architectural Digest*. December 10, 2024. First accessed December 12, 2024.

Paula Alvarez de Toledo and Marine Delaloy
10 Interview with Paula Alvarez de Toledo and Marine Delaloy via email. November 18, 2024.

Iris Apfel
11 Iris Apfel quoted in Jeffrey Podolsky's "Iris Apfel: 'There's no glamour or mystery any more.'" *Standard*. December 3, 2012. First accessed December 22, 2024.

Olimpiada Arefieva
12 Interview with Olimpiada Arefieva via email. November 18, 2024.

Valentina Audrito
13 Valentina Audrito quoted in Hayley Curnow's "DIA WA Forum: Culture, design, society." Architecture, Au. May 2013. First accessed March 11, 2025.

Gae Aulenti
14 Gae Aulenti quoted in Sally Loane's "Dialogue with an architect." *Sydney Morning Herald*. November 9, 1993.
15 Anon. "Letter from Europe." *New Yorker*. April 25, 1988.

Talitha Bainbridge
16 Interview with Talitha Bainbridge via email. December 6, 2024.
17 Interview with Talitha Bainbridge via email. March 26, 2025.

Neydine Bak
18 Camille Khouri. "A Well Told Tale – Verhaal Studio." The Local Project. First accessed December 17, 2024.
19 Neydine Bak quoted in Amrita Singh's "Meet the Interior Designer: Neydine Bak, Verhaal Studio." SheerLuxe Middle East. May 3, 2024. First accessed November 30, 2024.

Elvira Bakubayeva and Aisulu Uali
20 NAAW quoted in "FIKA Cafe." *ArchDaily*. March 25, 2024.

Sandra Benhamou
21 Sandra Benhamou quoted in Claire Sartin's "Interior designer Sandra Benhamou's feel-good Parisian apartment." *Elle Decoration*. February 3, 2021. First accessed January 20, 2025.

Falguni Bhatia and Priyanka Itadkar
22 Interview with Priyanka Itadkar and Falguni Bhatia via email. January 6, 2025
23 Nuriyah Johar. "This Sprawling Mumbai Home Takes Cues from the Neotenic Design Trend." *Design Pataki*. July 8, 2021. First accessed November 30, 2024.

Justina Blakeney
24 www.justinablakeney.com/decor

Cini Boeri
25 Cini Boeri quoted in Suzanne Slesin's "Milanese women: Dominant in design." Clarion-Ledger. February 12, 1981.
26 Cini Boeri Quoted in Doris Herzig's "Flexibility, Italian style." *Newsday*. September 4, 1969.

Sheila Bridges
27 Sheila Bridges. www.sheilabridges.com/product-category/harlem-toile/

Tiffany Brooks
28 Tiffany Brooks quoted in Sophia Herring's "Tiffany Brooks Interiors: Meet the AD100 2023." *Architectural Digest*. November 29, 2022. First accessed January 16, 2025.

Athena Calderone
29 Athena Calderone. "My Brooklyn Townhouse Design Process." *Eyeswoon*. First accessed January 9, 2025.

Nina Campbell
30 Nina Campbell quoted in Jan Moir's "Nina's Colour Clash with The Savoy." *The Daily Telegraph*. July 24, 1996, p.15

Madeleine Castaing
31 Madeleine Castaing quoted in Anon's "From the archive: an interview with Madeleine Castaing" (1966). *House & Garden*. July 10, 2020. First accessed December 21, 2024.

Khuan Chew
32 Khuan Chew quoted in Sarah Joseph's "Stunned by Burj Al Arab's striking interiors? See the design journey behind this landmark." Emirates Woman. April 16, 2024. First accessed February 5, 2025.

Rachel Chudley
33 Interview with Rachel Chudley via phone. October 4, 2024.

Sibyl Colefax
34 John Weston. "Private View of the Art World." *Sunday Telegraph*. November 25, 2001.

Erica Colpitts
35 Erica Colpitts quoted in Anon's "The Watson." Archello. First accessed February 14, 2025.
36 Interview with Erica Colpitts via email. November 15, 2024.

Sybil Connolly
37 Patricia M Jenkins. "Sybil Connolly's *In an Irish House*." Irish Literary Society. First accessed December 22, 2024.

Ilse Crawford
38 Ilse Crawford quoted in Guy Dittrich's "Revisiting Ilse Crawford's design for the Ett Hem, still Stockholm's chicest hotel." *House & Garden*. October 11, 2018.

Kana Cussen
39 grisanticussen.com
40 Ibid.

Aline Asmar d'Amman
41 Aline Asmar d'Amman quoted in Christine Schwarz Hartley's "Interior Designer Aline Asmar d'Amman Shares Her Inspirations." Galerie. Winter 2017. First accessed December 18, 2024.

Barbara D'Arcy
42 Barbara D'Arcy. *Bloomingdale's Book of Home Decorating*. HarperCollins. 1973.

Alex Dauley
43 www.unitedindesign.com

Pallavi Dean
44 Pallavi Dean quoted in Giovanna Dunmall's "10 Questions with…ROAR Founder Pallavi Dean." Interior Design. September 28, 2020. First accessed January 15, 2025.

Chiara Di Pinto and Arianna Lelli Mami
45 Interview with Arianna Lelli Mami and Chiari di Pinto via email. December 5, 2024.

Nicole Dohmen
46 Nicole Dohmen quoted in Anon's "Nicole Dohmen from Atelier ND designs the Residence stand during PAN Amsterdam." Residence. November, 2022.

Dorothy Draper
47 dorothydraper.com/history

Nathalie and Virginie Droulers
48 Interview with Nathalie and Virginie Droulers via email. November 9, 2024.

Eugenia Errázuriz
49 Eugenia Errázuriz quoted in Joanna Banham's *The Encyclopaedia of Interior Design*. Routledge. 1997, p.458.
50 John Richardson quoted in Ben Weaver's "Three Muses of Modernism." London List. First accessed December 19, 2024.
51 Eugenia Errázuriz quoted Jody Shields's "The Queen of Clean." *New York Times*. October 11, 1992.

Mica Ertegun
52 James Reginato. "Mica Ertegun the Nonagenarian Style Legend Who Shows No Sign of Stopping." *Vanity Fair*. April 27, 2017. First accessed November 28, 2024.

Stefanie Everaert and Caroline Lateur
53 bartlunenburg.com/Doorzon-2017

Claudina Flores
54 Claudina Flores quoted in Ben Dreith's "Nine Independent Studios Shaping Design in Guadalajara." *Dezeen*. May 28, 2024. First accessed December 17, 2024.

Kesha Franklin
55 Kesha Franklin quoted in Jessica Cumberbatch Anderson.'s "House Tour: Colin Kaepernick's California Bachelor Pad Defies Stereotypes." *Elle Decor*. January 10, 2018. First accessed November 11, 2024.

Sandra Githinji
56 Interview with Sandra Githinji via email. November 1, 2024.
57 www.sandragithinji.com/about

Laura Gonzalez
58 Laura Gonzalez quoted in Dana Thomas's "Inside Chic Designer Laura Gonzalez's Cheerfully Maximalist Paris Atelier." *AD Magazine*. August 7, 2023. First accessed November 29, 2024.

Adrienne Górska de Montant
59 María Pura Moreno. "The Cinéac movie theatres of Adrienne Górska and Pierre de Montaut: to adapt a 'type'." *VLC arquitectura*. Vol. 5, Issue 2 (October 2018). 59–89, p.65.

Eileen Gray
60 Eileen Gray quoted in Peter Adam's *Eileen Gray: Architect/Designer*, Adam Biro, 1987, p. 305.

Camilla Guinness
61 Camilla Guiness quoted in Laura Rysman's "How to Host a Relaxed, Italian-Style Late Lunch." *New York Times*. August 12, 2015.

Victoria Hagan
62 Suzanne Slesin. "Fun (Some of It Serious) at Kips Bay." *New York Times*. April 26, 1990.
63 Victoria Hagan quoted in John Loring's "Victoria Hagan." *Architectural Digest*. December 31, 2001. First accessed December 24, 2024.
64 Suzanne Slesin. "Fun (Some of It Serious) at Kips Bay." *New York Times*. April 26, 1990.

Rania Hamed
65 Ali Morris. "Weathered rocks inform interior of Orijins coffee shop by VSHD Design." *Dezeen*. July 11, 2022. First accessed November 30, 2024.
66 Ibid.

Olga Hanono
67 Olga Hanono quoted in Judith van Vliet's "Living Beautifully with Olga Hanono." The Color Authority. November 23, 2021. First accessed January 30, 2025.
68 Ibid.

Cecil Hayes
69 The History Makers interview with Cecil Hayes. April 18, 2002. www.thehistorymakers.org/biography/cecil-hayes-40

Ana Milena Hernández Palacios
70 Interview with Ana Milena Hernández Palacios via email. September 20, 2024.

Beata Heuman
71 Emily Tobin."Heuman Resources." *The World of Interiors*. January 2023.

Min Hogg
72 Min Hogg quoted in Jan Moir's "'I'm an unabashed, unabated snooper'." *Daily Telegraph*. January 2, 2001.
73 Ibid.

Nicole Hollis
74 Nicole Hollis quoted in Stacey Shoemaker Rauen's "Nicole Hollis." Hospitality Design. March 16, 2021. First accessed January 15, 2025.
75 Ibid.

Rossana Hu
76 www.neriandhu.com/en/works/urban-sanctuary-artyzen-new-bund-31-shanghai

Barbara Hulanicki
77 Emma Soame quoted in Ellen Himelfarb's "Biba (sans Barbara) lives!" *National Post*. January 14, 2006.

Polly Jessup
78 Maggie Lidz. *Polly Jessup: Grande Dame of Palm Beach Decorators*. D Giles Ltd. 2025.
79 Anne-Marie Shiro. "Grande Dame of Palm Beach Decorators." *New York Times*. March 5, 1987.

Betty Joel
80 Betty Joel quoted in Lizzie Broadbent's "Betty Joel (1894–1995)." *Women Who Meant Business*. September 22, 2021. First accessed December 2, 2024.

Annabel Karim Kassar
81 annabelkassar.com/ella-funt

Rita Konig
82 Lucie Young. "Rita Konig has subtly enhanced the airy interiors of this Manhattan house." *House & Garden*. May 5, 2024. First accessed January 15, 2025.

Agata Kurzela
83 Interview with Agata Kurzela via email. October 11, 2024.
84 Ibid.

Roísín Lafferty
85 Róisín Lafferty. roisinlafferty.com/our-story
86 Róisín Lafferty. roisinlafferty.com/projects/lovers-walk

Joanna Lavén
87 Interview with Joanna Lavén via email. December 6, 2024.
88 Ibid.

Eleanor Le Maire
89 Dorothy Jurney. "Woman with a Design." *Miami News*. January 11, 1948, p.64.
90 "Studebaker Brings New Trend to Automotive Color Styling." *The Sunday News*. November 22, 1953, p.74.

Na Li
91 hollowayli.com/project/bermonds-locke-apartment-hotel

Hilary Loh
92 Kenny Tan. "Interview with Hilary Loh: More than just a show." Sixides. First accessed February 13, 2025.
93 address.style/3-orchard-by-the-park-by-2nd-edition

Margaret Lord
94 Margaret Lord quoted in Anon's "Sydney is shabby and down-at-heel". *Sydney Morning Herald*. August 26, 1956.
95 Margaret Lord quoted in Dale Plummer's "If you are thinking of redecorating." *The Sydney Morning Herald*. September 16, 1973.
96 Ibid.

Fiona Lynch
97 fionalynch.com.au/about
98 fionalynch.com.au/workshop/about

Margaret Macdonald Mackintosh
99 Cynthia Green. "The Glasgow Sisters Who Pioneered Art Nouveau's Glasgow Four." JStor Daily. December 19, 2017. First accessed December 19, 2024.
100 Perilla Kinchin. *Taking Tea with Mackintosh: The Story of Miss Cranston's Tea Rooms*. Pomegranate Communications Inc. 1998, p.41.

Yasmina Makram
101 Interview with Yasmina Makram via email. December 9, 2024.

Eva Marguerre
102 Interview with Eva Marguerre via email. December 3, 2024.
103 Ibid.

Syrie Maugham
104 Joan Kron. "Syrie Maughani Style: The Twenties Come Ghosting Back." *New York Times*. December 1, 1977.
105 1stDibs Editors. "Decorators to Know: Syrie Maugham." 1stDibs.com. December 21, 2019. First accessed December 19, 2024.

Eleanor McMillen Brown
106 Carol Vogel. "Eleanor Brown is Dead at 100." *New York Times*. February 1, 1991. First accessed November 28, 2024.
107 Eleanor McMillen Brown quoted in Jane Geniesse's "60 Years of Interior Decorating: A Career of Elegant Rooms." *New York Times*. December 16, 1982, p.12.
108 Eleanor McMillen Brown quoted in "Marilyn Hoffman's "The Taste Maker Behind the McMillen Style." *Christian Science Monitor*. December 1, 1982. First accessed December 2, 2024.

Dorothée Meilichzon
109 Dorothée Meilichzon quoted in Sophie Cullen's "An interview with Dorothée Meilichzon, Founder of Chzon and one of the trendiest hotel designers in Paris." *Hotel Journal*. May 18, 2024.

Diana Luxton Messara
110 Interview with Diana Luxton Messara. "The People's House: audio interviews." Museums of History New South Wales. First accessed January 15, 2025.

Jeannette Meunier Biéler
111 Anon. *The Journal of Canadian Art History*. Vol. XXV. 2004, p.133.

Yana Molodykh
112 Interview with Yana Molodykh via email. December 11, 2024.

Julia Morgan
113 William Hearst quoted in Elizabeth Stamp's "Everything You Need to Know About Hearst Castle." *Architectural Digest*. December 7, 2023. First accessed December 23, 2024.

Elsie Nanji
114 Interview with Elsie Nanji via email. November 13, 2024.

Georgia O'Keeffe
115 Georgia O'Keeffe. *Georgia O'Keeffe*. Penguin Books. 1977.

Tola Ojuolape
116 Interview with Tola Ojuolape via email. November 19, 2024.

Tosin Oshinowo
117 Tosin Oshinowo quoted in Ugonna-Ora Owoh's "10 Questions with Tosin Oshinowo." Interior Design. March 14, 2023. First accessed November 30, 2024.

Maria Osminina
118 mariaosminina.com/en/beige

Marie-Anne Oudejans
119 Marie-Anne Oudejans quoted in Dana Thomas's "A Fashion Star-Turned-Interior Designer Lives in This Opulent Indian Apartment." *Architectural Digest*. March 14, 2017. First accessed January 16, 2025.

Laura Panebianco
120 Interview with Laura Panebianco via email. December 20, 2024.

Sister Parish
121 Barbara Meyer. "Sister Parish's Legacy: Styling the Familiar." *Los Angeles Times*. October 29, 1994. First accessed December 22, 2024.

Charlotte Perriand
122 Charlotte Perriand. *A Life of Creation*. The Monacelli Press. 2003.

Kerry Phelan
123 Interview with Kerry Phelan via email. November 1, 2024.

Clodagh
124 Clodagh. www.clodagh.com/about/clodagh
125 Clodagh. *Total Design: Contemplate, Cleanse, Clarify, and Create Your Own Spaces*. Clarkson Potter. 2001.

Clara Porset
126 Anon. "Woman 'Exile' from Cuba Tells Tales of Horror." *Morning Call*. May 3, 1933.

Andrée Putman
127 Andrée Putman quoted in Marnie Burke's "André Putman's stark appearance." *San Francisco Examiner*. April 8, 1992.
128 Andrée Putman quoted in Patricia Leigh Brown's "Designer claims money has nothing to do with style." *Morning Union*. September 21, 1986.

Diana Radomysler
129 Interview with Diana Radomysler via email. October 22, 2024.
130 Ibid.
131 Ibid.

Chessy Rayner
132 Chessy Rayner quoted in Amy Larocca's "Playing Chessy." *New York Magazine*. August 26, 2002. First accessed February 6, 2025.
133 Ibid.

Suzanne Rheinstein
134 Suzanne Rheinstein quoted in Penelope Green's "Suzanne Rheinstein, 77, Designer of Classic American Interiors, Dies." *New York Times*. March 31, 2023.

Ruby Ross Wood
135 Christopher Petkanas. "Ruby, It's You." *New York Times*. March 30, 2010. First accessed November 28, 2024.
136 Adam Lewis. *The Great Lady Decorators*. Rizzoli. 2010.

Rabah Saeid
137 Rabah Saeid quoted in Janice Rodrigues's "Founder Rabah Saeid blends natural materials and thoughtful design to create spaces that are meant to be lived in." Luxehabitat. November 30, 2022. First accessed November 14, 2024.

Laura Sartori Rimini
138 Laura Sartori Rimini quoted in Ian Phillips's "From the Archive: Inside a Grand London Manse Reimagined by Studio Peregalli." *Elle Decor*. June 7, 2023. First accessed December 2, 2024.
139 Interview with Laura Sartori Rimini via email. December 17, 2024.

Gaby Schreiber
140 Ruth de Wynter. "Design Archives Online and The Plastics Age." V&A Archive. May 3, 2017. First accessed December 2, 2024.

Anastasia Schuler
141 Interview with Anastasia Schuler via email. November 14, 2024.

Margarete Schütte-Lihotzky
142 Margarete Schütte-Lihotzky quoted in Margarete Schütte-Lihotzky and Juliet Kinchin's "Passages from Why I Became an Architect." *West 86th: A Journal of Decorative Arts, Design History, and Material Culture*. Vol. 18, No. 1 (Spring–Summer 2011), pp.86–96, p.95.

Gillian Segal
143 Gillian Segal quoted in Camille Freestone's "In This Palm Beach Home, Each Room Has Its Own Personality." Coveteur. April 5, 2022. First accessed March 2, 2025.

Tekla Evelina Severin
144 Tekla Evelina Severin quoted in Charlotte Beach's "Tekla Evelina Severin Shakes Up Scandinavian Design with a Keen Eye for Color." *PRINT*. June 12, 2023. First accessed February 6, 2025.

Halina Skibniewska
145 Iwona Szustakiewicz. "Halina Skibniewska's Good Flat." *IOP Conference. Series: Materials Science and Engineering*. 603. 2019, p.1.

Lena Solovyeva
146 Interview with Elena Solovyeva via email. December 13, 2024.

Anna Spiro
147 Anna Spiro quoted in "Designer Anna Spiro's vivid Brisbane cottage indulges her love of mixing color & pattern." *House & Garden*. January 4, 2021. First accessed December 2, 2024.

Sara Story
148 Sara Story quoted in David Foxley's "Inside a Gramercy Park Home That's Taken Nearly Two years to Assemble," *Architectural Digest*, May 15, 2023.

Madeline Stuart
149 Madeline Stuart. *No Place Like Home: The Interiors of Madeline Stuart*. Rizzoli. 2019.

Rose Tarlow
150 Rose Tarlow quoted in Joni Webb's "Rose Tarlow." Cotedetexas.com. First accessed December 1, 2024.
151 Rose Tarlow quoted in Elaine Markoutsas's *Homes with Character: New Ways to Use Old Looks*. Clarion-Ledger. January 4, 2002, p.58.

Vritima Wadhwa
152 Interview with Vritima Wadhwa via email. October 18, 2024.
153 Ibid.

Kelly Wearstler
154 Kelly Wearstler quoted in Jane Englefied's "'I think my work stands out because I follow my gut' says Kelly Wearstler." *Dezeen*. April 23, 2024. First accessed December 2, 2024.
155 Ibid.

Edith Wharton
156 Edith Wharton. *The Decoration of Houses*. B.T. Batsford. 1898.
157 www.edithwharton.org/discover/edith-wharton

Candace Wheeler
158 Pioneer Designers. Daily Sentinel. American Press Association. December 10, 1892, p.4
159 Candace Wheeler quoted in "The Development of Art." *New York Daily Tribune*. October 6, 1897, p.5.

Jialun Xiong
160 Interview with Jialun Xiong via email. October 16, 2024.

INDEX

2nd Edition studio 155
3 Orchard By-the-Park 155, *155*
19 Town Restaurant 260, *260*
25hours Hotel Piazza San Paolino 183

A

A Interiors 135
"A Room for Mary Quant" *112*
Aalto, Aino 8, 12
Aalto, Alvar 8, 12, 13
Aalto, Elissa 13
Aalto Theatre 13
Aboukheir, Zeina 14
Abstract Home 184, *184*
Act of Quad, The 41
Acut Residence 69, *69*
Adelman, Lindsay 213
Africa Centre, The 10, *188–189*, 189
African (aesthetic) 102, 110, 116, 132, 181, 184, 189, 190, 241
Afro Minimalism 190
Aga Khan Award for Architecture 90
Agata Kurzela Studio 140
Agaton, Lotta 15, *15*
Agnelli, Gianni 16
Agnelli, Marella 16, *16*
Ahmed Mathias, Farah 17
AKA Furniture Company 53
Akkari, Selma 18
Al Moudira 14, *14*
Al Sowaidi, Aisha 19
Albers, Joseph 39
Albini, Franco 230
Alessi 247
Alía, Miriam 20, *20*
Aljoaib, Nebras 21
Altana Palazzo Pucci 31, *31*
Alvarez de Toledo, Paula 22
Amano Hotel 52
American Bar 55
American Country (aesthetic) 195
American Institute of Architects 178
American Institute of Interior Designers 168
Americana 7
Amity Street Residences 18, *18*
Andrei, Anda 37
Andric, Nada 23
Anna Spiro Designs 234
Apartment by the Colonnade *64*
Apartment Nessi 196, *196*
Apartment ST 148, *148*
Apfel, Carl 24
Apfel, Iris 9, 24, *24*
Aptitude Café 60
Architects' Journal 70
architecture
 Art Deco 55, 72, 84, 104, 124, 138, 176
 Beaux-Arts 31, 258
 Classicism 83
 Edwardian 75
 Georgian 68, 186, 243
 Greek Revival 54, 211
 Japanese 32, 41
 Modernist 8, 89, 104, 132, 185, 187, 205, 209, 231
 Rationalism 58, 83
 Spanish Baroque 10, 216
 Spanish Colonial Revival 178
 Victorian 130, 176
Architectural Clearing House 81
Architectural Digest 95
Architecture Interior Design studio 128
Arefieva, Olimpiada 25
Argyll House 65, *65*
Armani/Casa 180
Art Nouveau 145, 159, 181
Art of Beautiful Living, The 114
Arte Povera 82
Artek 12, 197
Articolo Studios 96
Artistic Apartment 25, *25*
Arts & Architecture 85
Arts and Crafts Movement 28, 40, 53, 69, 112, 136, 173, 237
Arts and Crafts Workshop (Mexico) 93, *93*
Artyzen NEW BUND 31 Hotel 123, *123*
ASD Studio 224
Ashby, Sophie 10, 26, 75
Ashley, Laura 7, 28
Aspe, Sofía 29, *29*
Atelier About Architecture 256
Atelier MKD 84
Atelier ND Interiors 79
Audrito, Athena 30

Audrito, Franco 30
Audrito, Valentina 30
Aulenti, Gae 16, 31
Australian Home Beautiful 144, 157
Australian Home Builder, The 144
avant-garde 8, 38, 86, 87, 152, 183, 252
Avedon, Richard 16
Azuma, Rie 32
Azuma, Takamitsu 32

B

b-arch 43
Bainbridge, Michael 33
Bainbridge, Talitha 33, *33*
Bak, Nadine 34
Bakhirka, Kateryna 94
Bakubayeva, Elvira 35
BAMBU Beach House 80, *80*
Bar Bête 150, *150*
Bar Palladio 192, *192*
Barbara Hulanicki Design 124
Baroque 71, 107, 220
Bataille, Claire 36, *36*
Bauhaus 17, 39, 132, 209, 222, 263
Baxter International Inc. 200, *200*
BAYN Café 217, *217*
Beetle Under the Leaf House *252*
Behune, Kelly 37
Bell, Clive 38
Bell, Vanessa 38
Bella Freud House 233, *233*
Belle Époque 87
Benhamou, Sandra 39
Bergöö Larsson, Karin 40
Bergson, Maria 9
Bermonds Locke 151, *151*
Betty Joel Ltd. 129
Bhatia, Falguni 41
Bianchi, Natalia 42, *42*
Biba 9, 124
Bignami, Sabrina 43
Bilú Riviera 221
Bill Blass Apartment 208, *208*
Black Arts Movement 150
Black Folks in Design 10, 150
Blakeney, Justina 10, 44
Blewcoat School, The *26–27*
Blomgren, Veronika 25
Bloomingdale's 9, 74, 251
Bloomsbury Group 38
Blumenfeld, Erwin 16
Bo Bardi, Lina 10, 45, 185, 207
Boeri, Cini 46
Bone Studio 161
Book of Home Decorating 28, 74
Boronkay, Linda 47
Brandolini, Muriel 48, *48*
Breer, Sally 49, *49*
Breuer, Marcel 137, 262
Bridgehampton Getaway *146–147*, 147
Bridges, Sheila 10, 50
Brisbane Cottage 234, *234*
Brooklyn Townhouse 54
Brooks, Tiffany 51
Brugman, Til 8
Brutalism 123, 161
Bruzkus, Ester 52
Buddha Room, The 55, *55*
Bullocks Wilshire Store 149, *149*
Bülow-Hübe, Sigrun 53
Burj Al Arab 61, *61*
Burj Khalifa 23, *23*
BVBA Ibens & Bataille 36

C

Calderone, Athena 54
calligraphy, Islamic 135
Campbell, Nina 55, 139
Campbell and Birley 55
Candy & Candy 98
Capellaro, Alessandro 43
Carl Larssen-gården 40, *40*
Carré Blanc 232, *232*
Cartier 103, 235
Carulla, Cristina 56, *56*
Casa Amesti 86, *86*
Casa de Vitro (Glass House) 45, *45*
Casa do Passadiço 214
Casa do Passadiço Lisbon showroom *214*
Casa Coa 216
Casa Foa 72, *72*
Casa nel Bosco 46
Casa Orlandi 43, *43*
Casabella 31, 183

Case Study House 8 85, *85*
Cassina 33, 164, 196, 247
Castaing, Madeleine 7, 57
CB2, Black in Design Collective 102
Cecil's Designs Unlimited 116
Celestino, Cristina 58
Celtic Revival 159
Ceylon et Cie 186
Chagall State Hall 97
Charles, Vicky 59
Charles & Co. 59
Charleston House 38, *38*
Charlotte Moss & Co. 179
Chehab, Ghida 60
Chen, Lea 261
Chew, Khuan 61
Chou, Ray 62
Chu, Vera 62
Chudley, Rachel 63
Churchill, Winston 143
CHZON studio 172
Cienciálová, Petra 64
Classic English Interiors 55
Clermont Residence 17, *17*
Clodagh 202
Colefax, Sibyl 65, 167
Colefax and Fowler 55, 65, 115, 143, 243
collections
 Black in Design 102
 Bloomsbury Room 28
 Hue 181
 Le Uova di Leon 30
 Moon Collection 253
 Object/Modules 232
 Oriental Treasures 261
 Sister 26
 Token 129
Colombo, Joe 112
Colpitts, Erica 66
Colter, Mary 67
Colwood House 66, *66*
Commune 229
Connolly, Sybil 68
Cortina, Gloria 69
"cottagecore" 28
Cowles Publication Office 137
Crawford, Ilse 59, 70
Creager, D'lisa 213
Cubism 104, 249
Culture in Architecture 73
Cumming, Rose 7, 71
Cumming Residence 71, *71*
Cussen, Kana 72

D

d'Amman, Aline Asmar 9, 73
D'Arcy, Barbara 9, 74
Dadaism 223
Dalí, Salvador 167
Dauley, Alex 10, 26, 75
Day, Robin 112
de Portzamparc, Christian 140
de Soissons, Louis 128
De Stijl 8, 223, 249
de Wolfe, Elsie 7, 24, 76, 215
Dean, Pallavi 77
Decoration of Houses, The 258
Delaloy, Marine 22
The Delineator magazine 215
Design Miami Art Fair 147
Dhvani Bhanushali Residence 228, *228*
Di Pinto, Chiara 78, *78*
Diana, Princess of Wales 28
Didion, Joan 178
Ditau Interiors 241
Dixon, Tom 47
d.Mesure 230
Dog House 256, *256*
Dohmen, Nicole 79, *79*
Domestic Bliss 139
Domino magazine 139
Domus 97
Donna Karan 70, 95, 113
Doorzon Interior Architects 89
Dosekun-Adjei, Olayinka 80
Draper, Dorothy 7, 9, 81, 195
Dries, Sophie 82, *82*
Droulers, Nathalie and Virginie 83, *83*
Droulers Architecture 83
Dru, Marika 84
Dzen Space Club 94, *94*

E

E-1027 105, *105*
Eames, Charles 85, 137, 173
Eames, Ray 85, 173
Eastern/ East Asian (aesthetic) 62, 71, 90, 115, 123, 153, 239, 255
Ebur 110
Ecart International 206
Eclectic Patio 165
EFM Design 96
Elicyon 98
Elizabeth Metcalfe Interiors 175
Elkins, Frances 86
Ella Funt 132, *132*
Elle Decor 169
Elle Decoration 70, 230
Elsa Gullberg Textil og Inredningar AB 108
Emaar Properties 23
English Country (aesthetic) 55, 107, 134, 143, 180, 243, 250
environmental design 93, 104, 141, 231, 260
ergonomics 12, 100, 137
Errázuriz, Eugenia 9, 87, *87*
Ertegun, Mica 8, 88, *88*, 208
Ester Bruzkus Architekten 52
Estudio Claudina Flores 93
ETC.etera 49
Ett Hem House 70, *70*
Everaert, Stefanie 89
Extradesign Selection 43
EyeSwoon 54

F

FADD Studio 17
Fadillioğlu, Zeynep 90
Fahmy, Shahira 91
Featherston, Mary 92
Feldman, Simone 111
Fendi 58
FG Private Residence 190, *190*
FIKA Café 35, *35*
Fiona Lynch Office 158
Firmdale Hotels 134
Fitzroy House 158, *158*
Flamingo Room 34, *34*
Flores, Claudina 93
Ford House 127, *127*
Forma Private Dining Room 239
Fornace Brioni 58
Foster, Norman 255
Foster + Partners 99
FOURSPA IV 21, *21*
Fradina, Olga 94
Frankfurt Kitchen 225, *225*
Franklin, Kesha 95, *95*
Franklin Road House 154, *154*
Frattini Magnusson, Emanuela 96
French Classicism 145
French Vernacular 243
Furnishing Forward: A Practical Guide to Furnishing for a Lifetime 50
furniture
    bamboo sofa *32*
    Barcelona chair 209
    Bibendum chair 8
    Bocca Sofa 30
    Bonacina chairs 179
    Butaque chair 205
    Byobu screens 21
    Directoire furniture 171
    Due Più chair 252
    Eames Elephant chair 85
    Familyscape seating 37
    Fernando and Humberto Campana sofa 177
    Golden Universe Obsidian table 69
    Harry Bertoia metal chair 111
    Jay Spectre steamer lounge chairs 203
    Kikuyu *giturwa* stool 102
    La Chaise 85
    Ligne Roset Togo sofa 33
    Linea Floor lamp 252
    Louis XIV settee 111
    Mario Bellini chairs 164
    Mission-style furniture 67
    Nombe carved throne chair 37
    Ori globe lamp 10
    Plywood Group furniture 85
    Saarinen dining chairs 43
    Utrecht chair 33
    Furora, 264
futurism (aesthetic) 58, 61

G

Gad, Dora 97
Galería de Arte Mexicano 69
Gallery at Sketch 162, *162–163*
Ganache Dubai Hills 60, *60*
Gandhi, Charu 98
Garden Gallery Residence 153, *153*
GAS Moema 248
Gathe, Hanne 99, *99*
Gathe + Gram 99
Gehry, Frank 74, 128
Geller House III 262
geometric abstraction 8, 134, 176, 260
Geremia, Lauren 100, *100*
German Modernism 136, 176
gesamtkunstwerk 147, 159
Ghoniem, Yasmine 101
Ginori 1735 43
Githinji, Sandra 10, 102
Glamour 208
"The Glasgow Four" 159
The Gloss 142
Gomide, Regina 8
Gonzalez, Laura 103, *103*
Good Housekeeping 81
Górska de Mantaut, Adrienne 104
Gothic (aesthetic) 71, 178
GQ magazine 95
Gramercy Park Townhouse 236, *236*
Gray, Eileen 8, 105
The Great Home Transformation 75
"Great Lady Decorators" 7, 71, 215
Green Box, The 52, *52*
Green Massage Spa 62, *62*
Greenbriar Hotel 7, 81, *81*
Grisanti & Cussen 72
Gropius, Walter 137
Grossman, Greta Magnusson 106
Gruppo Zero 252
Guest, C.Z. 16
Guinness, Camilla 107
Gullberg, Elsa 108
Gupta, Shabnam 109
Gutierrez, Racha 110, *110*
Gwyneth Paltrow Home *212–213*

H

H+O 192
Habitat magazine 45
Hadid, Zaha 140
Hagan, Victoria 111
Halden Interiors 95
Hall, Peter 174
Hall Best, Marion 112
Hamed, Rania 10, 113
Hanono, Olga 114, *114*
Harley House 166, *166*
Harper's & Queen 169
Harper's Bazaar 68, 87, 167
Haussmann apartment 22, 39, 82
Haworth Hotel at Hope College 247, *246–247*
Hay, Elizabeth 115, *115*
Hayes, Cecil 116
Hearst Castle 178, *178*
Hecker Phelan Guthrie 201
Helg, Franca 46
Henri Martin II 84
Henrietta Experimental Hotel 172, *172*
Hernández Palacios, Ana Milena 117, *117*
Heuman, Beata 118, *118*
HGTV 51
Hickling, Briar 119
Hicks, Sheila 39
Hinoki Kogei 32
Hogg, Min 9, 120, *120*
Hojeij Deleuze, Dahlia 110, *110*
Hollis, Nicole 121, *121*
Holloway Li 151
Home Chic 162
Hong Kong Convention and Exhibition Centre 23
hooks, bell 10
Hopi House 67, *67*
Hoppen, Kelly 122, *122*
Hôtel de Crillon 9, 73
Hotel Josef 128, *128*
Hotel Villa d'Este 83
House & Garden 139, 211, 244
House Beautiful 106, 169
House Beautiful Whole Home Concept House 51, *51*
House in Good Taste, The 7, 76, 215
Hu, Rossana 123
Hudson Valley Cottage 50
Hulanicki, Barbara 9, 124
Human Dimensions of the House, The 46
Humanism 46
Hvidt, Malene 127, *127*
Hyla Architects 155

I

Ibens, Paul 36
Ilé-Ilà furniture 190
Image Interiors 142
The Independent 142
Inner Voice gallery 191
Interior Decoration 157
Interior Design Hall of Fame 23
Interiors (see *The World of Interiors*)
International Women in Design Conference 31
Ireland, Kathryn M. 126, *126*
The Irish Times 142
Isabella Blow Apartment 107, *107*
ISITA 156
Israel Museum 97
Itadkar, Priyanka 41
Italian Memphis Group 72, 183, 194
Italian Modernism 154

J

JanskyDundera 64
Japanese (aesthetic) 32, 40, 105, 125, 154, 210
Jaune Architecture 22
Jazz Lounge Beirut *218*
Jean Désert 105
Jencks, Charles 120
Jessup, Polly 127
Jessup Inc. 127
Jiřičná, Eva 9, 120, 128
Jobs, Steve 9, 128
Joel, Betty 7, 129
John Anthony 119, *119*
John Wardle Architects 158
Johnson, Tamsin 130
Joseph Dirand Architecture 22
Josh Brolin Residence 203, *203*
Jugend magazine 136
Jumeirah Beach Hotel 61
Jungalow 10, 44
Jungalow by the Mountain 44

K

K2India 138
Kahane, Melanie 8, 131
The Kahn's Residence 109, *109*
Karim Kassar, Annabel 132
Karméi restaurant 254, *254*
KCA International 61
Kemble, Celerie 133
Kemble Interiors 133
Kemp, Kit 134
Kennedy, Jacqueline 7, 68, 195
Khalid Mishaal bin Saud, HRH Anoud 135, *135*
Kips Bay Decorator Show House
    "2008" 179, *179*
    "A Dining Room of One's Own" 134
    "Salon of social consciousness" 111, *111*
Kit Kemp Design Studio 134
Kleinhempel, Gertrud 136
Klint, Kaare 53
Knesset 97, *97*
Knoll, Florence 9, 137
Knoll Associates 137
Knoll Planning Unit 137
Kohli, Sunita 138, *138*
Konig, Rita 55, 139, *139*
K.P.D.O. 201
Kurzela, Agata 140

L

L'Architecture d'Aujourd'hui 231
La Maison de Lèves 56, *56*
La Revue Moderne 176
La Ruota design firm 196
Laajisto, Joanna 141
Ladies' Home Journal 208
Lafferty, Róisín 142
Lagerfeld, Karl 73
Lancaster, Nancy 65, 143, *143*
Lane Poole, Ruth 144
Lanvin 95, 145
Lanvin, Jeanne 145, *145*
Lappia Town Hall 13
Larssen, Carl 40
The Last Swan 16
Lateur, Caroline 89
Lau, Amy 147
Lauren Santo Domingo Home 244, *244*
Lavén, Joanna 148
Le Corbusier 87, 105, 132, 199
Le Marie, Eleanor 9, 149
Lee, Little Wing 10, 150

283

INDEX

Lelli Mami, Arianna 78, *78*
Les Arcs 199, *199*
Li, Na 151
Li, Xiang 10, 152
Liaigre, Christian 82, *162*
Life magazine 68
Lindahl, Angela 153
Linehouse 119
Liwan Design Studios and Labs 19
Lladró 114
Lockhart, Katie, 154
Lodge at Yarralumla 144, *144*
Loh, Hilary 155
Lóios Apartment 198, *198*
Loong Swim Club 152, *152*
Loos, Adolf 8
López-Quesada, Isabel 156, *156*
Lord, Margaret 157
Lotje Roeselare 89
Lovers Walk House 142
Lucida Restaurant 91, *91*
Lynch, Fiona 158

M

MAC II 8, 88, 208
Macdonald Mackintosh, Margaret 159
Mackay, Elsie, 160
Maddock McMakin, Mimi 133, *133*
Mahakian, Natalie 161
Mahdavi, India 162
Mahindra Museum of Living History 182
Maison Louis Carré 13, *13*
Maison Métier 229, *229*
Maison Sarah Lavoine 204
Makram, Yasmina 164
Mandel apartment 22, *22*
Manor House 39, *39*
Marbury, Elisabeth 7, 76
Marguerre, Eva 165
Maria Chaya, Michèle 166
MARIAGROUP 166
Mark Twain House 259, *259*
Mas Creations 117
Masquespacio 117
Maugham, Syrie 167, *167*
Max Mara 113
Maximalist (aesthetic) 9, 29, 30, 42, 62, 81, 103, 142, 170, 183, 227, 234, 252, 257
McCartney, Stella 130
McCluskey, Ellen Lehman 168, *168*
McEvoy, Marian 9, 169, *169*
McLeod, Courtney 170, *170*
McMillen Brown, Eleanor 7, 171, *171*
McMillen Inc. 7, 171
Meilichzon, Dorothée 172
Merrill, Frances 173, *173*
Merrion Square House 68
Messara, Dian Luxton 174
Metcalfe, Elizabeth 175
Metropolitan Museum of Art 24, 81
Meunier Biéler, Jeannette 176, *176*
Michael Graves & Associates 123
Mid-century Modernism 8, 66, 78, 94, 101, 111, 123, 137, 147, 186, 187, 196, 221
Middle Eastern (aesthetic) 14, 110, 140, 166
Mies van der Rohe, Ludwig 137, 185, 200, 209
Minimalism 15, 18, 30, 36, 41, 46, 62, 64, 77, 87, 90, 113, 135, 139, 155, 158, 221, 224, 245, 251, 254, 258, 260, 261, 264
Modern Baroque 63, 81
Modernism 8, 87, 89, 104, 106, 108, 112, 130, 132, 135, 137, 141, 181, 185, 187, 190, 196, 200, 207, 209, 223, 226, 231, 249, 264
Mok, Alex 119
Molodykh, Yana 177, *177*
MoMA *Good Design* exhibition 85
Mondrian, Piet 8, 249
Monowai ship 157
Moore, Henri 175
Moore Park 175, *175*
Morgan, Julia 178
Morgans Hotel 206, *206*
Morris, William 173
Moss, Charlotte 179
Mott 32 restaurant 255, *255*
The Mount 258, *258*
Moyler, Joy 180
Mumbai Apartment 41, *41*
Mupangilaī, Kim 10, 181, *181*
Muqaddas, Rawan 18
Muqaddas Akkari Studio 18
Musée d'Orsay 31
Museum of Modern Art 16

Museum of Women in the Arts, India 138
Muuratsalo Experimental House 13

N

NAAW 35
Nakkash Design Studio 60
Nanji, Elsie 182, *182*
National Gallery of Victoria 92, *92*
Navone, Paola 183
Neri&Hu 119, 123
New Nordic 141
Newbold, Tanwa 184
Niemeyer, Anna Maria 185
Nina Campbell Interiors 55
Noli Katajanokka II 141, *141*
Notting Hill Home 250, *250*
Nouvel, Jean 82
Nu Mi Design House 184
Nussbaumer, Michelle 186, *186*

O

O'Keeffe, Georgia 187
Oceanfront condominium 116
Ogorchukwu Iyamah, Jacquelyn 10
Ojuolape, Tola 10, 189
Old Barn 180, *180*
Old World Weavers 24
Omega Workshops 38
ORA, Nursery of the Future 77, *77*
Orange Lane, The 109
Orijins 10, 113, *113*
Oshinowo, Tosin 190
Oshinowo Studio 190
Osminina, Maria 191, *191*
Ossino, Elisa 192
OTTO studio 183
Oudejans, Marie-Anne 193
OWO Raffles Residences 98, *98*

P

Paimio Sanatorium 12, *12*
Palácio da Alvorada 185, *185*
Palazzo dei Fiori 219, *219*
Palazzo Grassi 31
Palmette apartment 164, *164*
Panebianco, Laura 194, *194*
Parish, Sister 7, 8, 171, 195
Parisi, Luisa 196
Patio House 242
Peach, Sevil 197
Peacock Life 109
Penaguião, Mónica 198
Penthouse II 201, *201*
Perfect Darkness 192, *192*
Perriand, Charlotte 199, 207
Peterhans, Brigitte 200
Pfayfer & Fradina 94
Phelan, Kerry 201
[Phipps] Clodagh 202
Picasso, Pablo 87
Pierce, Louisa 203
Pierce & Ward 203
Plus One Architects 64
Poeira Interior Design 198
Polychrome House 101, *101*
Poniatowski, Sarah 204, *204*
Ponti, Gio 39, 46, 196, 207, 230, 252
Pop (aesthetic) 152, 162
Porset, Clara 205, *205*
Postmodernism 72, 175, 216
Potts Point Residence 130, *130*
Project 5 *253*
Project 810 254
Průchová, Kateřina 64
Putman, Andrée 9, 37, 206

Q

Quant, Mary 28
Queen Elizabeth 2 222
Queen magazine 120
Quitandinha Palace 81

R

Rachel Chudley Interior Design 63
Radomysler, Diana 207
Radziwill, Lee 16
Rainbow Room, Big Biba 124, *124*
Ralph Lauren 180
Rayner, Chessy 8, 88, 208
Razor House 37, *37*
Reath Design 173

Regency style 167, 210
Reich, Lilly 209
Residence 15
Retrouvius 233
Rheinstein, Suzanne 210, *210*
Richmond residence 47
Ridder, Katie 9, 211, *211*
Rietveld, Gerrit 8, 33, 233
Rietveld Schröder House 223, *223*
Right Meets Left Interior Design 170
Riihitie House 12
ROAR 77
Rogers, Richard 128
Romanek, Brigette 213
Romantic (aesthetic) 66, 76, 103, 107, 145, 203
Rosa-Violán, Lázaro 56
Rosas, Catarina 214
Rose Tarlow Melrose House *240*
Rose Uniacke Editions 245
Ross Wood, Ruby 9, 76, 215
Rossetti, Dante Gabriel 159
Royal York Apartment 131, *131*
Ruffino 43
Ruiz, Maye 10, 216

S

Saarinen, Eero 112, 137
Sackville-West, Vita 65
Sady Żoliborskie Estate *231*
Saied, Rabah 217
Saint Peter's Church 251, *251*
Sakhi, Tara 218
Sakhi, Tesse 218
Şakirin Mosque 90, *90*
Sally Breer World 49
Salon de Luxe 159, *159*
Salone de Mobile 30, 227
 "An Apartment of One's Own" 227
São Paulo Museum of Art 45
Sapey, Teresa 219
Sartori Rimini, Laura 220, *220*
Saynatsalo Town Hall 13
Scandinavian (aesthetic) 54, 99, 106, 108, 127, 153
Scarpa, Carlo 39
Schiaparelli, Elsa 87
Schiebeck, Katty 221
Schreiber, Gaby 222
Schröder, Truus 8, 223
Schuler, Anastasia 224, *224*
Schütte-Lihotzky, Margarete 225
Seascape 30, *30*
Sednaoui, Olivier 14
Segal, Gillian 226, *226*
Sentosa House 207, *207*
Servicio Continuo 56
SESC Pompéia 10, 45
Severin, Tekla Evelina 10, 227
"Shabby chic" 9, 120, 143
Shah, Darshini 228
Shamshiri, Pamela 229
Sheila Bridges Design, Inc. 50
Sheppard Robson 80
Shishang Architecture 261
Show Apartment, Park Lane 129, *129*
Show bedroom, Prima Esposizione Internazionale d'Art Decorativa Moderna 136, *136*
Singer Sargent, John 87
Sire, Elodie 230, *230*
Skaff, Claudia 166
Skibniewska, Halina 231
Skidmore Owings & Merrill 9, 23, 150, 180, 190, 200, 251
Smithsonian National Museum of African American History and Culture 150
Soares Pereira, Catarina 214
Soares Pereira, Cláudia 214
Society of Decorative Arts 259
Society of Interior Designers of Australia 112
Soho Farmhouse 151
Soho House 47, 59, 70
Solovyeva, Lena 232
Søndergårdspark Kitchen Design *238*
South London Home 75
Spacon & X 127
Spanish Revival 243
Speake, Maria 233
Spectrum Pty Ltd. 112
Spiro, Anna 234
Stanislas, Isabelle 235, *235*
Starck, Philippe 172
Steyn City Showhouse *241*
Story, Sara 236
Stravinsky, Igor 173
Struwig, Dewald 34
Stuart, Madeline 237, *237*
Studebaker Land Cruiser 9, 149

284

Studio & Projects 150
Studio Ashby 26
Studio Baab 60
Studio Besau-Marguerre 165
Studio Contra 80
Studio KO 22
Studio Lawahl 148
Studio MK27 207
Studio Panebianco 194
Studio Peregalli Sartori 220
Studio65 30
Studiolise 70
Studiopepe 78
Styled Habitat 217
Sunita Kohli Interior Designs 138
Surrealist (aesthetic) 63, 71, 81, 89, 118, 167
sustainability 33, 119, 126, 141, 194, 197, 202, 217, 232, 233, 253
Swan House 215
Swedish Modern 40
Sydney Opera House 174, *174*
Syrie Ltd. 167

T

Tafdrup, Ulla 238
Takenouchi, Naoko 239
Tamara de Lempicka Residence *104*
Tarlow, Rose 240
Taukobong, Nthabi 241
The Telegraph 139
Terence Conran 120
Terra Eatery 161, *161*
textile/wallpaper designs
    H55 13
    Harlem Toile de Jouy 10, 50
    Patio 13
    Pisa 13
    Zebrine 71
textiles, wall and floor coverings
    Karakami wallpaper 32
    Kente cloth 189
    Lee Jofa florals 180
    mashrabiya latticework 103
    mycelium panels 35
    Sunny Shag Up Rug 30
    tatami mats 32
    "tozzetti" tiles 96
    William Yeoward glass 210
    zellige tiles 242
Tiffany, Louis Comfort 259
Tiffany & Co. 68
Tocca 193
Toniton 227
Total Design 202
Townhouse 8 19, *19*
TRABDESIGN 242
Trombetta, Paola 242
Trousdale House 106, *106*
Tucker, Suzanne 243, *243*
Tucker & Marks 243
Tupker, Virginia 9, 244
Tsukihashi Maisonette, Hoshinoya resorts 32, *32*

U

U.A.E. Government offices 140
Uali, Aisulu 35
Uniacke, Rose 245, *245*
United in Design 10, 26, 75
Urquiola, Patricia 247

V

van Dijk, Noura 248
van Doesburg, Nelly 8, 249, *249*
van Doesburg, Theo 8, 249
Vanity Fair 71, 88
Vanrenen, Sarah 250
Veere Greeney 115
Vera Wang 95
Veranda magazine 180
Verhaal 34
Vermilion Zhou Design Group 62
Viceroy of India 160, *160*
Victoria & Albert Museum 28, 243
Victorian (aesthetic) 66
Vignelli, Lella 9, 251
Vigo, Nanda 252
Viipuri Library 12
Villa Tugendhat 209, *209*
Vineyard Family House 96, *96*
Vitra 197, 224
    "Citizen Office" 197, *197*
Vogue 16, 48, 76, 169, 180, 202, 204, 208, 215, 244
Volante, Ana 253
VSHD Design 113

W

Wadhwa, Vritima 254
Wanderlust: Interiors that Bring the World Home 186
Wang, Joyce 255
Wang, Ni 256
Wanstead Villa *63*
Ward, Emily 203
Warhol, Andy 16
Wearstler, Kelly 257, *257*
Well Done Interiors 25
Wells, H. G. 65
Wharton, Edith 258
Wheeler, Candace 7, 259
White House, The 7, 24, 68, 171, 195, *195*, 259
Wiener Werkstätte 108, 209
Women's Institute 28
Women's Pavilion 103
Women's Wear Daily 24, 169, 208
Wood-paneled office 108, *108*
Woods Bagot 47
Woolfe, Virginia 65, 134
Word of Mouth House 30
The World of Interiors 9, 70, 120
World's Fair 108, 131

X

X+LIVING Studio 152
Xiong, Jialun 260
Xuan, Chen 261

Y

Yatofu Studio 153
Yeats, W.B. 144
Yovanovitch, Pierre 82
YSG studio 101
Yves Saint Laurent 42, 206
Yu, Jane 262

Z

Zeynep Fadillioğlu Designs (ZF Designs) 90
Zhang Jie Studio 261, *261*
Zimbler, Liane 263, *263*
Žurek, Diana 264, *264–265*
ZWEI 33
ZWEI Finds 33

285

IMAGE CREDITS

Page 12 Photo: Gustaf Welin, Alvar Aalto Foundation. 1933; page 13 Photo: Martti Kapanen, Alvar Aalto Foundation. 1980s; page 14 Mark Anthony Fox; page 15 Erik Lefvander; pages 16 and 19 Francois Halard / Trunk Archive; page 17 Gokul Rao Kadam. Styled by Samir Wadekar; page 18 Sean Davidson; page 20 Manolo Yllera; page 21 Tamara Hamad; page 22 Yannick Labrousse; page 23 Nick Merrick; page 24 Roger Davies; page 25 Photography by Sergey Ananiev; pages 26–7 The Blewcoat School by Studio Ashby, photographed by Kensington Leverne; page 28 Laura Ashley IP Holdings and Charleston Trust. Featuring paintings by Tobit Roche; page 29 Montse Garriga Grau / Courtesy of Sofia Aspe; page 30 Studio Audrito; page 31 Ivan Terestchenko; page 32 © Hoshino Resorts; page 33 Photo: Lichtspiel (Adine Schweizer); page 34 Courtesy of Verhall Studio; page 35 Damir Otegen; page 36 Flanders Architecture Institute, archive Claire Bataille & Paul Ibens Design; page 37 Frank Frances / Art Department; page 38 Paul Massey / Condé Nast / © Estate of Vanessa Bell. All rights reserved, DACS 2025; page 39 Gaelle Le Boulicaut; page 40 Mattias Edwall; page 41 Design and ex-ecution by The Act of Quad, Mumbai. Photography by The Fishy Project; page 42 Francesco Dolfo; page 43 Photo: Nicolas Matheus; page 44 Justina Blakeney / Jungalow; page 45 Nelson Kon; page 46 Photograph Giancarlo Sponga. Courtesy Archivio Cini Boeri; page 47 Bermonds Locke by Holloway Li, photography by Edmund Dabney; pages 48, 63, 143 and 180 Simon Upton / Interior Archive; page 49 Laure Joliet; page 50 Laura Resen / OTTO (designed by Sheila Bridges); page 51 Emily Minton Redfield; page 52 Ester Bruzkus Architekten, photo: Robert Rieger; page 53 Sigrun Bülow-Hübe Fonds, John Bland Canadian Architecture Collection, McGill Libraries; page 54 Gieves Anderson / Trunk Archive; page 55 Fritz von der Schulenburg / The Interior Archive; page 56 Nacho Alegre; page 57 © Sotheby's / Art Digital Studio; page 58 De Pasquale Maffini; page 59 Douglas Friedman / Trunk Archive; page 60 Visualization by T7 Studios / Courtesy of Studio Baab; page 61 Benjamin Preece; page 62 Courtesy of Vermilion Zhou Design Group; page 64 Radek Úlehla; page 65 Photo from 1936 by E. J. Mason / Colefax & Fowler; page 66 Ema Peter Photography; page 67 National Park Service; page 68 David Davison; page 69 Photography Michael Calderwood; page 70 Magnus Marding; page 71 Courtesy of Sarah Cecil; page 72 Benjamín Moreno; page 73 Tom St Aubyn Photography; page 74 Stephan Jul-liard; page 75 Condé Nast / Tom Yee; page 76 Photo: David Almeida / Planting Fields Foundation; page 77 Courtesy of Design by Roar; page 78 Andrea Ferrari; page 79 Space Content Studio; page 80 Rubyspolaroid Photograph; page 81 Dorothy Draper & Co; page 82 Christophe Coenon; page 83 Pietro Savorelli; page 84 Alice Mesguich; page 85 © Eames Office, LLC. All rights reserved.; page 86 Mark Darley / Architectural Digest © Condé Nast Publications, Inc.; page 87 Harper's BAZAAR / Hearst Magazine Media, Inc / Photographs by François Kollar; page 88 ELLE Decor / Hearst Magazine Media, Inc / Photograph courtesy of MAC II; page 89 © Filip Dujardin; page 90 Hit-Photography.com; page 91 Nour El Refai, Architectural Photographer, www.nourelrefai.com; page 92 Photo © The Estate of Mark Strizic. Image courtesy National Gallery of Victoria, Melbourne; page 93 Pepe Molina; page 94 Yevhenii Avramenko; page 95 Christopher Stark; page 96 Simone Bossi; page 97 National Library of Israel / Jewish Womens Archive; page 98 Photographer: Patrick Williamson; page 99 Photographer: Filippa Tredal; page 100 Laure Joliet; page 101 Prue Ruscoe; page 102 Courtesy of CB2; page 103 © Inês Silva Sá / FAVORI; page 104 ©The Regents of the University of California, The Bancroft Library, University of California, Berkeley. This work is made available under a Creative Commons Attribution 4.0 license; page 105 CMN Dist. SCALA, Florence; page 106 Maynard L. Parker, photographer. Courtesy of The Huntington Library, San Marino, California.; page 107 Fritz von der Schulenburg; page 108 Photographer Sune Sundahl / Digitalmuseum # ARKM.1988-111-080401; page 109 Fabien Charuau; page 110 Matteo Verzini; page 111 Courtesy of Victoria Hagen; page 112 Caroline Simpson Library, Museums of History NSW. Photo © Estate of Mary White.; pages 113 and 161 Oculis Project; page 114 Courtesy of Olga Hanono; page 115 Neon Studio; page 116 Tim Rebar; page 117 Luis Beltran; page 118 Beata Heuman; page 119 Jonathon Leijonhufvud; page 120 James Mortimer, World of Interiors © Condé Nast; page 121 Douglas Friedman; page 122 Kelly Hoppen CBE, Interior Designer; page 123 Pedro Pegenaute; page 124 Justin De Villeneuve / Iconic Images; page 125 Philip Messmann; page 126 Tim Beddow; page 127 © Edsel and Eleanor Ford House 2025; page 128 Courtesy of Eva Jiřičná; page 129 The Stapleton Collection / Bridgeman Images; page 130 Photographer: Anson Smart; page 131 Pedro E. Guerrero / © Condé Nast; page 132 Seth Caplan; page 133 Jessica Glynn / JBSA; page 134 Kelly Marshall; page 135 Photo: Tamara Hamad / Harper's BAZAAR Arabia; page 136 Bayerische Staatsbibliothek München; page 137 Courte-sy of Knoll Archives; page 138 Amit Mehra, 2004; page 139 Paul Massey; page 140 Photo: Sebastian Böttcher; page 141 Courtesy of Studio Joanna Laajisto; page 142 Photographer: Ruth Maria / Courtesy of Róisín Lafferty; page 144 National Library of Australia; page 145 Nicolas Schimp / © Condé Nast; page 146–147 Thomas Loof / Art Department; page 148 Kristofer Johnsson; page 149 Jock Peters Papers, Architecture and Design Collection. Art, Design & Architecture Museum; University of California, Santa Barbara; page 150 Joseph DeLeo; page 151 Bermonds Locke by Holloway Li, photography by Edmund Dabney; page 152 SFAP; page 153 Photo by Wen Studio; page 154 David Straight; page 155 Studio Periphery; page 156 Miguel Flores-Vianna / Interior Archive; page 157 Photograph by Max Dupain. Collection: Powerhouse Museum. Margaret Lord Interior Design Archive. Gift of the Estate of the late Mr Vincent Wardell; page 158 Sharyn Cairns; page 159 Courtesy of The Hunterian; page 160 Reproduced by kind permission of P&O Heritage; pages 162–163 Edmund Dabney; page 164 Sherifa Hamid; page 165 Lucas Hardonk; page 166 Stephan Julliard; page 167 Chronicle / Alamy Stock Photo; page 168 Horst P. Horst / Getty Images; page 169 Don Freeman / Trunk Archive; page 170 Dane Tashima; page 171 Courtesy of Eleanor McMillen Brown; page 172 Courtesy of studio CHZON; page 173 Laure Joliet / This Represents; page 174 Daniel Boud; page 175 Photography by Younes Bounhar; page 176 Biéler's Archives / The Montreal Museum of Fine Arts; page 177 Vigo Jansons; page 178 Charles Davies / 500px / Getty Images; page 179 Pieter Estersohn / Art Department; page 181 Photo credit Gabriel Flores; page 182 Courtesy of Elsie Nanji; page 183 Paola Navone OTTO Studio; page 184 Courtesy of NU MI Design House Team; page 185 Architect Gonzalo Viramonte; page 186 Douglas Friedman / Trunk Archive; page 187 © Georgia O'Keeffe Museum / DACS 2025; pages 188–189 Felix Speller; page 190 Photo cred-it: David Timibra; page 191 Maria Osminina / Photography by Pavel Osminin; page 192 Giorgio Pos-senti; page 193 Henry Wilson; page 194 Thomas de Bruyne; page 195 Tom Leonard / Getty Images; page 196 Courtesy Archivio Design Ico Parisi, Como; page 197 Courtesy of Sevil Peach Architec-ture+Design; page 198 Ricardo Junqueira; page 199 Archives Charlotte Perriand / © ADAGP, Paris and DACS, London; page 200 © Ezra Stoller / Esto.; page 201 Photographed by Anson Smart; page 202 Art Gray; page 203 Photography by Michael P. H. Clifford; page 204 Nicolas Matheus; page 205 Courtesy of Side Gallery; page 206 Deidi von Schaewen; page 207 Studio MK27; page 208 Horst P. Horst / Condé Nast via Getty Images; page 209 Igor Sefr / CTK / Alamy Live News; page 210 Pieter Estershon / Art Department; page 211 Eric Piasecki / OTTO; pages 212–213 Yoshihiro Makino / Condé Nast; page 214 Francisco Almeida Dias; page 215 Courtesy of Atlanta History Center; page 216 Photography: Leandro Bulzano; page 217 Courtesy of Styled Habitat; page 218 Leava Saudargaite; page 219 Thomas Pagani; page 220 Vincent Leroux; page 221 Courtesy of Katty Schiebeck; page 222 Isabelle Prondzynski; page 223 Stijn Poelstra; page 224 Ekaterina Fussinger; page 225 Photo: J.F. / Museum der Dinge; page 226 Nick Mele; page 227 Photography: Maria Teresa Furnari; page 228 Photographer: Talib Chitalwala; page 229 Photog / OT-TO; page 230 Elodie Sire; page 231 Architektura-1963-nr-1-2 / Photo: Z. Kapuścik; page 232 Ilya Klimov; page 233 Michael Sinclair; page 234 Tim Salisbury; page 235 Matthieu Salvaing; page 236 Joshua McHugh; page 237 William Abranowicz; page 238 Laura Stamer; page 239 Studio Periphery; page 240 Derry Moore; page 241 Ivan Geurtse; page 242 Image courtesy of @TRAB; page 243 Roger Davis / OTTO; page 244 Noe DeWitt / OTTO; page 245 Simon Upton; pages 246–247 Kendall McCaugherty, Hall+Merrick Photographers; page 248 Photo: GJ / Courtesy of Noura van Dijk; page 249 Adam Štech; page 250 Mike Garlick Photography; page 251 Photo by Marco Anelli 2018; page 252 Courtesy Nanda Vigo Heirs / © Adam Štech; page 253 Courtesy of Ana Volante; page 254 Avesh Gaur; page 255 Photo by Edmon Leong; page 256 Haiting Sun; page 257 Joyce Park; page 258 Eric Limon; page 259 Smith Archive / Alamy Stock Photo; page 260 Image / photo credit to Ye Rin Mok; page 261 Jonathan Leijonhufvud; page 262 Paul Warchol photography; page 263 Photo by ullstein bild / ullstein bild via Getty Images; page 264–265 Courtesy of Diana Żurek.

Every reasonable effort has been made to acknowledge the ownership of copyright for photographs included in this volume. Any errors are inadvertent and will be corrected in subsequent editions provided notification is sent in writing to the Publisher.

ABOUT JANE HALL

Dr. Jane Hall is the inaugural recipient of the British Council Lina Bo Bardi Fellowship (2013) and a founding member of the Turner Prize-winning architecture collective Assemble. Jane completed a PhD at the Royal College of Art where her research considered the legacy of modernist architects in Brazil and the UK in the immediate postwar period. She is a Bye-Fellow at King's College, the University of Cambridge (2024–), specializing in the intersections of gender and architecture, and the author of two books, *Breaking Ground: Architecture by Women* (2019) and *Woman Made* (2021).

Many friends and colleagues have supported the research behind this book, and *Making Space* is richer for it. The ideas it explores have been shaped by wide ranging conversations with generous contributors from around the world. The content is not an exhaustive account, but rather a starting point reflecting the ongoing dialogues shaping an ever-changing discipline. Thanks to all the designers featured in these pages, many of whom kindly and generously took the time to answer my questions. I'm also grateful to my students in the History of Art Department at Cambridge University on whom I road tested much of the framing of the project. Finally, thanks to Helen Issler, David Hall, Rachel Hall, Owen Watson, and Goldie for their support and encouragement along the way.

Phaidon Press Limited
2 Cooperage Yard
London
E15 2QR

Phaidon Press Inc.
111 Broadway
New York, NY 10006

Phaidon SARL
55, rue Traversière
75012 Paris

phaidon.com

First published 2025
© 2025 Phaidon Press Limited

ISBN 978 1 83729 008 6

A CIP catalogue record for this book is available from the British Library and the Library of Congress.

All rights reserved. No part of this publication may be reproduced, stored in a retrieval system or transmitted, in any form or by any means, electronic, mechanical, photocopying, recording or otherwise, without the written permission of Phaidon Press Limited.

Commissioning Editor: Emilia Terragni
Senior Editor: Sophie Hodgkin
Production Controller: Zuzana Cimalova
Design: Ariane Spanier Design

The Publisher would like to thank Sarah Bell, Jane Birch, Jocelyn Miller, Jodie Parachini, and Phoebe Stephenson for their contributions to the book.

Printed in Slovenia